STUDY GUIDE TO ACCOMPANY
PRINCIPLES OF MACROECONOMICS

RICHARD W. TRESCH
Boston College

Prepared by
LYNDA RUSH
California State Polytechnic University-Pomona

West Publishing Company
Minneapolis/St. Paul ▲ New York ▲ Los Angeles ▲ San Francisco

WEST'S COMMITMENT TO THE ENVIRONMENT

In 1906, West Publishing Company began recycling materials left over from the production of books. This began a tradition of efficient and responsible use of resources. Today, up to 95% of our legal books and 70% of our college texts and school texts are printed on recycled, acid-free stock. West also recycles nearly 22 million pounds of scrap paper annually—the equivalent of 181,717 trees. Since the 1960s, West has devised ways to capture and recycle waste inks, solvents, oils, and vapors created in the printing process. We also recycle plastics of all kinds, wood, glass, corrugated cardboard, and batteries, and have eliminated the use of Styrofoam book packaging. We at West are proud of the longevity and the scope of our commitment to the environment.

Production, Prepress, Printing and Binding by West Publishing Company.

COPYRIGHT © 1994 by   WEST PUBLISHING CO.
                                    610 Opperman Drive
                                    P.O. Box 64526
                                    St. Paul, MN 55164–0526

All rights reserved
Printed in the United States of America
01 00 99 98 97 96 95 94   8 7 6 5 4 3 2 1 0

ISBN 0–314–04212–1

CONTENTS

Part I: Introduction

1. The First Principles of Economics 1
2. Solving the Economic Problem 9
3. Society's Economic Problem 17
4. Markets, Prices, and the United States Economy 25
5. The Laws of Supply and Demand 33
   Sample Test 43

Part II: Introduction to Macroeconomic Theory and Policy

6. The Macroeconomic Policy Goals I:
      Long-Run Economic Growth and Full Employment 47
7. The Macroeconomic Policy Goals II:
      Price Stability and Stable International Economic Relations 55
8. The National Income and Product Accounts 63
9. Modeling the Macro Economy: New Classical and New Keynesian Perspectives 69
   Sample Test 77

Part III: National Income Determination, Fiscal Policy, and Unemployment

10. National Income Determination 81
11. The Spending Multiplier, Fiscal Policy, and Unemployment 89
12. Automatic Stabilizers, Net Exports, and Budget Deficits 97
13. Business Cycles: The Multiplier-Accelerator Model and the Real Business Cycle 105
    Sample Test 113

Part IV: Money and Monetary Policy

14. The Nature of Money and Banking: First Principles 117
15. The Monetary System of the United States 123
16. Monetary Policy 129
17. Fiscal Policy, Monetary Policy and the Macroeconomic Policy Goals 137
    Sample Test 145

Part V: The Role of Prices and the Problem of Inflation

18. Aggregate Supply and Aggregate Demand 151
19. Controlling Inflation and Other Policy Issues 159
    Sample Test 165

Part VI: International Economic Issues

20. International Trade and Barriers to Trade 169
21. International Finance 175
22. The Developing Countries 181
    Sample Test 187

Part VII: Government in the U.S. Economy

23. The Role of Government in the U.S. Economy and Government Expenditures 191
24. Government Revenues, the Principles of Taxation, and the Economics of Democracy . 199
    Sample Test 207

Answer Key 211

Chapter 1
The First Principles of Economics

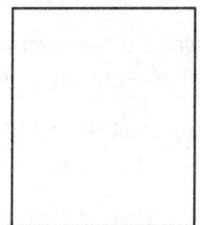

LEARNING OBJECTIVES

CONCEPTS TO LEARN

The three-part economic problem   Interdependence
Three key players in the economy   Opportunity cost
Economic exchange

CHAPTER REVIEW

Chapter 1 introduces the student to the concept of what economics is really about. Economics is a social science that is based on fundamental principles of analysis that can be used to study society and social relationships. Every economic problem can be broken down into a three-part structure of objectives, alternatives, and constraints. Then, the problem is to choose among competing alternative choices when there are scarce resources. In other words, to quote Mick Jagger "you can't always get what ya want." However, the economic framework does help you make the best possible choices under a given set of circumstances. And, when you make choices the economic framework provides a mechanism to evaluate the relative benefits and costs of selecting a particular alternative. Learning the economic framework and learning how to apply the methodology to study society and relationships takes time and will be the focus of the remainder of the text.

1. Objectives, alternatives, and constraints are the three-part structure of the economic problem.

2. The Law of Scarcity refers to the problem that exists because there are a limited amount of resources at any given point in time.

3. Economics is the study of allocating scarce resources among competing wants or choices by exchange.

4. Individuals, business firms, and government are the three key players in an economy. All three key players are confronted by the economic problem. Individuals consume goods and services as well as providing labor for the production process. Business firms produce goods and services for sale and also purchase labor from individuals and goods and services from other business firms. Government also produces and purchases goods and services. In addition, government redistributes income among individuals and business firms.

5. The principle of interdependence is based on the idea that the impact of a particular economic choice will affect and be affected by other economic alternatives.

6. The true economic cost of making a choice is the opportunity cost because economic decisions are interdependent. Opportunity cost is the value of the next best alternative.

7. Economic exchange allows individuals, business firms, and government agencies to solve their economic problems.

A FEW HELPFUL TIPS

Hopefully, the economic framework will appear logical and therefore "easy". However, students often get confused by all of the new economic jargon and somehow get the logic twisted in the process. First, make sure you have a good grasp of the terminology and then think through the logic of the economic problems you are trying to solve. The worst strategy is to try to memorize economics. It fails every time. The BEST way to learn economics is to analyze the problems systematically and not to just brush over a problem just because it appears " easy" on the surface. Once you start logically working your way through the economic problems you're on your way to learning economics.

QUICK STUDY GUIDE

	T/F	Mult. Choice	Short Answer	Problems
Economic Problem	2, 7	4. 7, 10	1, 4	6, 9
Opportunity Cost	3, 6	3, 5, 6, 8	2, 3	1, 2, 3, 5, 8, 9, 10
Scarcity	2		4	2, 10
Factors of Production	1, 8	1, 9	5	

PRETEST

Answer the following questions to test your initial understanding of the material in this chapter:

1. Suppose you have four hours of free time and you choose to go to the movies instead of studying economics. Explain the three-part economic problem that you solved.
2. Universities are often forced to make a decision between raising tuition or laying off faculty members. Explain the three-part economic problem.
3. Explain why an economic problem would not exist if you had an unlimited amount of time to study for an exam.
4. Describe the three factors of production as they relate to a university.
5. Suppose you decide to go to the beach instead of going to work. What's the opportunity cost of going to the beach?
6. What is the opportunity cost of a television network's decision to broadcast non-stop coverage of the aftermath of a plane crash instead of showing the regularly scheduled broadcast?
7. Why would you consider an owner of a new computer software company to be an entrepreneur?
8. When are opportunity costs equal to zero?
9. Explain why opportunity costs are positive when choosing to watch a movie on network television at home rather than spending $7.00 to go to the movies at a local theater.
10. List at least three examples of when government is a producer and when government is a consumer of goods and services.

TRUE/FALSE PRACTICE QUESTIONS

1. The factors of production only include land and capital.   T   F
2. In the absence of scarcity, there is no economic problem.   T   F
3. Positive opportunity costs require an interdependence of choices.   T   F
4. A skydiver is an example of an entrepreneur.   T   F
5. Individuals consume goods and services but are not factors of production according to economists.   T   F
6. The opportunity cost of watching television on a Sunday evening is zero.   T   F
7. Economic problems always involve monetary transactions.   T   F
8. Capital refers to plant and equipment required to produce goods and services.   T   F
9. Economists view government as a consumer of goods and services but not as a producer.   T   F
10. Economic exchange always requires a monetary transaction.   T   F

MULTIPLE CHOICE QUESTIONS

Choose the best option for the following questions.

1. Which of the following is NOT considered a factor of production?
    a. land
    b. labor
    c. money
    d. capital

2. Which one of the following individuals is the best example of an entrepreneur?
    a. a mountain climber
    b. an owner of a new gourmet take-out restaurant
    c. the manager of twenty engineers designing the space station
    d. a stockbroker

3. The opportunity cost of going to work on the weekend instead of going skiing are
    a. the actual wages earned.
    b. the price of ski lift tickets, transportation, and lodging.
    c. the value of the satisfaction received from skiing.
    d. the wage rate times the number of hours that would have been spent skiing.

4. The three parts of the economic problem include
    a. objectives, monetary concerns, and alternatives.
    b. objectives, alternatives, and constraints.
    c. individuals, monetary concerns, and business.
    d. individuals, government, and business.

5. Profits are the difference between the revenues obtained from selling goods and services and
    a. opportunity costs.
    b. the costs of producing goods and services not including opportunity costs.
    c. the costs of producing goods and services including opportunity costs.
    d. labor costs.

6. The economic costs of painting your own house are equal to
    a. the costs of paint and equipment used to complete the work.
    b. the value of your hourly wages at your "regular job."
    c. the costs of paint, equipment, and the value of the next best use of your time.
    d. the value of the next best use of your time.

7. Which of the following options is not an example of an economic problem?
    a. choosing between going to Hawaii and Mexico during spring break
    b. the government's decision to fund a school lunch program
    c. determining the balance in your checkbook
    d. choosing to go to work instead of going to the movies

8. Which of the following options is not an example of an opportunity cost?
    a. the value of foregone wages while you attend college
    b. the value of your leisure time when you are at work

c. the cost of a movie ticket
   d. the wages that could be earned working for another firm

9. Economists define capital as
   a. factories.
   b. factories, buildings, and machinery.
   c. factories and buildings.
   d. factories, machinery, and labor.

10. The consumer's economic problem is
    a. to maximize their income.
    b. to maximize their level of satisfaction given their scarce resources.
    c. to maximize their level of satisfaction.
    d. to maximize the monetary value of goods they purchase.

SHORT ANSWER QUESTIONS

Fill in the blanks in the following statements.

1. Every economic problem has a three-part structure that consists of _____, _____, and _____.

2. _____ costs refer to the value of the next best alternative.

3. Opportunity costs are the result of the _____ of economic decisions.

4. Economics is the study of the allocation of _____ through the process of _____.

5. Land, _____, capital and _____ are the factors of production.

PROBLEMS

1. Suppose that your college tuition is $4500 per year, books and school supplies cost $1000 per year and that you paid an additional $7200 for room and board in the dormitory. Assume you earn $5200 per year at a part-time job during the calendar year when you attend college and $15,800 per year if you did not attend college. What is the true economic cost of attending college?

2. While water is a scarce resource in the western United States, farmers often select growing techniques that require large amounts of water. What is a possible explanation for why farmers choose water intensive technologies?

3. President Clinton's National Service program for students will pay a portion of the costs of attending school and a small stipend in return for two years of community service. What are the opportunity costs for students enrolled in the program? What are the opportunity costs for the federal government?

4. Explain how the purchase and sale of goods and services can simultaneously benefit both consumers and producers.

5. Suppose the cost of hiring a contractor to build a fence around your yard is $1100 including materials and labor. Your father proposes that you both take off three days of work to save him some money. Assume that you can purchase the materials for $450 and that you normally earn $50 per day and he earns $200 per day. In this example, is your father making the best economic decision? Why or why not?

6. Explain how an individual's decision to save income affects the consumer's economic problem.

7. Economists assume that profit is the predominant goal of American business, describe additional objectives of firms.

8. Describe the opportunity costs that are ignored by individual commuters when they decide not to carpool.

9. Identify the elements of the economic problem when you decide to go to a party with your friends rather than study for an economics exam.

10. Most people would like to live in a cleaner environment. What are some of the opportunity costs of decreasing pollution in an advanced economy like the U.S.?

POST-TEST

Answer the following questions to determine how well you have learned the material in the chapter and to determine those areas where you need to focus your studies.

1. Explain why the principles of interdependence and opportunity costs follow directly from the structure of the economic problem.

2. Explain why each of the following *is or is not* an example of an economic problem.
    1. The House and Senate's decision to cut education spending to decrease the federal deficit
    2. The choice between attending a low-cost state university versus an expensive private school
    3. Preparing for an exam when your time is unlimited

3. Explain the opportunity costs of the following economic decisions:
    1. Changing your own flat tire on the highway
    2. Ordering a hamburger at a fast-food outlet
    3. Buying a new sweater instead of a book for school

4. Use examples to describe how the government is both a producer and a consumer of goods and services.

5. Suppose you live in San Francisco and attend school in Washington D.C. The round trip airfare is $500 but you have been offered a "free ride" across country with a friend. The car trip will cost you $100 for your share of the motel expenses and your friend will pay for the gas. Explain your economic problem and the circumstances that may lead you to choose to skip the "free ride."

6. Explain whether or not the following individuals meet the criteria to be labeled entrepreneurs.
    1. College professors
    2. An owner of a new fast-food restaurant specializing in low fat, healthy foods
    3. The manager of a large corporate marketing department

7. Explain why an economic problem does not exist if scarcity does not exist.

8. How will the Law of Scarcity affect your decision to attend summer school next year?

9. A doctor has to decide whether or not to hire a physician's assistant. If the physician's assistant is hired the doctor will be able to see 10 additional patients a day who on average pay $50 per visit. Use economic principles to explain why the doctor will hire the assistant if the pay is less than $2500 per week (assume there are no additional costs of treating 10 additional patients).

10. Explain why entrepreneurs may be overstating firm profits if they do not pay themselves salaries.

Chapter 2
Solving The Economic Problem

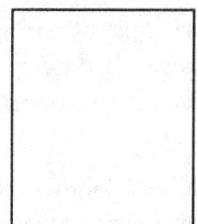

LEARNING OBJECTIVES

CONCEPTS TO LEARN

Process equity: Equality of opportunity	The margin in economic analysis
End-results equity: Horizontal equity	Positive and normative economics
An economic model	Microeconomics and macroeconomics

CONCEPTS TO RECALL

The economic problem	Opportunity cost
Interdependence	Scarcity

CHAPTER REVIEW

Chapter 2 focuses on the properties that characterize the best possible solution to the economic problem, the use of models in economic analysis, normative versus positive analysis, and the difference between microeconomics and macroeconomics. Efficiency and equity are the two criteria used by economists to judge solutions to economic problems. The efficiency criterion means that individuals make the best possible choice to meet their objectives and the equity criterion focuses on fairness. The second section of the chapter describes how models are used in economic analysis. Models are used by economists to study the effects of an individual variable on an economic event. The third section includes a discussion of the distinction between normative and positive economics, and finally, the fourth section focuses on the difference between micro- and macroeconomics. All of these concepts will be used throughout the book.

1. Efficiency implies that the best possible choice for an economic problem will be selected. If there is only one objective, efficiency will result in an outcome as close to the objective as possible. When there's no natural limit, then efficiency means maximizing the objective. When there is more than one objective, the Law of Substitution holds: a solution is efficient if moving closer to one objective requires moving away from the other objective.

2. Equity is a standard used to judge both the end results and the process of an economic problem. End-results equity is a measure of the fairness of economic outcomes. Process equity is a measure of whether or not the rules under which the economy operates are fair.

3. Economists generally agree that the principle of horizontal equity, the equal treatment of equals should be a criteria for end-results equity. Economic policies and events will have winners and losers. End-results equity measures the relative benefits and costs of those who gain and those who lose.

4. Process equity is accepted by almost all economists. This principle requires that individuals have equal access to whatever economic opportunities that they are willing and able to pursue.

5. True equality of opportunity is likely to result in horizontal equity.

6. Economic models are used to analyze and discover the cause and effects of economic variables on real world economic events. One economic variable is changed at a time while holding all other variables constant in order to isolate its effects on the model.

7. Marginal analysis is used to study the effects of small changes in an economic variable. It is important to analyze effects on the margin in order to solve for efficient economic solutions.

8. Normative economics is based on value judgments made by individuals. There are no right or wrong normative judgments and they cannot be proved or disproved.

9. Positive analysis is based on factual information and is used to describe how the actual conditions of exchange determine economic outcomes. Real world data can be used to support or negate a positive economic statement.

10. Microeconomics is the study of individual consumers, business firms, and government. Microeconomists study the incentives for exchange and the outcomes.

11. Macroeconomists study the economy as a whole and focus on the overall level of economic activity. Full employment, price stability, long-run economic growth, and stability in international economic relations are the four objectives used to judge the performance of the overall economy.

A FEW HELPFUL TIPS

While most of the text will focus on positive economics, it is important not to lose sight of equity issues. You will need to develop your own conclusions regarding equity issues raised by the economic models you are learning. Remember, you can produce evidence to support or negate a positive economic statement but, there is no right or wrong normative criteria. You need to develop your own normative criteria as you progress in your studies of economics. A more mundane concern for the beginning economics student is learning marginal analysis. It's an important concept that is used repeatedly by economists. Remember, isolate one variable at a time, and then evaluate how an incremental change in that variable will affect your economic model. A common error among beginning students is to change a number of variables all at once and then it is impossible to analyze the effects of any individual variable. Also, while the definition of macro- and microeconomics is pretty straightforward, the line is often a bit hazy. There are a number of economic problems that will straddle that line.

QUICK STUDY GUIDE

	T/F	Mult. Choice	Short Answer	Problems
Equity	2, 4, 10		1, 5	1, 2, 3, 7, 8, 10
Positive vs. Normative Economics		9		6
Economic Efficiency	10		2	3, 9, 10
Microeconomics vs. Macroeconomics	9	1, 8, 10	4	5

PRETEST

Answer the following questions to test your initial understanding of the material in this chapter:

1. Read the following statements and determine if they meet the standards of horizontal equity.
   a. A flat tax rate on all individuals regardless of their income level
   b. Allowing the same amount of time to take an exam for all students
   c. Allowing students with reading disabilities additional time to take an exam

2. Affirmative action hiring programs are intended to open up doors for women and minorities that have been closed due to discrimination. How would you judge affirmative action programs based on process and end-result equity criteria?

3. Explain the equity issues raised by the following examples.
   a. Allowing all students an additional fifteen minutes to complete an exam
   b. Discounts for senior citizens at a local restaurant
   c. Tax breaks for homeowners

4. Suppose you are managing a small yogurt shop. You currently hire three employees, two wait on customers and the third prepares inventory, cost, and sales information. A new computer software package that costs $3000 will prepare and summarize all of this data as the clerks enter their sales into the computer/cash register. If all three employees are paid $1000 per month how should you decide whether or not to continue hiring three employees or buy the new software?

5. State whether the following are microeconomic or macroeconomic issues.
   a. Farm labor wage rates
   b. U.S. unemployment rates
   c. Local property taxes

6. State whether the following are normative or positive economic statements.
   a. Poverty rates in the U.S. are too high
   b. One in five children in the U.S. are living below the official poverty line
   c. Long-term interest rates are too low

7. How does the Law of Substitution apply to replacing bank tellers with Automated Teller machines?

8. Suppose the government proposes a new tax plan that will redistribute income from the richest 5% of the people to those in lower income groups but will also result in some inefficiencies in the economy. What economic argument can be used to support the new tax plan in light of the resulting inefficiencies?

9. The Food Stamp program issues coupons to low income individuals that can be exchanged for food at authorized retail outlets. An alternative proposal is to pay individuals a cash supplement equal to the value of the food coupons. Evaluate both methods of supplementing low income individuals' food consumption using the principle of consumer sovereignty.

10. In the U.S., individual income tax rates rise as taxable income rises. Does the U.S. income tax policy violate horizontal equity criteria?

TRUE/FALSE PRACTICE QUESTIONS

1. The principle that individuals are best able to judge their own self-interests is Consumer Sovereignty.   T   F
2. Horizontal equity requires equal treatment of unequals.   T   F
3. Full employment occurs when all individuals are employed.   T   F
4. Process equity occurs when the final economic outcomes are fair.   T   F
5. Full employment has not been a major policy goal in the U.S.   T   F
6. Price stability has not been a major policy goal in the U.S.   T   F
7. An individual without a job who is not looking for work is not unemployed.   T   F
8. A stable dollar refers to the relative prices of goods and services within the domestic economy.   T   F
9. An analysis of the effects of a gas tax on carpooling is an example of a microeconomic model.   T   F
10. Economic outcomes can NOT be both efficient and equitable at the same time.   T   F

MULTIPLE CHOICE QUESTIONS

Choose the best option for the following questions.

1. An analysis on the effects of a reduction in interest rates on the long-term growth rates in the economy is an example of a
   a. microeconomics model.
   b. macroeconomics model.
   c. normative model.
   d. process equity model.

2. The Humphrey-Hawkins Act of 1978 requires
   a. horizontal equity in all federal programs.
   b. consumer sovereignty.
   c. federal policies to promote maximum employment, growth, and purchasing power.
   d. equality of opportunity.

3. Full employment occurs when
   a. everybody has a job.
   b. the unemployment rate is below 5%.
   c. the unemployment rate is below 3%.
   d. all people who want to work have a job.

4. A model analyzing the effects of federal subsidies paid to the tobacco industry is an example of a
   a. microeconomics study.
   b. macroeconomics study.
   c. normative study.
   d. a process equity model.

5. Isolating the effects of increasing tax rates on the growth in tax revenues is an example of
   a. end-results equity.
   b. marginal analysis.
   c. consumer sovereignty.
   d. horizontal equity.

6. Price inflation occurs when
   a. the value of the dollar increases relative to foreign currencies.
   b. there is a persistent increase in the prices of most goods and services.
   c. there is a persistent increase in the prices of only a small number of goods and services.
   d. the cost of living continues to fall.

7. The value of a nation's imports to exports relative to other countries is the
   a. margin rate.
   b. consumer sovereignty problem.
   c. balance of trade.
   d. exchange rate.

8. A study reporting that unemployment rates for African Americans under the age of 25 are equal to 40% is an example of
   a. macroeconomics.

b. normative economics.
   c. positive economics.
   d. the law of substitution.

9. A U.S. Senator's comment that the unemployment rate for African Americans is too high is an example of
   a. normative economics.
   b. positive economics.
   c. marginal analysis.
   d. process equity.

10. The study of long-run economic growth of the economy is an example of a
    a. microeconomic problem.
    b. macroeconomic problem.
    c. normative problem.
    d. process equity problem.

SHORT ANSWER QUESTIONS

Fill in the blanks in the following statements.

1. Horizontal equity is a principle of _____ which requires that _____ be treated equally.

2. Efficiency means that the Law of _____ holds: moving _____ to one objective means moving farther away from at least one other objective.

3. _____ is the principle that individuals are best able to judge their _____ interests.

4. _____ is the study of individual economic agents and exchanges between them.

5. End-results equity is a criterion for judging whether _____ are fair while process equity judges whether the _____ of the economy are fair.

PROBLEMS

1. President Clinton initially proposed a broad based BTU (British Thermal Unit) tax based on the energy used in the production of all goods and services. Later he compromised with Congress to replace it with a tax on gasoline. Discuss the horizontal equity issues of both tax proposals.

2. Presidents Clinton, Bush, and Reagan have argued in favor of lowering taxes on capital gains for long-term investments, (the difference between the purchase and sales price of an investment), to spur economic growth. Assuming that the tax break will spur economic growth, what are the possible equity trade-offs of the policy change?

3. In the past, large numbers of residents of the U.S. have had no health care insurance. What kinds of efficiency and equity arguments can you make to support universal health coverage?

4. Explain why some people may still not have jobs when the economy is at full employment.

5. Which of the following are examples of microeconomic and which are examples of macroeconomic topics?
   a. Determining the effect of floods in the Midwest on wheat prices
   b. The growth rate of the Vietnamese economy
   c. Unemployment rates in Eastern Europe

6. Label the normative and positive economic examples on the following list.
   a. Interest rates are too high
   b. Unemployment rates have been reduced by 2% in the last quarter of the year
   c. Inflation is not as important of a problem as high unemployment

7. California property tax rates are based on property values frozen at 1979 levels. However when a property is sold it is reassessed at a value equal to the sales price. Owners of identical homes often pay substantially different property taxes (i.e. one neighbor may pay $5000 per year and another who has lived in the home for twenty years may only pay $1000). What are the equity issues surrounding the California property tax policy?

8. Suppose Congress proposes to tax earned income (income obtained from working) at a lower rate than other types of income. What are the equity issues of such a tax proposal?

9. How does efficiency criteria change when you evaluate a single objective versus multiple objectives?

10. Why might the majority of people be in favor of a proposal that redistributes income from the wealthy to the poor even in the case when economic inefficiencies occur?

POST-TEST

Answer the following questions to determine how well you have learned the material in the chapter and to determine those areas where you need to focus your studies.

1. What is the difference between full employment and zero unemployment?

2. Explain how the Law of Substitution is a test of efficiency.

3. Describe some of the limitations of only using an efficiency criterion when evaluating an economic problem.

4. Which of the following are examples of normative economics and which are examples of positive economics?
   a. Taxes on cigarettes are too low
   b. The annual growth rate was 3% last year
   c. The percentage of wealth owned by the top 1% grew in the 1980s

5. Which of the following are microeconomic examples and which are macroeconomic examples?
   a. A study on the high unemployment of teenagers
   b. A study evaluating the effects of lowering the income tax rate on economic growth
   c. An analysis of the effects of child care subsidies on the employment rates of welfare parents

6. Why is horizontal equity a necessary condition for end-result equity?

7. Explain why equality of opportunity and unequal outcomes are not inconsistent ideas.

8. Describe three examples of government policies that interfere with the principle of consumer sovereignty.

9. Explain why each of the following examples *does or does not* violate the principle of horizontal equity.
    a. Discount tickets for movie matinees
    b. Flat income tax rates regardless of income levels
    c. Charging "in-state" students a lower tuition rate than "out-of-state" students

10. Describe the two dimensions of equity, end-results and process equity.

Chapter 3
Society's Economic Problem

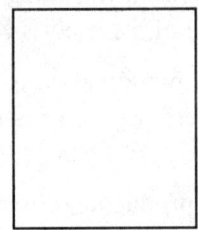

LEARNING OBJECTIVES

CONCEPTS TO LEARN

Society's economic problem	The four fundamental economic questions
The production possibilities frontier	Long-run economic growth
The elements of an economic system	Pure market capitalism
	Centrally planned socialism

CONCEPTS TO RECALL

The economic problem	Efficiency
Opportunity cost	Equity
Interdependence	

CHAPTER REVIEW

Chapter 2 describes society's economic problem and focuses on the difficult choices made to solve their economic problem. Societies face a standard economic problem of working towards achieving a set of objectives given a number of alternatives and constraints. Assuming a society's objectives are to maximize efficiency and equity the fundamental questions are: What? How? For Whom? and Now vs. the Future? The economic choices faced by a society can then be examined using a simple model called a production possibilities frontier. Finally, the chapter includes an examination of the differences between centrally planned and market based economic systems.

1. The economic objectives of a humanistic society are efficiency and equity.

2. Society's economic alternatives can be expressed by the following four fundamental economic questions:
   a. The What or Output question: What goods and services should a society produce and in what amounts?
   b. The How or Input question: How should firms produce goods and services?
   c. The For Whom or Distribution question: Who receives the goods and services?
   d. The Now versus the Future question

3. The quantity and quality of a nation's resources along with available production technologies are constraints that determine the outcome of a society's economic problem.

4. A production possibilities frontier is a two-dimensional diagram that shows the combinations of goods and services that is potentially efficient to produce given a limited amount of resources and available technology.

5. A society can not produce beyond its production possibilities frontier; and if it is producing at a point in the interior of the frontier it is operating inefficiently.

6. The shape of the production possibilities frontier demonstrates the opportunity costs of producing more of a particular good or service. These opportunity costs mean that increases in the production of one good will require a decrease in the production of other goods.

7. Long-run economic growth will increase the production of goods and services in an economy that can graphically be represented by the production possibilities frontier shifting outward away from the origin.

8. An increase in the quality or quantity of a nation's resources or a technology change can lead to growth.

9. Investments in physical and human capital (education and training) are the keys to economic growth. New capital tends to make the factors of production more productive and new technologies are usually linked to the new capital.

10. The opportunity cost of economic growth is the value of the foregone consumption that is necessary to increase investment.

11. Four principal characteristics of an economic system that determine economic performance are: the delegation of decision making authority; the methods for processing and coordinating economic information; the ownership of capital and land; the incentives used to encourage consumers and producers to pursue society's objectives.

12. Real world economies lie somewhere on the theoretical spectrum between a pure market capitalist and a centrally planned socialist system.

13. Pure market capitalist systems decentralize economic decisions to individual consumers and firms, use a market price system to process and coordinate economic information, allow private

ownership of land and capital, and rely on material incentives. Individual freedom, responsiveness to consumer's desires, and efficiency in the allocation of scarce resources are the principal strengths of a capitalist system.

14. Centrally planned socialist systems centralize decision making authority, use a national plan to process and coordinate economic information, have public ownership of capital and land, and rely on both moral and material incentives. Principal strengths include the ability to formulate and pursue national objectives, a fairly equal income distribution, and a full employment guarantee.

A FEW HELPFUL TIPS

Don't get in the trap of labeling a system based on only a part of the story. It is important to remember that pure market capitalism and pure centrally planned socialism are theoretical models of how an economy can be structured. There are no real world examples of either of these economic systems. While the U.S. is closer to pure market capitalism there are some elements of the American economy that are consistent with a socialist system. Also, just because equity concerns are based on normative criteria it does not mean that they should be ignored or are unimportant to economists. The four fundamental economic questions incorporate both efficiency and equity objectives.

	QUICK STUDY GUIDE			
	T/F	Mult. Choice	Short Answer	Problems
Four Fundamental Questions		1	1	
Production Possibilities Frontier	9, 10	2, 3, 8	2, 4, 5	2, 3, 7, 8, 9
Economic Growth	6	6		5
Capitalism vs. Socialism	1, 7, 8	4		4, 6

PRETEST

Answer the following questions to test your initial understanding of the material in this chapter:

1. What are the four fundamental economic questions that every society must answer?
2. What are the differences and similarities between a pure market capitalist and centrally planned socialist economy's approach to the four fundamental economic questions?
3. What is the income distribution problem?
4. What is the efficiency dimension of the income distribution problem?
5. Use a production possibilities frontier to describe the U.S. government's decision to cut back defense expenditures in the 1990's.
6. Use a production possibilities frontier to show what happened to wheat and corn production in the Midwest during the devastating floods in the summer of 1993.

7. Explain the effects of a nationwide education program on the nation's output using a production possibilities frontier.
8. What are the characteristics of an economy based on pure market capitalism?
9. What are the characteristics of an economy based on a centrally planned socialist system?
10. How will reductions in current consumption levels affect long-term growth in an economy?

TRUE/FALSE PRACTICE QUESTIONS

1. Land and capital are owned by the private sector in a centrally planned socialist system. T F
2. The market value of knowledge and skills is defined as human capital. T F
3. The percentage of the population that joins the labor force is the employment rate. T F
4. A stock variable is one that can be measured over time. T F
5. Labor productivity is the amount of output produced per worker. T F
6. Increases in current consumption and long-term economic growth are inversely related. T F
7. Both moral and material incentives are used in a centrally planned socialist system. T F
8. Only material incentives are used in a pure market capitalist system. T F
9. An increase in labor productivity will NOT affect a production possibilities frontier. T F
10. A decrease in natural resources can be shown by a movement along a production possibilities frontier. T F

MULTIPLE CHOICE QUESTIONS

Choose the best option for the following questions.

1. Which of the following is NOT one of the four fundamental economic questions for a society?
   a. how or input question
   b. for whom or distribution question
   c. what or output question
   d. capitalism versus socialism

2. An increase in labor productivity throughout an economy will
   a. cause the production possibilities frontier curve to shift inward.
   b. cause the production possibilities frontier curve to shift outward.
   c. cause a movement along a production possibilities frontier.
   d. not result in any changes to the production possibilities frontier.

3. An outward shift of the production possibilities curve could be caused by all of the following options EXCEPT
   a. a new technology.
   b. immigration.
   c. shifting production from one sector to another.
   d. educational investments.

4. Property rights in a pure centrally planned economic system are held by
   a. private individuals.
   b. government and private individuals.
   c. government.
   d. corporations.

5. Human capital investments will result in
   a. an outward shift of a nation's production possibilities frontier.
   b. a movement along a nation's production possibilities frontier.
   c. an inward shift of a nation's production possibilities frontier.
   d. no change in the production possibilities frontier.

6. A reduction in current consumption levels will
   a. lead to a decrease in growth and future production levels.
   b. lead to an increase in growth and future production levels.
   c. not have an impact on growth or future production levels.
   d. mean less investment in the economy.

7. In the U.S. the ultimate answer to the output question is made primarily by
   a. government.
   b. a central planning committee comprised of business and government leaders.
   c. consumers.
   d. producers.

8. A bowed out production possibilities frontier represents
   a. opportunity costs.
   b. distribution of the goods and services.
   c. economic efficiency.
   d. flow variables.

9. Capital in an economy is
   a. an example of a flow variable.
   b. the available land in an economy.
   c. an example of a stock variable.
   d. constant over time.

10. Moral incentives encourage behavior in society by means of
    a. market forces.
    b. governmental legal sanctions.
    c. personal social responsibility.
    d. the market economy.

SHORT ANSWER QUESTIONS

Fill in the blanks in the following statements.

1. Increasing opportunity costs along a _____ frontier means that producing more of one output requires _____ the production of another good.

2. A(n) _____ shift of the production possibilities frontier implies that more _____ can be produced in an economy.

3. The economic objectives of a humanistic society are _____ and _____.

4. An economy operating inside its production possibilities _____ is operating _____.

5. Investments in human _____ will cause the production possibilities frontier to shift _____.

PROBLEMS

1. President Clinton's Secretary of Labor Robert Reich is a proponent of increasing federal expenditures for training and education. Use a production possibilities frontier to explain the effects on output in the economy.

2. Draw a production possibilities frontier for bagels and muffins. Answer the following questions about the production possibilities frontier.
    a. Draw a point representing an output level that is unobtainable.
    b. Draw a point representing an output level that is inefficient.
    c. Explain the opportunity cost of shifting output from bagels to muffins using the graph.
    d. Suppose output was initially at a point on the frontier. Explain how the economy could move to an unobtainable point.

3. In the 1980's the federal government increased defense spending and in the 1990's defense expenditures have been cut. Use the production possibilities frontier to explain the opportunity cost of the defense increases in the eighties and the cuts in the nineties.

4. How might the answer to the distribution question differ in a pure market capitalist vs. a centrally planned socialist country?

5. What trade-offs exist between current consumption and economic growth?

6. What are some of the obstacles that the Eastern European countries are likely to encounter as they move towards an economic system based on market capitalism?

7. Economists have generally viewed immigration as a significant factor in the growth of the U.S. economy. Explain using the production possibilities frontier how output levels are affected by immigration.

8. Many economists credit the "GI Bill" (a program that paid veterans' college expenses) for the sustained economic growth in the U.S. after World War II. Use the production possibilities frontier to explain how the program may have increased economic growth today.

9. Why is the opportunity cost of increasing production zero if the economy is operating inside its production possibilities frontier?

10. Savings rates are much higher in Japan than in the U.S. How would you expect this difference in saving rates to affect long-term growth rates in the two economies?

POST-TEST

Answer the following questions to determine how well you have learned the material in the chapter and to determine those areas where you need to focus your studies.

1. Describe the equity and efficiency issues that are raised by the four fundamental economic questions.
2. How will long-term growth change if current consumption rates increase?
3. Use a production possibilities frontier to describe the effects of the war in the former Yugoslavian Republic on the economies of Serbia, Bosnia and Croatia.
4. During the 1980's the Reagan/Bush administrations and Congress increased defense spending and decreased domestic spending. Use a production possibilities frontier to demonstrate the opportunity cost of the defense spending increases.
5. How might a country increase the amount of health care services without incurring any opportunity costs?
6. Suppose an economy is on its production possibilities frontier and wants to increase the quantity of education. Describe both the short and long run effects using a production possibilities frontier to support your answer.
7. Describe the principal strengths of a pure market capitalist system.
8. Describe the principal strengths of a centrally planned socialist system.
9. What is the opportunity cost of increasing investment to increase economic growth rates?

Chapter 4
Markets, Prices, and the Economy

LEARNING OBJECTIVES

CONCEPTS TO LEARN

A market	The economic function of prices
The principle of comparative advantage	The circular flow of economic activity
Highlights of the U.S. economy	

CONCEPTS TO RECALL

Characteristics of pure market capitalism	Economic exchange
Interdependence	

CHAPTER REVIEW

Chapter 4 examines how markets operate in highly developed economies. Specialization in production, the circular flow of economic activity, and the size and diversity of modern market economies are the three characteristics of highly developed economies that use a pricing mechanism. The overview presented in this chapter will prepare you to go on and study the specifics of how market based economies function in the remainder of the book. The chapter also includes a discussion of the major economic and demographic changes in the U.S. economy since 1950.

1. Markets are institutional arrangements that allow buyers and sellers to voluntarily exchange goods and services and factors of production.

2. Markets have distinct product and geographic dimensions and occur in a wide variety of institutional settings. Economists define markets by product or factors of production. Transactions costs of a market exchange determine the geographic dimensions of a market.

3. Economic growth and the division of labor go hand in hand. Labor becomes increasingly specialized as an economy grows to take advantage of economies of scale, lower production costs per unit as output expands.

4. Money is used to ease market exchanges in an economy with a high degree of specialization and economic growth. In the absence of money all exchanges would be by barter.

5. Countries benefit from international trade and specialization due to the law of comparative advantage. Ricardo's law of comparative advantage is based on differences in the opportunity costs of production. It is always in a country's best interest for countries to specialize in the areas where they have a comparative advantage in production and trade for products where they have a comparative disadvantage.

6. All markets are interrelated due to the circular flow of the economy. Individuals buy consumer products and sell their labor to firms in factor markets. Firms sell goods and services and then also must buy labor from individuals. Hence, the circular flow of the economy which also includes government as both consumer and producer. Exports and imports are the only exceptions to the circular flow in the economy.

7. Prices are used to coordinate millions of market exchanges in diverse modern market economies.

8. Households, business, government, and the foreign sectors are the four main subsectors of the economy.

A FEW HELPFUL TIPS

Don't forget that economic transactions are all linked to each other given the circular flow of the economy. Money is just the conduit that enables large numbers of transactions in an advanced economy. When money transfers from households to government it does not disappear. The government then uses the money to buy goods and services from businesses and individuals. Likewise, money can be used to speed transactions between individuals and firms. When the money passes hands from individuals to firms it reenters the system when firms purchase inputs. Money has no intrinsic value it is used as a means of exchange in market transactions.

Markets, Prices, and the Economy

QUICK STUDY GUIDE				
	T/F	Mult. Choice	Short Answer	Problems
Circular Flow	8	6	1, 5	
Comparative Advantage	5	1		1
The U.S. Economy	1	7, 8, 9, 10		6, 7, 8, 9
Markets	4, 6	5		4

PRETEST

Answer the following questions to test your initial understanding of the material in this chapter:

1. Describe four methods of defining a market.

2. Explain how the division of labor can result in economies of scale.

3. Suppose one country is very efficient with respect to producing computer hardware and another country is relatively more efficient at producing computer software. What economic law explains why they should specialize in production and trade?

4. Draw a circular flow of the U.S. economy that shows the flow of goods and services in the economy.

5. Describe the two economic roles for household members in the circular flow of the economy.

6. Describe the two economic roles for firms in the circular flow of the economy.

7. Suppose you decided to become a self-employed economic consultant after completing your education. Why might you decide to organize your business as a corporation rather than a single proprietorship? What are the advantages and disadvantages of the two firm structures?

8. Describe some of the most important economic and demographic changes in the U.S. since 1950.

9. What evidence exists to support the statement that whites fare much better economically in the U.S. than African Americans?

10. How have the work experiences of women changed since 1950?

TRUE/FALSE PRACTICE QUESTIONS

1. A grand piano is an example of a durable good. T F
2. The process of specialization is called the division of labor. T F
3. Producing smaller quantities at a lower cost is an example of economies of scale. T F
4. Barter arrangements are exchanges that occur without money regardless of the size of the transaction. T F

5. The law of comparative advantage is an argument for trade restrictions between countries.   T   F

6. The total dollar value of the flow of activity in product markets is equal to the national product.   T   F

7. A disadvantage of the corporate structure is double taxation by the government.   T   F

8. The government is not part of the circular flow of the economy.   T   F

9. Interest payments on the national debt are transfer payments.   T   F

10. In 1990, women on average earned two-thirds as much as men.   T   F

MULTIPLE CHOICE QUESTIONS

Choose the best option for the following questions.

1. The law of comparative advantage implies that a country should specialize in the production of those goods with
   a. lower opportunity costs and trade for other goods produced by countries with higher opportunity costs.
   b. higher opportunity costs and trade for other goods produced by countries with higher opportunity costs.
   c. lower opportunity costs and trade for other goods produced by countries with lower opportunity costs.
   d. higher opportunity costs and trade for other goods produced by countries with lower opportunity costs.

2. A budget deficit is the
   a. total amount of money the government owes.
   b. a positive difference between tax revenues and government expenditures.
   c. situation when a government's revenues exceed its expenditures.
   d. the difference between imports and exports.

3. Which of the following is NOT an example of a consumer durable?
   a. a computer
   b. a corned beef sandwich
   c. a car
   d. a CD player

4. Which of the following is NOT a characteristic of a corporation?
   a. a legal entity that is distinct from the owners of the firm
   b. it allows owners to transfer shares of stock
   c. single taxation advantages
   d. limited liability for business losses

5. The division of labor is profitable because it
   a. increases the circular flow.

b. generates economies of scale.
   c. leads to lower unionization rates.
   d. keeps wages low.

6. Exceptions to the circular flow of the economy are
   a. imports and exports.
   b. government expenditures.
   c. taxes.
   d. transfer payments.

7. The most common type of firm in the U.S. is the
   a. corporation.
   b. partnership.
   c. single proprietorship.
   d. limited partnership.

8. Which of the following industries accounts for the largest percentage of total output in the U.S.?
   a. finance, insurance, real estate
   b. services
   c. manufacturing
   d. government

9. The majority of purchasers of the final output of the U.S. are
   a. consumers.
   b. government agencies.
   c. firms.
   d. the foreign sector.

10. The U.S. is the world's largest exporter of
    a. petroleum and petroleum products.
    b. perfume and cosmetics.
    c. agricultural products.
    d. consumer electronics.

SHORT ANSWER QUESTIONS

Fill in the blanks in the following statements.

1. National income is the total dollar value of the flow of economic activity through _____ markets and _____ is the flow through product markets.

2. _____ are goods that typically last less than one year.

3. A budget surplus occurs when _____ exceed _____.

4. _____ occur when costs rise proportionately less than output as production _____.

5. Individuals have dual roles as _____ of final goods and services and suppliers of _____ of production to business firms.

PROBLEMS

1. Suppose you and your friend are alone on a tropical island in the middle of the Pacific Ocean. The only products you can produce on the island are fish and carved coconuts. You can catch 8 fish in a day or carve 5 coconuts and your friend can only catch 5 fish in a day but can carve 12 coconuts. Use the law of comparative advantage to explain how you could both be better off by trade.

2. Suppose that the family incomes for the individuals living in your dorm suite are as follows:
   Family A $85,000
   Family B $35,000
   Family C $22,000
   Family D $65,000
   Family E $120,000

   What is the median income of the families? How does the median income compare to the average income level?

3. List four examples of durable goods and four examples of non-durable goods.

4. What are the three characteristics of a modern economy that place special burdens on prices?

5. Describe a modern day example of a case where the specialization of labor leads to economies of scale and greater economic growth.

6. What are the major revenue sources for federal, state, and local governments?

7. What types of transfer payments are made by the U.S. government?

8. President Clinton's 1993 budget bill called for an approximate $500 billion in deficit reduction. Why won't the federal debt decline as a result of the bill?

9. What evidence exists to support the allegation that women have suffered from labor market discrimination?

10. What are the five principles of the corporate structure?

POST-TEST

Answer the following questions to determine how well you have learned the material in the chapter and to determine those areas where you need to focus your studies.

1. What are the advantages and disadvantages of a corporation over a single proprietorship?

2. Define the national debt and national deficit and explain how the deficit could fall while the debt continues to rise.

3. Which were the leading growth sectors in the U.S. economy between 1950 and 1990?

4. Label each of the following either a durable or non-durable good.
   a. a swimming pool
   b. computer dating services
   c. a Prince concert

d. tickets to Steven Spielberg's latest movie
   e. a big screen TV

5. Describe the role of government in the circular flow of the economy.

6. What is the median per capita income of the following 5 countries?
   Country A $39,000
   Country B $18,000
   Country C $2,100
   Country D $11,000
   Country E $1,500

7. Women have increasingly entered the labor force since 1950 but their wages still lag behind men. What evidence is there of a wage gap and what is a possible explanation for the difference?

8. Suppose the U.S. has a comparative advantage in agricultural production over Mexico. Why might it still be in both countries' best interest for Americans to trade manufactured goods for agricultural products produced in Mexico?

9. What is the difference between national income and national product?

10. Describe the three types of government transfer payments.

Chapter 5
The Laws of Supply and Demand

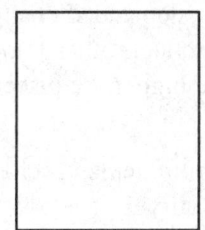

LEARNING OBJECTIVES

CONCEPTS TO LEARN

The Laws of Supply and Demand	Factors that shift the demand and supply curves
Market equilibrium	The elasticity of demand and supply

CONCEPTS TO RECALL

The consumer's and the firm's three-part economic problems	The margin in economic analysis
Opportunity cost	A market

CHAPTER REVIEW

Chapter 5 focuses on the Laws of Supply and Demand. An understanding of the Laws of Supply and Demand is essential in order to proceed with economic analysis. Regarding Demand, economists assume that consumers want to achieve the greatest possible utility among competing alternative choices of goods and services given their limited incomes. The Law of Demand says that price and quantity demanded are inversely related, other things being equal; the lower the price the greater the quantity demanded. Market demand curves are downward sloping. Regarding supply, firms maximize their profits by producing the output at which price equals the marginal costs of production. Since marginal costs increase as output increases, the Law of Supply says that price and quantity supplied are directly related, other things equal; the higher the price the greater the quantity supplied. Market supply curves are upward sloping. Other factors that affect market supply are the prices of other products supplied by the firm, production technologies, factor prices, and taxes. Chapter 5 explores the role of supply and demand in determining price and output in the market. A stable equilibrium price and quantity is reached at the intersection of the market demand and supply curves. Shifts in demand and/or supply change the equilibrium. The demand and supply curves shift when one of the "other things" affecting demand or supply changes, such as income (demand shifter) or input prices (supply shifter). The final section of Chapter 5 discusses the elasticity of demand and supply. Elasticity is a measure of the responsiveness of the quantity demanded or the quantity supplied to a change in price.

1. Quantity demanded is the amount of a product that consumers are willing to buy at a given price over a specific time period.

2. Demand schedules show how quantity demanded changes as price changes. Quantity demanded is inversely related to the price of the product, other things equal. Demand schedules and demand curves obey the Law of Demand: the higher the price the lower the quantity demanded, and vice versa.

3. Demand Curves are graphs derived from demand schedules that show how the quantity demanded declines as prices increase. Demand curves generally have a negative slope. Always measure quantity on the x-axis and price on the y-axis and remember that demand curves slope downward.

4. The substitution and income effects of a price change explain the Law of Demand. The substitution effect is a relative price effect. When the price of a good falls, that good is now cheaper relative to all other goods. The substitution effect says that consumers tend to substitute in favor of goods that have become relatively cheaper. The income effect is a purchasing power or real income effect. When the price of a good falls, consumers now have more purchasing power. They tend to buy more of all normal goods, including the good whose price has fallen. Therefore, when the price of a good falls, other things equal, both the substitution and income effects tend to increase the quantity demanded.

5. Market demand schedules are the summation of individual demand schedules and market demand curves are the horizontal summation of individual demand curves.

6. Movements along a demand curve reflect changes in the price of the good, other things equal.

7. Shifts in demand curves reflect non-price changes in the marketplace. Changes in income, population, tastes, and the prices of substitute and complement goods are principal factors that can cause shifts in demand curves.

8. The quantity of a good supplied is determined by the price of the product, the prices of other products supplied by the firm, production technologies, factor prices, and taxes.

9. Supply schedule shows the quantity supplied as prices change. A supply curve is a graph of a supply schedule.

10. To maximize their profits, firms produce the output at which marginal cost, the additional cost of producing one more unit, equals price. Since marginal costs increase as output increases, firms will only increase their production if the price also increases. The Law of Supply states that, other things equal, the higher the price the greater the quantity supplied.

11. A market supply schedule is the summation of all of the individual firms' supply schedules. The market demand curve is the horizontal summation of all of the individual firms' supply curves.

12. Market supply curves shift when there are changes in the prices of other products, factor prices, technology, the number of firms in the market, and other events that affect costs and supply decisions.

13. Equilibrium prices and quantity are at the intersection of market demand and supply curves.

14. When the price is higher than the equilibrium level an excess supply will exist and prices will come down. And when the price is lower than the equilibrium level an excess demand will exist forcing the price to increase. At the equilibrium the quantity demanded equals the quantity supplied at a unique price.

15. Shifts in the demand or supply curve will change the equilibrium price and quantity. An increase in demand will increase the equilibrium price and quantity while a decrease in demand will bring the equilibrium price and quantity down. Increases in supply will bring the equilibrium price down and quantity up. Decreases in supply will reduce the equilibrium quantity and increase price.

16. Price changes analyzed in supply and demand diagrams are real price changes that have already been adjusted for inflation.

17. The elasticity of demand is a measure of how responsive quantity demanded is to a change in the price of the product. The ratio of the percentage change in quantity demanded to the percentage change in price is used to compute a measure of demand elasticity (written as an absolute value). Demand is elastic if the ratio is greater than one; unit-elastic if the ratio equals one; and inelastic if the ratio is less than one. The elasticity of supply is defined the same way, with the percentage change in quantity supplied used instead of the percentage change in quantity demanded (and without expressing the ratio as an absolute value for supply elasticity).

18. Price changes will either increase or decrease Total Revenue (price × quantity) depending on the elasticity of demand. When demand is elastic, a drop in price significantly increases the quantity demanded and as a result total revenue increases. The increases in quantity demanded more than offset the price cut. When demand is inelastic, total revenue declines if price is lowered because the quantity demanded will not increase by enough to offset the price cut.

19. Elasticity of demand will be affected by the necessity for a good, the availability of substitutes, the passage of time, and whether or not it is expensive. The greater the perceived need for the good, the less elastic the demand.

20. Supply elasticity is determined by production technologies, substitutability in production, and the amount of excess capacity in industry, and the passage of time.

21. The elasticity of demand and supply will determine how much of an effect a shift in demand or supply has on the equilibrium. For example, in the case where demand is very elastic any shift in demand will result in a relatively small change in the equilibrium price and a large change in quantity.

A FEW HELPFUL TIPS

One of the most common errors made by beginning economics students is to confuse movements along a demand or supply curve with shifts in these curves. REMEMBER, a change in price implies a movement along a demand or supply curve, whereas a change in any other factor affecting demand or supply causes the demand or supply curve to shift to the right or to the left. The best way to really learn how demand and supply curves work is to solve sample problems, draw your own graphs, and make up your own hypothetical situations to analyze their effects on demand and supply. Similarly, the best way to really understand how the equilibrium price and quantity are determined in the market is to sit down and practice how shifts in demand and supply affect the outcome. The "invisible hand" of the market is a logical idea, but don't just assume that it is so obvious that you can "do it in your head." It's very easy to turn the logic around and get it all wrong. Remember, analyze one change at a time and then analyze the effects. Make sure you don't confuse shifts in the curves versus movements along the curves.

QUICK STUDY GUIDE

	T/F	Mult. Choice	Short Answer	Problems
Demand and Supply Curves	1, 3		2, 6	1, 4, 6
Demand, Supply Shifts, vs. Movements	2, 4, 5, 7, 8, 10	1, 2, 3, 4, 10	1, 3, 4	2, 3, 5, 7
Elasticity	9, 10	6, 7, 8, 9, 10		1, 8, 9, 10
Market Equilibrium and Changes in the Equilibrium	6, 7, 8, 10	3, 4, 5, 10	4, 5, 6	5, 6, 7

PRETEST

Answer the following questions to test your initial understanding of the material in this chapter:

1. The music industry spends millions of dollars advertising their recording artists each year. Explain how advertising will affect the market demand for CDs.

2. Suppose the following two individual demand schedules represent the market for frozen yogurt cones in a given week.

Prices	Quantity Demanded by Elizabeth	Quantity Demanded by Katie
$3.00	2	0
$2.50	3	2
$2.00	4	4
$1.50	5	6

    Draw Elizabeth and Katie's individual demand curves, determine the market demand schedule, and then draw the market demand curve. Who has the more elastic demand for yogurt, Elizabeth or Katie?

The Laws of Supply and Demand

The following is a supply schedule for an individual firm manufacturing sweatshirts that will be used in questions 3 and 4:

Price	Quantity
$10	70
$20	150
$30	230
$40	310

3. Draw a supply curve for the firm.

4. Compute the elasticity of supply when the price changes from $10.00 to $20.00.

5. Use graphs to explain the effect on the strawberry supply for the following examples:
   a. An early frost that ruins 20% of the crop
   b. An increase in the competitive market price
   c. New labor laws that require health benefits for farm workers
   d. A new mechanical strawberry picker that reduces costs

6. Suppose the sushi market is initially at an equilibrium price and output level and a national magazine does an article warning of the health dangers of eating raw fish (most sushi chefs use raw fish). Show the effects on the equilibrium using supply and demand graphs.

7. Explain how a drought in the Midwest ruining 20% of the supply of wheat will affect the equilibrium price and quantity of bread. Use supply and demand curves to support your answer.

The following supply and demand schedules will be used for questions 8 and 9:

Price	Quantity Demanded	Quantity Supplied
$10	100	50
$15	75	75
$20	50	100
$25	25	125

8. Draw the supply and demand curves and label the market equilibrium.

9. When the price is $20.00 explain how the market forces will move the market towards the equilibrium. Use graphs to support your explanation.

10. Department stores appear to have "sales" on clothing almost every week while they have "sales" on linens much less often. How do you suppose the demand elasticities of clothing versus linens affect the department stores' decisions to conduct promotional sales on the two product lines?

TRUE/FALSE PRACTICE QUESTIONS

1. Demand curves are positively sloped because of the Law of Demand.   T   F
2. A coffee price increase will lead to an increase in the demand for tea.   T   F
3. Market demand is the horizontal sum of individual demand curves.   T   F

4. A reduction in labor costs will cause a supply curve to shift outward to the right. T F

5. An increase in costs due to higher energy prices will cause the supply curves for bagels to shift upward to the left. T F

6. An excess supply will exist when the price exceeds the equilibrium level. T F

7. An increase in demand will generally cause price to increase and output to decrease. T F

8. When demand and supply both increase, the quantity exchanged will increase and price may either increase or decrease. T F

9. When demand is elastic, a drop in price will decrease total revenues. T F

10. When supply is more elastic a decrease in demand will have a larger effect on output. T F

MULTIPLE CHOICE QUESTIONS

Choose the best option for the following questions.

1. Suppose a new study is published in *The New England Journal of Medicine* that concludes that drinking cranberry juice can lead to weight loss. The demand for cranberry juice is likely to
   a. shift to the left.
   b. shift to the right.
   c. remain the same.
   d. become more elastic.

2. A supply curve for Eric Clapton audio cassettes would shift to the left for all of the following reasons except
   a. increases in the cost of recording tape.
   b. lower fees for "backup" musicians.
   c. Clapton negotiates a higher guaranteed royalty rate for each tape.
   d. Higher advertising costs.

3. A storm demolishes the peach crop. As a result, the equilibrium price
   a. is likely to increase and the quantity will decrease.
   b. is likely to increase and the quantity will increase.
   c. is likely to decrease and the quantity will decrease.
   d. is likely to decrease and the quantity will increase.

4. An increase in the demand for wine occurs after a medical study is released praising the positive effects of drinking one glass of wine each day. At the same time the supply of wine decreases due to an early frost. As a result, the new equilibrium
   a. quantity of wine exchanged is indeterminate and the price will increase.
   b. quantity of wine exchanged is indeterminate and the price will decrease.
   c. price is indeterminate and the quantity will increase.
   d. price is indeterminate and the quantity will decrease.

5. When an excess demand exists the
   a. equilibrium price will increase and the quantity will decrease.
   b. equilibrium price will increase and the quantity will increase.
   c. equilibrium price will decrease and the quantity will decrease.
   d. equilibrium price will decrease and the quantity will increase.

6. Suppose the university is trying to increase revenues from student tuition. An increase in tuition will accomplish this goal if
   a. demand is elastic.
   b. demand is perfectly elastic.
   c. demand is inelastic.
   d. demand is perfectly inelastic.

7. Insulin used for diabetics is an example of a
   a. perfectly elastic good.
   b. perfectly inelastic good.
   c. elastic good.
   d. inelastic good.

8. If the percentage quantity demanded for a good changes by more than the percentage price for a particular good
   a. demand is elastic.
   b. demand is inelastic.
   c. demand is perfectly inelastic.
   d. none of the above.

9. The elasticity of supply
   a. will decrease over time.
   b. will not change over time.
   c. will increase over time.
   d. may either increase or decrease over time.

10. An increase in supply will have a larger effect on price if the
    a. demand is more elastic.
    b. supply is more elastic.
    c. demand is more inelastic.
    d. demand is perfectly elastic.

SHORT ANSWER QUESTIONS

Fill in the blanks in the following statements.

1. An increase in the population of Aspen, Colorado is likely to cause the demand for housing to shift to the _____.

2. A Market supply curve is the _____ summation of _____ supply curves.

3. An increase in operating costs will cause a firm's supply _____ to shift to the _____.

4. An increase in demand will cause the price to _____ and the quantity exchanged to _____.

5. A market equilibrium occurs when the quantity supplied _____ the quantity _____.

6. Real price changes are those that have been adjusted for _____.

PROBLEMS

1. The demand schedule for tickets to a series of five concerts on campus is as follows:

Price	Quantity Demanded
$200	200
$150	400
$100	600
$50	800
$25	900

   a. Draw the demand curve for the example.
   b. Compute the elasticities of demand for changes between the prices listed in the demand schedule.
   c. Solve for the total revenue at each price on the demand schedule.
   d. Compute the changes in total revenue when the price decreases from $200 to $150 and when it changes from $100 to $50. Explain why total revenue changes in the opposite directions for these same dollar amount reductions in price.

2. Explain the effects on the demand curve for video rentals of the following:
   a. an increase in the price of rentals
   b. an increase in incomes
   c. an advertising campaign for cable movie channels
   d. an increase in the price of admission to local movie theaters

3. Draw a diagram to show how the following would affect the supply of sunglasses:
   a. New federal regulations requiring a 10% increase in protection from ultraviolet rays for all sunglasses sold in the U.S.
   b. A decrease in the price of plastic
   c. An increase in the wage rates for sunglass designers

4. Suppose a firm is producing at an output level where marginal costs are rising and are equal to $10.00. If the competitive market price is $14.00 what advice would you have for the firm?

5. Use supply and demand graphs to explain why the reluctance of large grocery store chains to open stores in poor neighborhoods leads to higher food prices in these depressed areas.

Use the following demand and supply schedules for a hamburger "combo" meal to answer questions 6 and 7:

Price	Quantity Demanded	Quantity Supplied
$5.00	500	5,500
$4.00	2,000	4,500
$3.00	3,500	3,500
$2.00	5,000	2,500

6. Draw the Demand and Supply curves for "combo" meals and label the equilibrium price and quantity.

7. How would the equilibrium change if demand decreased by 500 meals at each price after a period of high unemployment in the area? Explain your answer using demand and supply curves.

8. Draw demand curves that represent goods that are elastic, inelastic, perfectly elastic, and perfectly inelastic. Then, list examples of at least three goods that would fit in each of these categories.

9. Suppose the price of raspberries and milk both increased by 20%. Explain why you would expect a much smaller change in the quantity demanded of milk.

10. In the early 1970's oil prices rose dramatically and the quantity demanded declined but only by a relatively small amount. However, in the 20 year period since then, the demand for gasoline has dropped significantly even though the price of gasoline adjusted for inflation has not increased. How can you explain this result? Use graphs to support your answer.

POST-TEST

Answer the following questions to determine how well you have learned the material in the chapter and to determine those areas where you need to focus your studies.

1. Use graphs to show how the demand curve for rap musician MC Hammer CDs shifts in the following cases:
   a. Rap music becomes unpopular
   b. A music store chain slashes 20% off all merchandise in the store
   c. Incomes rise for 16-30 year olds
   d. A music store chain slashes 20% off of rap group Criss Cross CDs and tapes

The following are gasoline demand schedules for Lillian and Kurt during one week. Use the information in the schedules to answer questions 2 and 3:

Price	Quantity Demanded by Lillian	Quantity Demanded by Kurt
$2.00	16	22
$1.50	17	24
$1.00	18	26
$0.50	19	28

2. Suppose the market consists of only Lillian and Kurt. Create a market demand schedule and graph the market demand curve.

3. Compute the elasticities of demand along the market demand curve.

4. If President Clinton's health care reform is successful, the costs of medical care should be reduced. Health care benefits are a major cost for employers including computer software firms. How will these projected cost savings affect the supply of computer software?

5. How will the government restrictions on the logging of old growth forests affect the supply of timber in the U.S.?

6. Explain why the market will return to an equilibrium level of output if an excess supply exists.

7. Suppose the demand for eggs decreases due to a salmonella scare and at the same time chickens lay a record number of eggs. Use supply and demand curves to explain the effects on price and quantity.

8. Use demand and supply curves to explain the effects on the equilibrium price and quantity of laptop computers of a new technology that lowers production costs.

9. Suppose the university increases the price of living in the dormitories. Use demand and supply curves to describe the effects on the local market for apartment rentals.

10. State whether you would expect the following goods to have elastic or inelastic demand curves.
    a. Aspirin
    b. Milk
    c. Movie tickets
    d. Big Screen Televisions

Part I–Sample Test

Introduction

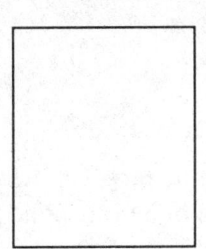

1. According to an economist, what is capital?
   a. The plant and equipment required to produce goods and services. One of the primary factors of production.
   b. The money required to buy goods and services.
   c. The space required to produce goods and services. One of the primary factors of production.
   d. The people required to produce goods and services. One of the primary factors of production.

2. What is "the economic problem?"
   a. A one-part problem consisting only of solutions.
   b. A three-part problem consisting of objectives, alternatives, and constraints.
   c. A three-part problem consisting of capital, consumers, and constraints.
   d. A three-part problem consisting of investment, innovation, and consumption.

3. What is economics?
   a. The science of how consumers allocate scarce resources.
   b. The study of how best to allocate scarce resources. Alternatively, the study of the allocation of scarce resources through the process of exchange.
   c. A business guide as to how to allocate scarce resources. Alternatively, the study of the allocation of scarce resources by business.
   d. The study of how scarce resources are consumed and bought and sold.

4. What are factors of production?
   a. The money that producers use to purchase goods and services, consisting of labor, capital, land, and material inputs.
   b. The resources or inputs that producers use to produce goods and services, consisting of labor, capital, land, and material inputs.
   c. The outputs that producers use to produce goods and services, consisting of labor, capital, land, and material outputs.
   d. The resources or inputs that consumers use to purchase goods and services, consisting of labor, capital, land, and material.

5. The principle that individuals are best able to judge their own self-interests.
   a. purchaser's choice
   b. consumer sovereignty
   c. buyer's desire
   d. market forces

6. In the context of a solution of an economic problem, what is efficiency?
   a. A criterion for judging the solution of an economic problem that refers to creating a perfect objective.
   b. A criterion for judging the solution of an economic problem that refers to making the choices that best meet the objectives.
   c. A criterion for judging the solution of an economic problem that refers to structuring variables to meet objectives.
   d. A criterion for judging the solution of an economic problem that refers to using government influence to best meet the objectives.

7. What is macroeconomics?
   a. The study of the economy "in the large;" analyzes the overall performance of the economy.
   b. The study of the economy "in the large;" analyzes the economic problems of individual economic agents and the exchanges between them.
   c. The study of the economy "in the small;" analyzes the overall performance of the economy.
   d. The study of the economy "in the small;" analyzes the economic problems of individual economic agents and the exchanges between them.

8. Operating at "the margin" in economics
   a. refers to the effects of a large change in an economic variable.
   b. refers to the effects of a small change in an economic statistic.
   c. refers to the effects of a small change in an economic variable.
   d. refers to the effects of a small change in a price.

9. One of the four fundamental economic questions that every society must answer, and which asks how the economy produces its goods and services, is the
   a. Now vs. the Future Question.
   b. What or Output Question.
   c. How or Input Question.
   d. For Whom or Distribution Question.

10. A persistent increase in the economy's potential for producing goods and services.
    a. long-run planning
    b. long-run economic growth
    c. consistent growth level
    d. growth planning

11. Incentives that encourage behavior for the good of society and may be enforced with legal sanctions.
    a. material incentives
    b. moral incentives
    c. maternal incentives
    d. tangible incentives

12. What are the production possibilities of an economy?
    a. The economy's capacity for producing goods and services assuming that it produces them efficiently.
    b. The economy's capacity for consuming goods and services.
    c. The economy's capacity for producing goods and services but not at the most efficient cost.
    d. The government's capacity for producing goods and services assuming that it produces them efficiently.

13. What are property rights?
    a. government ownership of the factors of production
    b. stockholder's ownership of production
    c. the ownership of the factories of production
    d. the ownership of the factors of production

14. The movement of goods and services and factors of production through the product and factor markets is called
    a. the circular flow.
    b. the squaring of business.
    c. exploitation.
    d. zigzag of commerce.
    e. the Phillips effect.

15. The process by which labor becomes more and more specialized is called
    a. economies of scale.
    b. unionization.
    c. division of labor.
    d. barter of labor.

16. The demand curve will shift to the right when
    a. the price of complementary goods increase.
    b. the price of substitute goods decrease.
    c. incomes increase and the good is a normal good.
    d. all of the above
    e. none of the above

17. Equilibrium in a supply and demand model occurs where
    a. all consumers are happy with the outcome.
    b. all producers are happy with the outcome.
    c. prices are set by the government.
    d. the price at which the quantity demanded equals the quantity supplied.

18. The price elasticity of demand is
    a. the change in quantity divided by the change in price.
    b. the percentage change in quantity divided by the percentage change in price.
    c. the change in price divided by the change in quantity.
    d. the percentage change in price divided by the percentage change in quantity.

19. The substitution effect occurs as the result of a change in
    a. the price of another product.
    b. the taste for the product.
    c. the income of the consumer.
    d. the appearance of a new product.
    e. the improvement of a product.

20. Under normal circumstances, which of the following has the *least* price elastic demand?
    a. desserts
    b. ice cream
    c. Bill's ice cream
    d. Bill's vanilla ice cream

21. When there is excess demand for a product
    a. the government should control prices.
    b. the price is above the equilibrium price.
    c. producers are unwilling to sell the product.
    d. consumers are not correctly curbing their appetites.

22. The real price of the good adjusts the money price by
    a. the seller's markup.
    b. the amount of taxes.
    c. the general level of prices.
    d. the shipping and handling charge on the product.

23. With normal supply and demand, the equilibrium price of a product will surely increase if
    a. supply increases.
    b. demand increases.
    c. both demand and supply increase.
    d. both demand and supply decrease.

24. As the period of time considered increases
    a. demand become more price inelastic.
    b. supply becomes more price inelastic.
    c. supply becomes more price elastic.
    d. demand price elasticity does not change.

Chapter 6
The Macroeconomic Policy Goals I: Long-Run Economic Growth and Full Employment

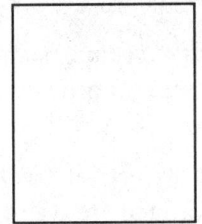

LEARNING OBJECTIVES
CONCEPTS TO LEARN

Macroeconomic policy goals	Full employment
Cyclical unemployment	Frictional/search unemployment
Structural unemployment	The natural rate of unemployment
The rule of 72	

CONCEPTS TO RECALL

Long-run economic growth	Circular flow of economic activity
Laws of supply and demand	

CHAPTER REVIEW

Chapter 6 begins with the three fundamental questions of macroeconomics. Then, the chapter focuses on the macroeconomic goal of long-run economic growth. Finally, the chapter ends with a discussion of a full employment goal.

1. What factors determine the circular flow of the economy?

2. How does the circular flow of economic activity relate to the four macroeconomic policy goals: long-run economic growth; full employment; price stability; and stability in economic relations with foreign countries.

3. What role can government take to affect the circular flow of the economy in order to achieve macroeconomic policy goals?

4. The potential for long-term growth is increased by pushing the production possibilities frontier outward over time.

5. Long-term economic growth can be promoted by increasing investment in physical and human capital (education).

6. The maximum level of economic growth is probably around four percent a year.

7. The overall economic health of a nation over time is a function of long run economic growth. Even relatively small differences in the rate of growth can have significant effects on a nation's standard of living.

8. Unemployed individuals are those who are actively seeking work and are unable to find a job and those who have been temporarily laid off and are waiting to be called back to work.

9. Average unemployment rates have increased in each decade since the 1950s. Unemployment rates are higher for blacks and teenagers.

10. The three types of unemployment are cyclical, frictional (or search), and structural.

11. Cyclical unemployment is affected by the good and bad times in the overall economy. Fiscal and monetary policy can be effective tools in changing cyclical unemployment. Sticky wages account for much of the cyclical unemployment in the economy. Wages are sticky because both employees and employers are likely to resist lower wages. Wages remain high even when the demand for labor decreases. Since the market does not clear, the costs of sticky wages are lost jobs. Three popular explanations for sticky wages are: workers want to preserve relative wages in a hierarchical structure; the insider/outsider theory which assumes that experienced workers want to maintain their high wages and prefer a system of layoffs which are more likely to affect those with less experience; employers that rely on internal labor markets keep wages high in order to improve worker morale, reduce high labor turnover costs and increase productivity. Job losers account for the majority of those individuals that are cyclically unemployed.

12. Frictional and search unemployment are a function of a lack of information about employment opportunities. Frictional unemployment occurs when individuals move from one sector of the economy to another. These shifts are a result of the constant changing mix of available employment opportunities. Search unemployment occurs when job leavers, reentrants, and new

The Macroeconomic Policy Goals I: Long-Run Economic Growth and Full Employment

entrants to the labor market search for the best job opportunities before they accept a job. Frictional/search unemployment is not sensitive to cyclical economic changes.

13. Structural unemployment occurs when workers with specific skills are no longer needed in the economy or when specific geographic areas experience economic downturns. Structural unemployment is not sensitive to cyclical economic changes.

14. The natural rate of unemployment is consistent with an economy operating on its production possibilities frontier. The natural rate is equal to structural unemployment plus frictional/search unemployment.

15. Unemployment has psychological as well as economic costs.

A FEW HELPFUL TIPS

When you hear someone discussing the unemployment problem or policies make sure you clarify the type of unemployment. For example, policies that are effective for cyclical unemployment are not going to have an impact on structural unemployment.

QUICK STUDY GUIDE

	T/F	Mult. Choice	Short Answer	Problems
Macroeconomic Goals	8			2, 7, 10
Rule of 72		5	5	8
Natural Rate	1, 7	8	2	1, 3, 4, 6
Defining Unemployment	2, 4, 10	1, 4, 6, 7	3	

PRETEST

Answer the following questions to test your initial understanding of the material in this chapter:

1. How is unemployment defined in the U.S.?
2. What rates of economic growth are considered excellent, good, fair or poor in the U.S.?
3. How long will it take the output of an economy to double if the growth rate is equal to 2%?
4. What have the trends in long-term economic growth been in the U.S. since World War II?
5. Compute the unemployment rate when the labor force in the U.S. is equal to 125 million people, 6 million individuals are actively seeking work and 1 million people are discouraged workers who are no longer looking for work.
6. What is cyclical unemployment and why does it occur?
7. Define structural unemployment and explain why policies aimed at cyclical changes in the economy are unlikely to have any effect on the problem.

8. Why are wages sticky?

9. Define frictional/search unemployment and explain why both employers and employees may benefit from search.

10. Define the natural rate of unemployment.

TRUE/FALSE PRACTICE QUESTIONS

1. Economists have reached a consensus that the natural rate of unemployment has fallen since the 1970s.   T   F

2. Layoffs in the defense sector are an example of cyclical unemployment.   T   F

3. Unemployment rates for blacks are significantly higher than those of whites.   T   F

4. Structural unemployment is equal to search plus frictional unemployment.   T   F

5. Wages are sticky downward.   T   F

6. Small changes in economic growth rates will have little effect on long-term growth.   T   F

7. The economy is on the production possibilities frontier when unemployment is at the natural rate.   T   F

8. The economy will double in 18 years if the annual growth rate is 3%.   T   F

9. The labor force includes all those individuals over 16 years of age who are actually working.   T   F

10. The major category of unemployed workers are new entrants to the labor force.   T   F

MULTIPLE CHOICE QUESTIONS

Choose the best option for the following questions.

1. Suppose there are 100 million individuals in the labor force and 4 million are structurally unemployed, 1 million are frictionally unemployed, and 2 million are cyclically unemployed. The unemployment rate in the economy is
   a. 5%.
   b. 7%.
   c. 2%.
   d. 1%.

2. When wages are sticky and the demand for labor decreases
   a. wages will decline.
   b. unemployment will increase.
   c. unemployment will decrease.
   d. wages and unemployment remain constant.

3. Black unemployment rates are
   a. the same as white unemployment rates.
   b. less than white unemployment rates because of Affirmative Action programs.
   c. two and one-half times the rates for whites.
   d. five times the rates of whites.

4. Which of the following individuals is *not* structurally unemployed?
   a. a laid off defense worker in the 1990s
   b. a 55 year old former steel mill worker in Ohio
   c. a new college graduate looking for work
   d. an elevator operator replaced by automation

5. When the growth rate is 4%, the economy will double in
   a. 18 years.
   b. 32 years.
   c. 60 years.
   d. 24 years.

6. When discouraged workers stop looking for jobs the unemployment rate
   a. remains constant.
   b. increases.
   c. decreases.
   d. can either increase or decrease.

7. When there is an economic downturn, frictional employment is likely to
   a. increase.
   b. decrease.
   c. either increase or decrease.
   d. not change much.

8. The natural rate of unemployment is equal to
   a. the frictional rate plus the cyclical rate.
   b. the structural rate plus the cyclical rate.
   c. the cyclical rate plus the discouraged workers.
   d. the frictional/search rate plus the structural rate.

9. When the economy is performing well job search time is likely to
   a. increase.
   b. decrease.
   c. either increase or decrease.
   d. not change.

10. Which of the following decades had the highest unemployment rates?
    a. 1950s
    b. 1960s
    c. 1970s
    d. 1980s

SHORT ANSWER QUESTIONS

Fill in the blanks in the following statements.

1. Average annual growth rates during the 1980s were _____ than those in the 1970s.

2. The natural unemployment rate is equal to the _____ plus the _____.

3. _____ are those individuals who drop out of the labor force due to frustration after long periods of unemployment.

4. When unemployment levels and wages remain high, wages are _____.

5. When the annual growth rate is 2% the economy will _____ in _____ years.

PROBLEMS

1. How have changes in the employment patterns of women affected the natural rate of employment in the U.S. since the 1950s?

2. The largest number of military base closures in the early 1990's was in the San Francisco Bay area. Unemployment rates in the area increased as a result of the base closures. How would you define this unemployment and explain the effects of cyclical economic changes on this particular problem?

3. How have demographic changes in the U.S. affected the natural rate of unemployment?

4. Why might the natural rate of unemployment decline and why might it actually increase over the next ten years?

5. During the 1982-83 recession many economists argued that the natural rate of unemployment had risen and things were not really as bad as they seemed. What are some of the possible explanations for their opinion?

6. Critics of the Reagan administration argued that the decreases in unemployment in 1986-87 negates the arguments of those who believed that the natural rate of unemployment had increased. What are the main arguments of those economists who believe the natural rate is falling?

7. Explain how the official unemployment rate understates the problems of joblessness in the U.S.

8. How long will it take the economy to double in size if the annual growth rate in the economy is a booming 6%?

9. How do supporters of the insider/outsider theory explain sticky wages?

10. What factors are likely to result in increases in frictional/search unemployment?

POST-TEST

Answer the following questions to determine how well you have learned the material in the chapter and to determine those areas where you need to focus your studies.

1. Explain why some economists believe the official unemployment rate overstates the problems in the economy.

2. Describe three examples of structural unemployment in the U.S.

3. Describe three examples of frictional/search unemployment in the U.S.

4. What arguments can be made to support a downward trend in the natural rate of unemployment in the 1990s?

5. What arguments can be made to support an upward trend in the natural rate of unemployment in the 1990s?

6. What is the relationship between internal labor markets and sticky wages?

7. Suppose the demand for auto workers declines by 10% and the wages remain at the same level as a result of a long-term union contract. What are the likely effects on auto workers?

8. Why might only tenured professors fight against wage cuts?

9. Compute the unemployment rate in an economy with a labor force of 200 million when 8 million individuals are structurally/frictionally unemployed, 1 million are discouraged workers, and 2 million are cyclically unemployed.

10. What types of unemployment are likely to respond to macroeconomic policies geared at cyclical changes in the economy?

Chapter 7

The Macroeconomic Policy Goals II: Price Stability and Stable International Economic Relations

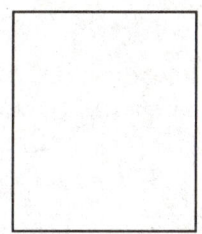

LEARNING OBJECTIVES

CONCEPTS TO LEARN

Inflation	Consumer price index
Hyperinflation	Fischer equation
Imports and exports	The balance of trade
Dollar depreciation/appreciation	

CONCEPTS TO RECALL

Circular flow of economic activity	Laws of supply and demand

CHAPTER REVIEW

Chapter 7 focuses on inflation in the economy. The first section defines inflation and the methods used to measure inflation. Then, the chapter evaluates the effects of inflation on different sectors of the economy. The final section introduces the balance of trade and how the amounts of imports and exports can affect the stability of a currency.

1. Inflation occurs when there are continuous increases in the price level.

2. The rate of inflation is tracked by the federal government by analyzing the changes in the cost of a "typical market basket of goods" over time. A price index establishes a base year which is currently 1987. Comparisons of the costs in any year can then be made to the cost of the "market basket" in the base year. Inflation rates are equal to the percentage change in the price index. The actual index is computed by taking a weighted average of the "market basket" in a given year, dividing it by the weighted average in the base year and multiplying it by 100. The Consumer Price Index, CPI, the Producer Price Index, PPI, and the Gross Domestic Product deflator, GDP, are the price indexes most commonly reported.

3. The CPI is used to evaluated the effects of inflation on households and is used to adjust wages, pensions, and transfer payments. The "market basket" includes only consumer goods and services.

4. The PPI tracks the finished products component of the prices of producer inputs and finished products sold wholesale.

5. The GDP deflator includes all goods and services in the economy and is used to evaluate inflation levels for the circular flow of the economy.

6. Government's need to keep inflation low to prevent hyperinflation, stop efficiency losses and prevent haphazard redistributions of purchasing power. Hyperinflation exists when prices change by very large amounts in very short time period. When hyperinflation occurs the confidence in the economic system erodes and exchange can revert to a barter system.

7. Inflation can be unbalanced, unadjusted or unanticipated. Inflation is unbalanced if prices of individual goods and services are increasing at different rates. Unadjusted inflation occurs when economic contracts or the tax system are not indexed for price level changes. Unanticipated inflation occurs when everyone is surprised by the rate of changes in prices. All three conditions are related and usually all occur during most inflationary periods. Inefficiencies and changes in income distribution are the results of these three conditions.

8. If an inflation is balanced, fully adjusted, and anticipated the only costs would be the "shoe leather" costs of managing money and the "menu" costs of changing price lists. These costs are relatively low.

9. Inefficiencies arise during an unbalanced inflation because of the changing relative prices of different products in the market. Excess supply will occur in markets that are experiencing high inflation and excess demand will occur in markets where prices are rising more slowly. Redistribution of income occurs because it will have a greater impact on those individuals who consume more of the goods with fast rising prices.

10. Unadjusted inflation occurs because individuals and firms respond to changes in the price level at different times. Long-term contracts with adjustments for the cost of living often are often based on different time periods. Lags in adjustments result in economic inefficiencies. Taxes are not fully adjusted for inflation and as a result individuals' tax liabilities are often affected by price level changes. Capital gains taxes do not take into account the amount of the capital gain that can be explained by inflation. As a result, capital markets are distorted and the result is inefficiency.

The Macroeconomic Policy Goals II: Price Stability and Stable International Economic Relations

11. Those individuals who have entered into long-term contracts with infrequent adjustments for inflation and those living on fixed incomes will particularly suffer from unanticipated inflation. Debtors/borrowers will gain at a cost to creditors/loaners during inflationary periods. Unanticipated inflation increases the amount of uncertainty in the economy and leads to inefficiencies.

12. Economists disagree regarding the actual costs of inflation. Robert Lucas argues that costs are relatively small and are confined to shoe leather and menu costs. All other costs are a result of other factors according to Lucas. Stanley Fischer believes that the costs of inflation should be measured within the context of the institutional framework of the economy. Fischer believes these costs can be quite high but are avoidable.

13. Imports are the ends of trade and exports are the means to the end. Countries will only be willing to buy imports if the trading party buys exports.

14. Most countries are forced to have a zero balance of trade where imports exactly equal exports. If imports exceed exports the other country will have excess amounts of the nation's currency. The net exporting country may not be willing to hold onto excess currency and may refuse to trade.

15. A currency appreciates when its value increases relative to other currencies. Depreciation occurs when the relative value declines. The values of a nation's currency relative to other countries currencies is affected by the balance of trade. When a country has a positive trade balance, the demand for its currency will increase driving up its value. Countries with negative trade balances will see their currencies depreciate.

16. The U.S. does not have to maintain a zero trade balance because individuals throughout the world are willing to hold dollars because they are an internationally accepted means of exchange. The U.S. has not achieved either a stable dollar or a balance of trade in the last 20 years.

A FEW HELPFUL TIPS

Students typically get confused about the relationship between the value of the dollar and the balance of trade. Remember, when Americans buy more goods from abroad than we sell, we need to trade our dollars for other currencies. The supply of dollars in world currency market increases and the demand does not change. As a result, the value of the dollar will go down relative to other currencies. If Americans sell more abroad than it buys just reverse the logic.

QUICK STUDY GUIDE				
	T/F	Mult. Choice	Short Answer	Problems
Defining Inflation		7	1, 2, 3, 4, 5	6
Real vs. Nominal Values	3	2, 6		
CPI	1	1, 5		1, 4, 9
Depreciation/Appreciation	4, 9	9, 10		10

Chapter 7

PRETEST

Answer the following questions to test your initial understanding of the material in this chapter:

1. What is the difference between inflation and hyperinflation?
2. What are the differences between the CPI, PPI, and GDP deflator?
3. Suppose a "typical market basket of goods" included the following goods. Compute the CPI for year one and year two assuming year one is the base year.

Units of Goods Purchased in a Year	Year One Price per unit	Year Two Price per unit
52 gallons of milk	$2.50	$3.00
100 bags of taco chips	$2.25	$2.00
2 pairs of blue jeans	$32.00	$45.00
5 T-shirts	$12.20	$15.00

4. Which types of consumers in question 3 are affected the most by the inflation from year 1 to year 2?
5. Why does inflation created inefficiencies in the economy?
6. Describe the redistributional effects of inflation.
7. Compute the rate of inflation if the CPI rises from 225 to 245.
8. How will inflation affect the real rate of interest?
9. Explain why the value of the dollar goes up when the U.S. trade balance is positive.
10. Why do most countries have to maintain a balance of trade?

TRUE/FALSE PRACTICE QUESTIONS

1. The base year for the CPI is equal to zero.   T   F
2. An increase in taxes on cigarettes will lead to inflation in the economy.   T   F
3. Nominal interest rates rise with inflation.   T   F
4. A negative balance of trade will increase the value of a countries' currency.   T   F
5. Capital gains taxes are not adjusted for inflation.   T   F
6. Lenders may experience losses during inflationary periods.   T   F
7. The U.S. has maintained a zero balance of trade over most of the last 20 years.   T   F
8. No one benefits from inflation.   T   F
9. The value of a currency is directly related to the balance of trade.   T   F
10. Inflation has no effect on income distribution.   T   F

The Macroeconomic Policy Goals II: Price Stability and Stable International Economic Relations 59

MULTIPLE CHOICE QUESTIONS

Choose the best option for the following questions.

1. What is the rate of inflation when the CPI increases from 320 to 335?
   a. 5.2%
   b. 4.6%
   c. 3.8%
   d. 6.1%

2. Suppose the CPI = 120 and the price of a taco is $1.25 this year. How much would the taco cost in the base year?
   a. $1.25
   b. $2.00
   c. $1.04
   d. $1.00

3. If the price level increases the GDP deflator will
   a. increase.
   b. decrease.
   c. either increase or decrease.
   d. remain constant.

4. Which of the following is not a price index?
   a. CPI
   b. GDP deflator
   c. PPI
   d. NNP

5. The current base year for the CPI is
   a. 1972.
   b. 1990.
   c. 1993.
   d. 1987.

6. If the nominal rate of interest is 7% and the anticipated inflation rate is 5%, the real rate of interest is
   a. 12%.
   b. 2%.
   c. 5%.
   d. 7%.

7. Menu costs of inflation refer to
   a. retail food prices
   b. restaurant menus
   c. changing price lists
   d. computer menus

8. Which of the following are *not* adversely affected by inflation?
   a. AFDC recipients

b. borrowers
c. pensioners
d. those paying taxes on capital gains

9. If the U.S. balance of trade is positive the value of the dollar will
   a. increase.
   b. decrease.
   c. either increase or decrease.
   d. not change.

10. When the value of the dollar increases U.S. exports will probably
    a. increase.
    b. decrease.
    c. either increase or decrease.
    d. not change.

SHORT ANSWER QUESTIONS

Fill in the blanks in the following statements.

1. Prices _____ increase during an inflation.

2. The core rate of inflation excludes _____, _____, and _____.

3. When new prices are quoted every hour the economy is experiencing _____.

4. _____ inflation occurs when prices of different goods and services rise at different rates.

5. _____ costs of inflation are the costs of managing our money during inflationary periods.

PROBLEMS

1. How will the CPI be affected if President Clinton's health care reform is successful in bringing down medical costs?

2. Who benefits from inflation?

3. Who loses during inflationary periods?

4. How is the CPI a poor measure of changes in the cost of living?

5. How would you evaluate the costs of an inflation that is primarily a result of higher food prices after floods in the Midwest?

6. Explain why a balanced, fully adjusted, fully anticipated inflation does not create a burden for the economy.

7. How will individuals with long-term labor contracts lose during unanticipated inflationary periods and how can they protect themselves during contract negotiations?

8. Who loses from a protectionist policy designed to protect the jobs of auto workers in Detroit?

The Macroeconomic Policy Goals II: Price Stability and Stable International Economic Relations

9. Suppose the following are the prices of goods and services for a market basket used in a price index. Compute the price index for the current and base years.

Units of a good purchased	Price of one unit in the base year	Price of one unit in the current year
52 magazines	$3.50	$3.75
25 books	$25.00	$27.50
yearly newspaper subscription	$360.00	$400.00
annual newsletter subscription	$20.00	$25.00

10. Who are the losers when the value of the dollar declines?

POST-TEST

Answer the following questions to determine how well you have learned the material in the chapter and to determine those areas where you need to focus your studies.

1. How do Stan Fischer and Robert Lucas disagree regarding the costs of inflation?
2. Who wins when the dollar of the value increases?
3. Who are the winners and losers during inflationary periods?
4. Compute the inflation rate when the CPI increases from 220 to 325.
5. How is the real rate of interest related to the inflation rate?
6. Explain the connection between the value of a currency and the balance of trade.
7. How do taxes in the U.S. fail to take into account inflation and what distortions occur as a result?
8. Why will inflation affect borrowers differently than lenders?
9. Why are welfare recipients more likely to be affected by inflation than others?
10. Why aren't cost of living adjustments guarantees that workers will be protected from inflationary costs?

Chapter 8
The National Income and Product Accounts

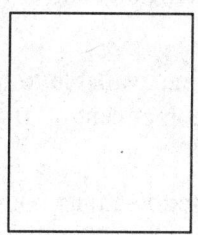

LEARNING OBJECTIVES

CONCEPTS TO LEARN

National income	Gross domestic product (GDP)
Value added	Consumption
Investment	Government purchases of goods and services
Net exports	The national income = national product accounting identity
The total saving = investment accounting identity	GDP deflator
Disposable income	

CONCEPTS TO RECALL

Circular flow of the economy

CHAPTER REVIEW

Chapter 8 focuses on the national income and product accounts for the United States. An understanding of national income accounting is important in order to be able to analyze how the macroeconomy operates. The national income and product accounts measure overall circular flow of economic activity.

1. National income and product accounts measure the circular flow of the economy. National income must always equal national product and it is a fundamental accounting identity.

2. Savings must equal investment. The three sources of saving are the private sector, government and the foreign sector. Personal savings of households and business saving or retained earnings account for private sector saving. The combined surpluses or deficits of federal, state, and local governments are equal to government saving. And, the difference between exports and imports is equal to foreign saving.

3. Total sales minus the costs of intermediate goods is equal to the value added of business firms in the circular flow of the economy.

4. Disposable income is the actual income available to households for consumption and saving. Consumption is the most important component of gross domestic product and personal savings finance business investment.

5. The GDP deflator is a price index used to adjust nominal GDP for inflation. Dividing the nominal GDP by the deflator and multiplying it by 100 will convert the dollars to the base year, 1987, price level.

6. GDP per capita is the best available measure of the overall economic well-being of a nation.

7. GDP is an incomplete measure of economic activity because it does not take into account the underground economy, the negatives of economic growth (i.e. pollution, congestion, etc.), quality changes in goods and services, changes in the amount of leisure time, and the distribution of income.

8. Real GDP has increased by 15 times since 1820. The standard of living may or may not be 15 times as high.

A FEW HELPFUL TIPS

Remember, since there is a circular flow of economic activity, the value of overall production must equal the income payments to labor, capital, and land. If national income does not add up to national product there has to be an error in the calculations.

QUICK STUDY GUIDE

	T/F	Mult. Choice	Short Answer	Problems
GDP	2, 6, 7	10	1, 2, 5	1, 2, 3, 4, 5, 6, 9
GDP deflator	10	5, 6, 7, 8		10
Savings and Investment	1, 4, 5, 9		4	8

PRETEST

Answer the following questions to test your initial understanding of the material in this chapter:

1. How will the amount of foreign saving change when exports decline?
2. How does the level of disposable income affect business investment?
3. What is the most important component of National Income? Define this component and explain how it fits in the circular flow of the economy.
4. Suppose the nominal GDP for a hypothetical country is $3360 billion and the GDP deflator is equal to 210. What is the real value of the GDP?
5. How does the GDP deflator differ from the CPI and why and when do we need to use these indices?
6. Why might a country be in decline even when GDP increases?
7. What is the underground economy and what is its impact on GDP?
8. How does the level of pollution in a country distort GDP figures?
9. Which of the following are final products and which are intermediate products?
   a. wheat
   b. bicycles
   c. air bags
   d. fast-food hamburgers
10. Explain the difference between investment and existing capital.

TRUE/FALSE PRACTICE QUESTIONS

1. A decrease in exports will increase foreign savings.   T   F
2. A proprietor's income is excluded from GDP.   T   F
3. A television set is an example of an intermediate good.   T   F

4. When a firm purchases a replacement computer it is counted as investment. T F
5. Net investment is equal to gross investment minus the capital consumption allowance. T F
6. An increase in transfer payments increases the GDP. T F
7. Indirect business taxes are not taken into consideration when calculating GDP. T F
8. Transfer payments are not included in disposable income. T F
9. Savings must equal investment. T F
10. Increases in inflation will increase the GDP deflator. T F

MULTIPLE CHOICE QUESTIONS

Choose the best option for the following questions.

1. Which of the following is NOT a final good?
    a. shoes
    b. jeans
    c. zippers
    d. backpacks

2. Which of the following is NOT an intermediate good?
    a. electrical conduit
    b. paint
    c. timber
    d. a home

3. Retained earnings are a portion of a firm's
    a. operating expense.
    b. profits.
    c. tax payment.
    d. depreciation account.

4. Transfer payments
    a. increase the GDP.
    b. are included in disposable income.
    c. increase NDP.
    d. are counted as investment.

5. If the GDP is equal to $4500 billion and the GDP deflator is equal to 180, the real value of GDP is
    a. $2200 billion.
    b. $2500 billion.
    c. $4500 billion.
    d. $1800 billion.

6. If the GDP is equal to $2400 billion and the GDP deflator is equal to 200, the real value of GDP is
    a. $960 billion.

b. $1200 billion.
   c. $1000 billion.
   d. $240 billion.

7. An increase in the rate of inflation will cause the real GDP to
   a. increase.
   b. decrease.
   c. increase then decrease.
   d. not change.

8. An increase in the rate of inflation will cause the nominal GDP to
   a. increase.
   b. decrease.
   c. increase then decrease.
   d. not change.

9. Value added is equal to
   a. sales minus depreciation.
   b. revenues minus depreciation.
   c. sales minus the cost of intermediate goods.
   d. total revenues minus total costs.

10. GDP is equal to
    a. C + I + G
    b. C + I + G + X
    c. C + I + G + (X − M)
    d. C + I

SHORT ANSWER QUESTIONS

Fill in the blanks in the following statements.

1. _____ is the value of final goods and services produced within a country regardless of who produced the goods.

2. GDP is the sum of Consumption + _____ + _____ + _____.

3. The _____ is the Bureau of Economic Analysis' estimate of the depreciation of the nation's capital stock.

4. Disposable income can be saved or _____.

5. An increase in net exports will cause GDP to _____.

PROBLEMS

1. Why is growth in GDP a good measure of the economic well-being of a country?

2. Why is growth in GDP an incomplete measure of the economic well-being of a country?

3. What is the difference between GDP and GNP?

4. How will trade agreements that increase both exports and imports affect GDP? Why?

5. Many undocumented workers currently receive their wages in cash. How would GDP be affected if these workers were allowed to work in this country legally?

6. How does human capital investment (education) affect GDP over time?

7. Why are intermediate goods excluded from GDP?

8. Explain why investment goods with short life-spans are likely to distort GDP growth figures?

9. Explain the effects of a Social Security increase on GDP.

10. What is the real GDP if the nominal GDP is equal to $5300 billion and the GDP deflator is equal to 310?

POST-TEST

Answer the following questions to determine how well you have learned the material in the chapter and to determine those areas where you need to focus your studies.

1. Why won't an increase in transfer payments increase the GDP?

2. Explain the effects of inflation on the real GDP.

3. What is the relationship between investment and savings in the circular flow of the economy?

4. How is an intermediate good different from a final good?

5. How would the legalization of marijuana affect the GDP?

6. What is the real value of GDP when the deflator is equal to 225 and the nominal GDP equals $550 billion?

7. How will an increase in imports affect the GDP?

8. Why won't increases in GDP necessarily help everyone in society?

9. Growth in GDP is often accompanied by increases in pollution. Explain how GDP figures can either understate or overstate the well-being of an economy as a result.

10. Describe three examples of non-market activities that are excluded from GDP calculations.

Chapter 9
Modeling the Macroeconomy: New Classical and New Keynesian Perspectives

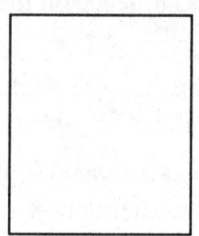

LEARNING OBJECTIVES

CONCEPTS TO LEARN

The business cycle	Fiscal policy
Monetary policy	New classical economics
New Keynesian economics	Aggregate Demand and Aggregate Supply
Aggregate Demand and Aggregate Supply shocks	

CONCEPTS TO RECALL

The three-part economic problem	Circular flow of economic activity
Laws of supply and demand	The macroeconomic policy goals
National income = national product accounting identity	

CHAPTER REVIEW

Chapter 9 focuses on how macroeconomists approach the three fundamental problems identified in Chapter 6. An introduction to building a simplified model of the macroeconomy is followed by an overview of the two leading models, the new classical model and the New Keynesian model. Both models are used in the analysis of the macroeconomy throughout the remainder of the text.

1. The three fundamental questions are: a) What determines the circular flow of economic activity? b) How does the level and composition of the circular flow relate to the four macroeconomic policy goals of long-run economic growth, full employment, price stability, and stability in economic relations with foreign nations? c) How can the government help achieve the macroeconomic policy goals through its fiscal and monetary policies, which influence the level and composition of the circular flow?

2. Developed economies follow a business cycle which consists of a pattern of booms and recessions over time. The intensity of the boom or recession will vary.

3. The Executive Branch of the federal government and the Congress are responsible for fiscal policy. Fiscal policy includes changes in government expenditures, transfer payments, or taxes. These budgetary changes can have an influence on the level and composition of the circular flow of the economy.

4. The Board of Governors of the Federal Reserve Bank are responsible for administering monetary policy. Monetary policy is changing the money supply to affect the circular flow of the economy.

5. Macroeconomic policy attempts to solve a three-part problem for the entire economy. The objectives are the four policy goals, the alternatives are fiscal and monetary policy, and the constraint is the economy itself.

6. Macroeconomic models are simplifications of highly developed economies. Even the most sophisticated models can not take into account all the nuances of the economy. The models are useful in predicting some events but are not foolproof.

7. Macro models are designed to explain the forces that determine the circular flow of the economy. The first equation in all macro models $Y = C^d + I^d + G^d + (Ex^d - Im^d)$ is a representation of the circular flow of product markets. The identity represents the aggregate supply and demand for final goods and services in the economy where Y represents national income, C^d equals consumption demand, I^d equals investment demand by business, G^d equals government demand for goods and services, and $(Ex^d - Im^d)$ represents the net demand of the foreign sector. The left hand side of the equation Y^d represents aggregate supply and the right hand portion represents aggregate demand.

8. Economists disagree about further specifications of the model and there are many variations that place different emphasis on the two sides of the market and the individual variables.

9. New Classical economists utilize the view of the Classical economists of the late 1800's and early 1900's that the macroeconomy is highly competitive and operates in accordance with the laws of supply and demand. The New Classical model implies that: a) competitive factor markets will force the economy to produce on the production possibilities frontier with zero unemployment of resources b) wages and prices are highly flexible and are the determinants of the supply and

demand for final goods and services c) the production possibilities frontier and the real domestic product are determined by the supply side of the economy d) changes in aggregate demand affect prices but not output since any change is temporary and the economy will shortly return to the production possibilities frontier e) fiscal and monetary policy are not necessary and the government should follow a steady and predictable course that businesses and households can count on when planning their economic affairs.

10. The classical model is often inconsistent with observations of the economy. Capitalist economies usually operate below the production possibilities frontier and experience high levels of cyclical unemployment. Changes in aggregate demand can affect output for long periods of time. Output responds first and price changes often follow. In a single competitive market prices change first and output follows.

11. The New Keynesians are descendants of John Maynard Keynes whose theories were developed during the Great Depression in the 1930's.

12. Keynes' four main ideas are: a) Wages and prices are sticky due to market imperfections and as a result the economy does not quickly return to the production possibilities frontier when there are changing conditions in the economy. The short-run adjustments can last years and national income is a more important determinant of the circular flow than wages and prices b) the economy responds to changes in aggregate demand and the supply side of the economy remains passive. When aggregate demand increases producers hire more resources and increase their production and when aggregate demand decreases the opposite occurs. The economy feeds on itself so that changes in national income due to changes in aggregate demand will lead to further changes in aggregate demand. c) Aggregate demand will not necessarily lead the economy to the production possibilities frontier. Given sticky wages and prices it is possible for the economy to operate at high levels of cyclical unemployment or at highly inflationary output levels for long periods of time. d) Fiscal and monetary policies can be used to affect the level of aggregate output and improve economic performance.

13. The New Keynesian model is a better predictor of how the economy reacts to changes in aggregate demand in the short run while the new classical model explains the effects of supply shocks better. Supply shocks occur when the costs of production or the ability to supply output is affected by a technical change or a change in the price of an important production input. Supply shocks affect both price and output at the macro level.

14. The differences between the New Classical and New Keynesian schools are over the short-run behavior of the economy. Both groups agree that in the long run the new classical approach is most appropriate for analyzing long-run growth, controlling inflation, and federal budget deficit control.

A FEW HELPFUL TIPS

Many beginning students confuse the analysis of the demand and supply for an individual market versus the macroeconomy. Remember, an increase in price means the price level for the entire economy changes. Relative price changes of individual products are caused by very different circumstances.

Also, the definition of short run is purposefully vague and is in dispute among economists. Keynes made the distinction between long and short run when he said, "In the long run we're all dead."

	QUICK STUDY GUIDE			
	T/F	Mult. Choice	Short Answer	Problems
New Keynesian Economics	5, 7, 8	3, 9	3, 5	3, 5, 8
New Classical Economics	1, 3, 4, 6	4, 7, 8, 10	4	1, 2, 4, 6
Aggregate Supply Shocks	9		1	9

PRETEST

Answer the following questions to test your initial understanding of the material in this chapter:

1. What are the goals of fiscal policy?
2. What are the goals of monetary policy?
3. Explain and define the first equation for a macro model representing the circular flow of the economy.
4. When will the circular flow of the economy reach an equilibrium?
5. What are the major assumptions of the New Classical economists regarding the macro economy in the short run?
6. What are the major assumptions of the New Keynesian economists regarding the macro economy in the short run?
7. How do New Classical and New Keynesians view the long run performance of the macro economy?
8. How well does the New Classical model predict what economists observe in the short and long run?
9. How well does the New Keynesian model predict what economists observe in the short and long run?
10. How do New Keynesian and New Classical economists differ on the usefulness of fiscal and monetary policy?

TRUE/FALSE PRACTICE QUESTIONS

1. New Classical economists predict that the economy will operate on the production possibilities frontier in the short and long run.   T   F
2. Keynes predicted long periods of unemployment in the short run.   T   F

3. New Classical economists argue that the aggregate supply curve in the short run is vertical at full employment.   T   F

4. The economy is demand driven in the short run according to the New Classical school of economists.   T   F

5. According to the New Keynesians an increase in Aggregate Demand will change prices but not output.   T   F

6. New Classical economists believe fiscal and monetary policy is unnecessary.   T   F

7. Sticky wages and prices prevent the economy from reaching the production possibilities frontier according to the New Keynesians.   T   F

8. An increase in government spending can increase output according to the New Keynesians.   T   F

9. Aggregate supply shocks are likely to have a rapid effect on prices and output in the short run.   T   F

10. Monetary policy is determined by the president of the U.S.   T   F

MULTIPLE CHOICE QUESTIONS

Choose the best option for the following questions.

1. Fiscal policy is the responsibility of
   a. Congress.
   b. the President.
   c. the Federal Reserve Bank.
   d. the Congress and the President.

2. Monetary Policy is the responsibility of
   a. the Congress.
   b. the President.
   c. the Federal Reserve Bank.
   d. the Congress and the Federal Reserve Bank.

3. New Keynesians would agree with all of the following except
   a. monetary policy is useful.
   b. wages and prices are sticky.
   c. the economy will adjust to its production possibilities frontier in the short run.
   d. fiscal policy is useful.

4. New Classical economists would agree with all of the following except
   a. the economy will reach full employment in the short run.
   b. the circular flow of the economy is determined by aggregate supply.
   c. fiscal policy is useless.
   d. monetary policy is useful.

5. The first equation of every macro model representing the circular flow of the economy is
   a. $Y = C^d + I^d$
   b. $Y = I^d + G + X^d$
   c. $Y = C^d + I^d + G^d$
   d. $Y = C^d + I^d + G^d + (Ex^d - Im^d)$

6. John Maynard Keynes wrote his General Theory during the
   a. 1920s.
   b. 1930s.
   c. 1940s.
   d. 1960s.

7. According to the New Classical approach a short-run increase in Aggregate Demand will cause
   a. prices and output to increase.
   b. prices to increase and output to stay constant.
   c. output to increase and prices to remain constant.
   d. prices to increase and output to decrease.

8. According to the New Classical approach a short-run decrease in Aggregate Demand will cause
   a. prices and output to decrease.
   b. prices to decrease and output to remain unchanged.
   c. output to decrease and prices to remain unchanged.
   d. prices to decrease and output to increase.

9. According to the New Keynesians a short-run decrease in Aggregate Demand will
   a. decrease output.
   b. decrease prices.
   c. increase output.
   d. not change output or prices.

10. New Classical economists believe the short-run Aggregate supply curve is
    a. vertical.
    b. horizontal.
    c. upward sloping.
    d. downward sloping.

SHORT ANSWER QUESTIONS

Fill in the blanks in the following statements.

1. An _____ shock is any event directly affecting producers' costs of production and market supply.

2. The _____ is the central bank for the U.S.

3. _____ and _____ policies are effective means of achieving economic goals according to the New Keynesians.

4. New Classical economists believe the economy always will operate on the _____.

5. _____ wages and prices stop the economy from reaching full employment in the _____ run according to the New Keynesians.

PROBLEMS

1. How do sticky wages and prices undermine the New Classical model of the macroeconomy?
2. Draw a graph to show the short-run effects of an increase in Aggregate Demand on the economy according to the New Classical approach. Explain your answer.
3. Draw a graph to show the short-run effects of an increase in Aggregate Demand on the economy according to the New Keynesian approach. Explain your answer.
4. Draw a graph to show the short-run effects of a decrease in Aggregate Demand on the economy according to the New Classical approach. Explain your answer.
5. Draw a graph to show the short-run effects of a decrease in Aggregate Demand on the economy according to the New Keynesian approach. Explain your answer.
6. Why wouldn't a New Classical economist recommend the use of fiscal policy in the short run?
7. What evidence on the performance of the economy is inconsistent with the New Classical approach?
8. What evidence on the performance of the economy is inconsistent with the New Keynesian approach?
9. Explain the likely effects on the macroeconomy of an across-the-board increase in oil prices. Use graphs to support your answer.
10. Describe U.S. actual output relative to the potential output over the last 15 years.

POST-TEST

Answer the following questions to determine how well you have learned the material in the chapter and to determine those areas where you need to focus your studies.

1. Explain the inconsistencies between actual output levels in the U.S. since 1977 and the New Classical approach.
2. How does the New Keynesian approach fail to explain the effects of supply shocks on the economy?
3. Graphically show the effects of an increase in consumer demand on prices and output according to the New Classical approach.
4. Graphically show the effects of an decrease in government demand on prices and output according to the New Classical approach.
5. What are the likely policy choices for a New Classical and a New Keynesian economist when the economy is experiencing a high rate of cyclical unemployment?

6. Why will sticky wages and prices prevent full employment in the short run?

7. What branches of government are responsible for fiscal and monetary policy?

8. How do the New Classical economists explain the effects of an Aggregate Supply shock?

9. Why are firms and individuals reluctant to tie prices and wages to the overall rate of inflation according to the New Keynesians?

10. Describe the theoretical split between the Bush/Reagan and Clinton economic advisors.

Part II–Sample Test

Introduction to Macroeconomic Theory and Policy

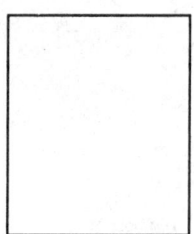

1. Unemployment that fluctuates with the state of the economy because of sticky wages is
   a. structural unemployment.
   b. cyclical unemployment.
   c. frictional unemployment.
   c. turnover unemployment.
   d. voluntary unemployment.

2. The rate of unemployment that places the economy on the production possibilities curve is
   a. actual unemployment rate.
   b. cyclical unemployment rate.
   c. frictional unemployment rate.
   d. structural unemployment rate.
   e. natural unemployment rate.

3. The theory which place all the risks of a business downturn on the younger, less experienced workers is
   a. the cyclical theory of unemployment.
   b. the laissez faire theory.
   c. the conspiracy theory.
   d. the insider/outsider theory.

4. The unemployment rate, expressed as a percent, is the ratio of
   a. unemployed workers to employed workers.
   b. unemployed workers to the adult population.
   c. unemployed workers to sum of employed plus unemployed workers.
   d. unemployed workers to the number of nonagricultural workers.

5. Long-run economic growth emphasizes the growth in
   a. actual output.
   b. the potential of the economy to produce goods and services.
   c. employment.
   d. the number of hours worked.
   e. demand.

6. The price level for the Gross Domestic Product is called the
   a. implicit price deflator.
   b. producer's price index.
   c. wholesale price index.
   d. ideal price index.
   e. global price index.

7. Bracket creep occurs when
   a. income increases with experience.
   b. income increases because of good luck.
   c. money income increases because of inflation.
   d. real income increases with capital accumulation.

8. The core rate of inflation is based upon
   a. the total consumer price index.
   b. the total producer price index.
   c. the GDP price deflator.
   d. a restricted market basket which excludes volatile items.
   e. inflation in the price of materials.

9. The difference between a nation's exports and its imports is called
   a. the balance of payment.
   b. the terms of trade.
   c. the balance of trade.
   d. the exchange rate.

10. An inflation in which prices are increasing very rapidly, causing people to lose confidence in the currency is called
    a. core inflation.
    b. hyperinflation.
    c. surprise inflation.
    d. structural inflation.
    e. stochastic inflation.

11. The value of final goods and services produced within a country during a period of time, whether by a country's own citizens or by citizens of other countries is the

a. Gross Domestic Product.
b. Gross National Product.
c. National Income.
d. Industrial Production.

12. Gross Domestic Investment includes
    a. purchases of new housing.
    b. purchases of new equipment.
    c. purchases of new building and structures.
    d. additions to inventories.
    e. all of the above

13. The chief difference between gross domestic product and net domestic product is
    a. corporate income taxes.
    b. personal income taxes.
    c. corporate consumption allowances.
    d. retained earnings.

14. Constant dollar Gross Domestic Product is
    a. is the same as Gross National Product.
    b. is the same as Domestic Income.
    c. is greater than Current dollar GDP when prices are greater than the base year.
    d. the actual dollar value of the GDP generated in that year.
    e. the value of the GDP generated in a year, but with prices from a base year.

15. Gross Domestic Product is called "gross" because
    a. the estimates are all rather inaccurate.
    b. no deduction is made for the capital worn out in producing the goods.
    c. the value of pornography is included in the total.
    d. no deduction is made for workers' commuting expenses.

16. The curve relating the price level to real GDP which slopes downward to the right is
    a. aggregate demand curve.
    b. demand curve.
    c. aggregate supply curve.
    d. supply curve.

17. An negative aggregate supply shock will
    a. cause a movement up along a fixed aggregate supply curve.
    b. cause a movement down along a fixed aggregate supply curve.
    c. shifts the aggregate supply curve to the right.
    d. shifts the aggregate supply curve to the left.

18. The new classical model of the economy is built upon the assumption that
    a. markets are competitive and economic agents rational.
    b. money wages are rigid.
    c. government has superior insight into the economy.
    d. prices are sticky.
    e. all of the above

19. The pursuit of the four macroeconomic goals
    a. can always be pursued simultaneously.
    b. is the primary responsibility of state government.
    c. may require the sacrifice of one goal to achieve another.
    d. is the responsibility of only Fiscal policy.
    e. is the responsibility of only Monetary policy.

20. The Federal Reserve System has primary responsibility for
    a. foreign trade.
    b. Federal government spending.
    c. Federal taxes.
    d. the money supply.

21. During the short run
    a. no resources can be varied in quantity employed.
    b. at least one resource is fixed in quantity employed.
    c. all resources can be varied in quantity employed.
    d. a period of less than one calendar year has elapsed.
    e. a period of less than one fiscal year has elapsed.

22. In the national income accounts, government purchases of new buildings is included as part of
    a. consumption purchases.
    b. investment purchases.
    c. government purchases.
    d. as negative taxes.

23. Which group believes that discretionary fiscal and monetary policies are likely to damage the economy?
    a. Classical School
    b. New Classical School
    c. Rational Expectations School
    d. all of the above
    e. none of the above

24. The one dimensional representation of the nation's production possibility frontier is
    a. the vertical aggregate supply curve.
    b. the horizontal aggregate supply curve.
    c. the vertical aggregate demand curve.
    d. the horizontal aggregate demand curve.

25. With respect to the desirability of government monetary and fiscal policy
    a. both New Classicals and New Keynesians see it as desirable.
    b. only New Classicals see it as desirable.
    c. only New Keynesians see it as desirable.
    d. neither New Classicals or New Keynesians see it as desirable.

Chapter 10
National Income Determination

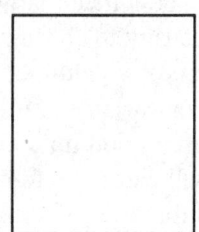

LEARNING OBJECTIVES

CONCEPTS TO LEARN

Consumption function	Saving function
Marginal propensity to consume	Marginal propensity to save
Life-cycle Hypothesis	Investment demand
Cost of capital	Equilibrium level of national income
The saving = investment equilibrium	

CONCEPTS TO RECALL

Circular flow of economic activity	New Keynesian economics
Aggregate Demand and Aggregate Supply	

CHAPTER REVIEW

Chapter 10 introduces a model with fixed wages and prices that can be used to analyze the effects of aggregate demand on the circular flow of economic activity from a New Keynesian perspective. The chapter includes a discussion of the determinants of consumption and investment demand and how these variables are important components of aggregate demand. Finally, the chapter concludes with a discussion of the equilibrium level of national income where actual saving always equals actual investment.

1. A simple model of the economy has an Aggregate Demand for goods and services that consists of investment demand by business firms and consumption demand of households.

2. Wages and prices are fixed in the simple model and firms have to predict the demand for their products and adjust their supply based on consumer demand. The product markets are in equilibrium when the level of national income equals the aggregate demand for goods and services.

3. According to John Maynard Keynes the level of household consumption was determined by a small component unrelated to income and a much larger component that varied with the current level of disposable income. The propensity to consume is the amount of consumption associated with varying levels of disposable income. Wealth, expectations about the future, the age distribution of the population, and other variables can all have an effect on consumption at all levels of disposable income. The consumption function is positively related to disposable income and a change in non-income factors will cause the function to shift up or down. (note: disposable income is measured on the x-axis and the level of consumption is measured on the y-axis)

4. The marginal propensity to consume, MPC, measures the change in consumption relative to a change in disposable income. Graphically, the MPC is represented by the slope of the consumption function. The MPC out of $1.00 will lie between 0 and 1.

5. The proportion of income that is not consumed is saved. The saving function is the mirror image of the consumption function. The marginal propensity to save, MPS, is the change in savings for a change in disposable income and $0 < MPS < 1$. Savings are positively sloped with respect to disposable income and the slope of the savings function equals the MPS. The MPC + MPS = 1 since whatever is not consumed out of income will be saved.

6. The aggregate consumption in the U.S. is consistent with the Keynesian consumption function. The short-run MPC is between .60 and .75 and the long-run MPC is .90.

7. The Life-Cycle Hypothesis is an alternate theory to explain consumption patterns. According to the Life-Cycle Hypothesis, individuals try to smooth out their consumption levels over their lifetimes. Lifetime consumption levels are adjusted when there are changes in current or expected wages, inherited wealth, government transfers or taxes that affect lifetime disposable incomes.

8. The Life-Cycle Hypothesis predicts workers will borrow money to consume when they first enter the labor force and when they reach a peak in the middle of their career they will pay off debts and save for their retirement. This strategy will allow an individual to have a constant level of consumption throughout their life. Temporary increases in income will not affect consumption while permanent changes will cause an individual to change their behavior. The MPC out of temporary changes in disposable income appears to be much smaller than the MPC out of

permanent changes in the U.S. The Life-Cycle Hypothesis also explains how wealth and age distribution can affect the consumption demand in an economy. However, the Life-Cycle Hypothesis under predicts the aggregate MPC in the U.S.

9. Investment demand in plant and equipment, inventory, and housing is NOT closely related to national income levels. The macro model presented in this chapter includes the assumption that these three components of investment demand are constant.

10. The desired stock of capital is determined by the firm's production technology and any change in demand will be related to changes in output or sales not the aggregate level of output.

11. Costs of capital are a function of the price of a unit of capital, interest rates, the rate of depreciation of capital, and the tax system. The government can influence investment in capital by changing corporate tax rates, depreciation allowances, and investment tax credits.

12. The relationship between the cost of capital and investment demand is difficult to determine due to the time lags between decisions to increase capital and the actual investment. Economists agree that changes in capital costs will affect the capital stock but they disagree as to whether the changes in the cost of capital have an immediate or important effect on investment demand.

13. Firms do adjust inventories to desired stocks of inventory in relatively short time periods. The Keynesian model assumes that firms attempt to maintain a desired inventory level. Then, when demand for goods and services are high and inventories are depleted firms will increase their output. And, when demand is low and inventories are above desired levels the firms will decrease their output.

14. An equilibrium in the economy occurs when the level of aggregate demand equals the level of national income. Graphically, the equilibrium is reached when the aggregate demand line, ADE, intersects the 45^0 emanating from the origin.

15. Aggregate demand is less than the economy's output when the national income level is beyond the equilibrium level. Inventories will exceed desired levels and firms will cut back their production moving the economy back towards the equilibrium output. When aggregate demand exceeds output the economy will be producing less than the equilibrium level. Inventories will be depleted and firms will expand their output pushing the economy towards the equilibrium level.

16. Savings demand will equal investment when the economy is producing at the equilibrium level of output. Actual savings must always equal actual investment but desired levels are equivalent only at the equilibrium level of output.

A FEW HELPFUL TIPS

Remember, when national income levels change it means that the economy is moving along the ADE curve and when any other components of aggregate demand change the curve will shift up or down. Also, the 45^0 line is intended to be used as a guidepost and has no inherent meaning. It just maps out those points where the ADE measured on the y-axis is equal to the level of national income.

QUICK STUDY GUIDE

	T/F	Mult. Choice	Short Answer	Problems
Consumption Function	1, 3, 4, 7	1, 2, 3, 4	1, 2	4, 5, 6, 7, 8
Life-Cycle Hypothesis	8	7		1
Investment Demand	2, 6, 9, 10	8	3, 5	3
Equilibrium Level of National Income	5	5, 6	1	2, 9, 10

PRETEST

Answer the following questions to test your initial understanding of the material in this chapter:

1. What is the relationship between national income and consumption in the simple Keynesian model?
2. Describe the relationship between national income and investment in the simple Keynesian model.
3. Describe the Life-Cycle Hypothesis of consumption.
4. How can government affect investment levels in the economy?

Use the following example to answer questions 5-8:

Disposable Income in Billion Dollars	Consumption Demand in Billion Dollars
0	400
1,000	1,200
2,000	2,000
3,000	2,800
4,000	3,600

5. What is the MPC in this economy?
6. What is the APC for each level of disposable income in this economy?
7. What is the marginal propensity to save in this economy?
8. What is the break-even level of consumption for this economy and at what levels will savings be positive and at what levels will savings be negative?
9. Draw a graph depicting an economy where ADE = C + I and show the national income level where the economy is at an equilibrium.
10. Use the same graph you drew in question 9 to explain why the economy will return to the equilibrium when national income is at a level beyond the equilibrium.

TRUE/FALSE PRACTICE QUESTIONS

1. Data on MPC levels in the U.S. are inconsistent with the Keynesian model.   T   F

2. In the short run the Keynesian model assumes that desired investment levels are independent of national income levels. T F

3. The effects of an increase in wealth can be shown by a movement along a consumption demand line. T F

4. An increase in MPC will cause the consumption line to shift downward. T F

5. When inventories are above desired levels firms will decrease their output. T F

6. Investment levels increase when national income increases in the simple Keynesian model. T F

7. When the MPC increases the MPS also increases. T F

8. The Life-Cycle Hypothesis predicts that only increases in permanent income will affect consumption. T F

9. Actual savings equals actual investment at all times. T F

10. Desired savings and investment levels are equal only at the equilibrium national income level. T F

MULTIPLE CHOICE QUESTIONS

Choose the best option for the following questions.

1. If the MPC is equal to .8 the MPS is equal to
   a. 1/.8
   b. .2
   c. 1.8
   d. .8

2. When the MPC increases the MPS
   a. increases.
   b. decreases.
   c. can increase or decrease.
   d. remains the same.

3. An increase in consumption demand will
   a. increase the equilibrium national income level.
   b. decrease the equilibrium national income level.
   c. either increase or decrease the national income level.
   d. not have an effect on national income.

4. A decrease in savings will
   a. increase consumption and the national income equilibrium level.
   b. decrease consumption and the national income equilibrium level.
   c. increase consumption and decrease the national income equilibrium level.
   d. not affect consumption.

5. When the economy is at a national income level beyond the equilibrium
   a. inventories are rising.
   b. inventories are falling.
   c. inventories can be rising or falling.
   d. inventories do not change.

6. If ADE is greater than national output
   a. inventories are rising.
   b. inventories are falling.
   c. inventories can rise or fall.
   d. inventories don't change.

7. According to the Life-Cycle Hypothesis a temporary increase in income will
   a. increase consumption.
   b. decrease consumption.
   c. either increase or decrease consumption.
   d. not affect consumption.

8. Which of the following is not a component of investment demand?
   a. housing stock
   b. inventories
   c. bank savings certificates
   d. plant and equipment

9. Which of the following will NOT cause the Consumption line to shift upward?
   a. an increase in national income
   b. an increase in MPC
   c. a decrease in MPS
   d. an increase in wealth

10. Which of the following will cause the ADE line to shift downward?
    a. a decrease in national income
    b. an increase in MPS
    c. inventory levels above the desired amounts
    d. consumption levels exceeding the equilibrium level.

SHORT ANSWER QUESTIONS

Fill in the blanks in the following statements.

1. The _____ links consumption levels to an age-earnings profile.

2. When the MPC increases the _____ will _____.

3. The three components of investment demand are _____, _____, _____.

4. An increase in wealth will shift the ADE line _____.

5. When inventories are _____ firms will expand their output and national income will _____.

PROBLEMS

1. How does the Life-Cycle Hypothesis differ from the simple Keynesian model of consumption?
2. Why will the equilibrium national income level actually decrease when savings increases?
3. The Federal government has been experimenting with investment tax credits for firms to encourage investment in depressed inner city areas. How would these credits affect the equilibrium level of national income?

Use the following example in questions 4-8:

Disposable Income in Billions of Dollars	Consumption Demand in Billions of Dollars
0	2,000
5,000	6,000
10,000	10,000
15,000	14,000
20,000	18,000

4. What is the MPC and MPS for this economy?
5. What is the APC at each level of disposable income?
6. Solve for the level of disposable income where savings are zero and draw a graph to describe the economy at that point.
7. Solve for the break-even level of income if Consumption Demand = $1000 billion when national income is zero. Also show your answer graphically.
8. How will the break-even level of consumption change if the consumption demand at zero disposable income increases by $1000 billion?
9. Suppose the economy is at a national income level above its equilibrium. Use graphs to explain how changes in inventory levels will help move the economy back towards the equilibrium level.
10. If there is a permanent change in wealth how will ADE be affected in the short and long run?

POST-TEST

Answer the following questions to determine how well you have learned the material in the chapter and to determine those areas where you need to focus your studies.

1. Describe the relationship between consumption and savings to the level of national income.
2. How do changes in permanent and temporary income affect consumption levels according to the Life-Cycle Hypothesis?
3. Explain the effects of an increase in MPC on savings, consumption, and the break-even point.

4. Why will national income fall when inventories exceed the desired levels?

5. Which components of investment demand are not affected by short-run changes in national income and why?

Use the following table for questions 6-9:

Disposable Income in Billions of Dollars	Consumption Demand in Billions of Dollars
0	4,000
20,000	22,000
40,000	40,000
60,000	58,000
80,000	76,000

6. Solve for the MPC and the MPS.

7. Solve for the APS at each level of disposable income.

8. What is the break-even level of consumption?

9. How will the break-even point change if consumption at a zero national income level increases to $6000 billion?

10. Suppose the economy is at a national income level below its equilibrium. Explain why national income is likely to increase.

Chapter 11
The Spending Multiplier, Fiscal Policy, and Unemployment

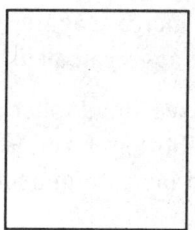

LEARNING OBJECTIVES

CONCEPTS TO LEARN

The macroeconomic policy problem	Spending multiplier
Tax multiplier	Transfer multiplier
Balanced budget multipliers	Recessionary and inflationary gaps

CONCEPTS TO RECALL

Production possibilities frontier	Circular flow of economic activity
Full employment	Fiscal policy
Consumption function	Saving function
Marginal propensity to consume	Marginal propensity to save
Equilibrium level of national income	

CHAPTER REVIEW

Chapter 11 focuses on how fiscal and monetary policy can be used to correct macroeconomic problems. Government is added to the simple model of the economy and the effects of changes in government spending and taxation on national income are analyzed. The strengths and weaknesses of fiscal policy are also discussed.

1. The equilibrium level of national income is not necessarily consistent with a desirable level. The economy can be at an equilibrium at a point in the interior or beyond the production possibilities frontier. If the economy is at an equilibrium in the interior unemployment will be a problem. When the economy is at an equilibrium beyond the frontier inflationary conditions will exist.

2. Fiscal and monetary policy follows a three-step process:
   a. Policy makers must establish a target level of national income based on the four macroeconomic policy goals of long run economic growth, full employment, low inflation, a balance of trade, and a stable value for the dollar.
   b. Policy makers need models that show the equilibrium level of income in the absence of any policy, how the economy will respond to specific fiscal or monetary policies, and how changes in the equilibrium will affect macroeconomic policy goals.
   c. Policy makers need to design fiscal and/or fiscal policies to meet target levels of national income. Expansionary policies increase aggregate demand and national income while contractionary policies decrease aggregate demand and national income.

3. Changes in aggregate demand will have a multiplier effect. A given dollar increase in aggregate demand will change the level of equilibrium level of income by more than the initial change. This multiplier effect occurs because each increase in demand will spur another increase in demand when national income rises.

4. In a simple model the multiplier = $M_{spending}$ = $1/(1-MPC)$. The product of a one dollar change (positive or negative) in aggregate demand times the multiplier equals the overall change in national income.

5. Changes in taxes, government spending or transfer payments are fiscal policy tools that can be used to change the equilibrium level of income.

6. Government expenditures are a component of aggregate demand in the economy so that the equilibrium condition is $Y = C^d + I^d + G^d$ or national income is the sum of consumption, investment and government demand.

7. The effects of increases in government spending on the equilibrium level of income are determined by the spending multiplier where $M_{spending} = 1/(1-MPC)$.

8. Changes in taxes and transfer payments affect aggregate demand because changes in disposable income will affect consumption and investment demand. Since taxes and transfer payments affect ADE indirectly the multipliers are smaller where $M_{taxes} = (-MPC)/(1-MPC)$ and $M_{transfer} = (MPC)/(1-MPC)$.

9. Recognition lags occur because it takes time for policymakers to recognize the need for fiscal or monetary policy. Lag times will vary depending on the ability to forecast macroeconomic performance.

10. Administrative lags occur between the time the problems are identified and legislative action is taken. Fiscal policy administrative lags often exceed a year.

11. Operational lags occur because once the policy has been approved it takes time to change the level of government expenditures or revenues and the multiplier process takes time.

12. Fiscal policy is not a practical tool for fine tuning the economy due to the lag problems. However, fiscal policy is effective in preventing major economic disasters like the great depression.

13. Temporary changes in taxes have historically had little effect on aggregate demand in the U.S. This result is consistent with the Life-Cycle Hypothesis of consumption.

A FEW HELPFUL TIPS

Remember when the economy is operating at a level below the desired level we want to give it a push, i.e. increase government spending or decrease taxes and when the economy is beyond its frontier just do the opposite.

QUICK STUDY GUIDE

	T/F	Mult. Choice	Short Answer	Problems
Multiplier Effects	3, 5	1, 2, 3, 4, 5	3, 4	4, 5
Fiscal Policy	1, 2, 4, 6, 7	8, 9, 10	1	1
Recessionary and Inflationary Gaps	9	6, 7	5	6, 7, 9
Policy Lags	8		2	10

PRETEST

Answer the following questions to test your initial understanding of the material in this chapter:

1. What are the fiscal policy options when the economy is operating within its production possibilities frontier?

2. How do changes in taxes affect aggregate demand and the equilibrium level of national income?

3. Why will fiscal policy be much more effective if the marginal propensity to save is lower?

4. Suppose the economy is at an equilibrium level of national income = $400 billion and the target level is actually $300 billion. What are the fiscal policy options when the mpc is equal to .8?

5. Suppose the economy is at an equilibrium level of national income at $1200 billion and the target level is $1600 billion. What are the fiscal policy options when the marginal propensity to consume equals .9?

6. Suppose that fiscal policy is constrained to balanced budget changes. If the economy is currently at an equilibrium level of national income at $1200 and the target level is $1600 billion what are the fiscal policy options when the marginal propensity to consume equals .9?

7. Why are balanced budget fiscal policies less effective?
8. Describe the types of lags common when implementing fiscal policy.
9. Use diagrams to show and explain an inflationary gap.
10. Use diagrams to show and explain a recessionary gap.

TRUE/FALSE PRACTICE QUESTIONS

1. A balanced budget fiscal policy will have a stronger dollar for dollar effect. T F
2. Tax increases are called for during recessions. T F
3. The multiplier effect increases when the mpc increases. T F
4. Changes in transfer payments have no effect on national income equilibrium. T F
5. The tax multiplier is smaller than the spending multiplier. T F
6. Government spending increases may help when the economy is operating within its production possibilities frontier. T F
7. Temporary changes in tax rates will have very large effects on the level of equilibrium income. T F
8. Fiscal policy is subject to few lag problems. T F
9. Tax cuts will increase inflation when the economy is already on its production possibilities frontier. T F
10. Target levels of national income are determined by the production possibilities frontier. T F

MULTIPLE CHOICE QUESTIONS

Choose the best option for the following questions.

1. When the mpc = .8 and government spending increases by $100 billion the equilibrium level of output will increase by
   a. $100 billion.
   b. $800 billion.
   c. $500 billion.
   d. $80 billion.

2. When the mpc = .9 and government spending increases by $50 billion the equilibrium level of income will increase by
   a. $500 billion.
   b. $450 billion.
   c. $45 billion.
   d. $50 billion.

3. When the mpc = .75 the spending multiplier equals
   a. 3.
   b. 4.
   c. 5.
   d. 3/4.

4. When the mps = .10 the tax multiplier is equal to
   a. 10.
   b. 9.
   c. 1.
   d. 5.

5. The balanced budget multiplier is equal to
   a. 0.
   b. the spending multiplier times the mpc.
   c. 1.
   d. the tax multiplier times the mps.

6. Which of the following is NOT an appropriate policy option to close a recessionary gap?
   a. decreasing taxes
   b. increasing government spending
   c. decreasing transfer payments
   d. expansionary monetary policy

7. If the economy is operating with an inflationary gap which one of the following is an appropriate policy option?
   a. decreasing taxes
   b. decreasing government spending
   c. an expansionary monetary policy
   d. increasing transfer payments

8. A temporary tax cut will
   a. increase aggregate demand.
   b. decrease aggregate demand.
   c. either increase or decrease aggregate demand.
   d. have little effect on aggregate demand.

9. A low mpc implies
   a. fiscal policy will not be as effective due to a low multiplier.
   b. fiscal policy will be more effective due to a low multiplier.
   c. fiscal policy will not be as effective due to a high multiplier.
   d. fiscal policy will be more effective due to a high multiplier.

10. Which of the following will NOT dampen the effectiveness of fiscal policy?
    a. a balanced budget requirement
    b. a small mpc
    c. a small mps
    d. long recognition lags

SHORT ANSWER QUESTIONS

Fill in the blanks in the following statements.

1. A balanced budget _____ implies that any increase in government spending means that _____ have to be _____ also.

2. A _____ is the time it takes for policy makers to determine there is a problem in the economy.

3. When the mpc _____ the _____ increases.

4. The tax multiplier is _____ than the spending multiplier.

5. An _____ exists when output is _____ the production possibilities frontier.

PROBLEMS

1. During the Great Depression of the 1930's what types of fiscal policy would you have used to correct the situation?

Use the following table to answer questions 2-9 (all numbers are in billions):

C^d	I^d	G^d	Aggregate Demand	National Income
200	100	100	400	0
1,100	100	100	1300	1,000
2,000	100	100	2,200	2,000
2,900	100	100	3100	3,000
3,800	100	100	4000	4,000
4,700	100	100	4900	5,000

2. Fill in the levels of aggregate demand on the chart.

3. What is the equilibrium level of income? Draw a graph and label the equilibrium point.

4. What is the value of the spending multiplier?

5. What is the value of the tax multiplier?

6. Suppose the full employment level of national income is $3000. What are the fiscal policy options?

7. Suppose the full employment level of national income is $5000. What are the fiscal policy options?

8. How would the equilibrium level of national income change if the investment demand declined to $50?

9. How would the equilibrium level of national income change if a $10 billion tax cut was implemented when there was a balanced budget requirement?

10. How do operational lags differ from administrative lags?

POST-TEST

Answer the following questions to determine how well you have learned the material in the chapter and to determine those areas where you need to focus your studies.

1. What are the economic policy options when the economy is operating beyond its production possibilities frontier?

2. How do increases in the marginal propensity to save change the effectiveness of fiscal policy?

3. Why are temporary changes in tax rates an ineffective method of changing the equilibrium level of national income?

4. Suppose the economy is at a full employment equilibrium, the mpc = .8, and investment demand increases by 100 billion. What is likely to occur in the economy and what are the appropriate fiscal policy options?

5. Suppose the economy is experiencing a recessionary gap equal to $50 billion and the mps = .1. What are the fiscal policy options that can be used to close the gap?

6. Suppose the economy is experiencing an inflationary gap equal to $200 billion and the mpc = .8. If there is a balanced budget requirement what are the fiscal policy options for correcting the problem?

7. What happens to the multiplier when the mps increases?

8. What are the implications of the Life-Cycle Hypothesis on fiscal policy?

9. Why is a balanced budget increase in government spending less effective in reducing unemployment than a deficit financed increase?

10. What is likely to happen to the equilibrium level of national income if transfer payments are increased? Support your answer using graphs.

Chapter 12

Automatic Stabilizers, Net Exports, and Budget Deficits

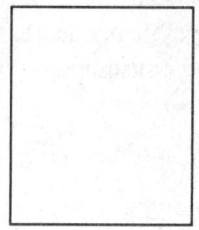

LEARNING OBJECTIVES

CONCEPTS TO LEARN

Automatic stabilizers	Marginal propensity to import
Cyclical budget deficit	Structural budget deficit
The burden of the federal debt	

CONCEPTS TO RECALL

Dollar appreciation/depreciation	Net exports
Total saving = investment accounting identity	Fiscal policy
Marginal propensity to consume	Equilibrium level of national income

CHAPTER REVIEW

Chapter 12 focuses on the feedback channels from national income to aggregate demand. The first section includes an analysis of automatic stabilizers in the economy; taxes, government transfer payments, business saving and import demand. The second section introduces the foreign sector into the macro model of the economy. The last half of the chapter focuses on the national debt including how the debt is defined and the effects of the debt on the economy and economic policy.

1. Automatic stabilizers in the economy lower the value of the multiplier and make the economy less sensitive to changes in aggregate demand.

2. Disposable income changes by a smaller amount than national income because income and sales taxes, transfer payments, and business saving act as automatic stabilizers. Since disposable income changes by a smaller amount there are smaller changes in consumption demand during each round of the multiplier process and the value of the spending multiplier is reduced.

3. Import demand is positively related to national income levels and is an automatic stabilizer. When national income rises, import demand increases and the expenditures on imports become sources of income for foreign producers. Shifting income abroad reduces disposable income and then consumption in the U.S. When national income falls, import demand falls and the opposite chain of events occurs.

4. Income taxes, business savings and import demand all increase when national income rises. These automatic stabilizers drain income and lower consumption demand during high growth periods in the economy. During recessionary periods these automatic stabilizers increase disposable income and consumption demand. Transfer payments decrease as national income rises. The decreases will lower both disposable income and consumption during inflationary periods and do the opposite during recessions.

5. The spending multiplier is reduced by approximately 40% by automatic stabilizers.

6. When the economy is operating at an output level close to its target, automatic stabilizers are helpful because they counteract any changes or shocks. However, automatic stabilizers will dampen the effects of fiscal or monetary policy tools when they are used to return an economy to target levels of output.

7. A more complete model of the economy includes the foreign sector by adding net exports, the difference between exports and imports. The model for the economy is $Y = C^d + I^d + G^d + (Ex^d + Im^d)$. The product markets are in equilibrium when aggregate demand equals the level of national income.

8. Export demand is determined by national income levels abroad but not by the level of national income in the U.S.

9. The federal deficit is affected by changes in national income and any discretionary changes in government purchases, transfer payments, or taxes.

10. The actual budget deficit can be divided into the structural budget deficit and the cyclical budget deficit. A structural budget deficit is an estimate how large the deficit would be if the economy was operating near or at its full employment level (i.e. at the natural rate of unemployment). The difference between the actual and structural deficits is the cyclical deficit, which tracks the effects of changes in the overall performance of the economy on the deficit.

11. The magnitude and direction of discretionary fiscal policy can be deduced by changes in the structural deficit. Increases in the structural deficit imply an expansionary policy and decreases imply a contractionary policy. The cyclical deficit increases when the economy slows down to the reduction in tax revenues and increases in transfer payments. During inflationary periods the cyclical deficit decreases because of increases in tax revenues and reductions in transfer payments.

12. Most economists do not support a balanced budget amendment to the Constitution because while it would promote fiscal discipline it would also reduce the effectiveness of fiscal policy when the economy needs some assistance.

13. Long-term structural deficits can be a burden to the economy if they are not used to finance productive public investment. Borrowing to pay for current expenditures is at the expense of future consumption when the debt is repaid. If the structural deficits finance education, research, or other productive investments they will not be a serious burden.

14. External debt is owed to those outside the U.S. and internal debt is owed to the country's own citizens. The majority of U.S. debt is internal debt.

15. External debt is a transfer of purchasing power to foreign citizens and the country will eventually have to pay it back with interest. External debt is similar to private debt.

16. Since internal debt is owed to a country's own citizens it does not drain resources out of the country and is not analogous to private debt. The burden of internal debt is due to the crowding out factor. Private saving does not increase by the full amount of the deficit (negative government saving) and as result the total amount of saving in the economy declines. Since actual savings must equal actual investment, total investment levels in the economy declines. Debt financed by the foreign sector reduces this burden but will eventually create a drain on the economy when the debt is repaid.

A FEW HELPFUL TIPS

Most beginning students confuse their own personal finances with the national debt. Remember, the government owes the majority of the debt to its own citizens. The U.S. government is using its own citizens' resources with a bit of help from the foreign sector to finance expenditures for education, health, defense, etc.

QUICK STUDY GUIDE

	T/F	Mult. Choice	Short Answer	Problems
Automatic Stabilizers	2, 3, 7		1	3
Import Demand	10	1, 7	2, 4, 5	1, 7, 8, 9, 10
Budget Deficits	4, 8	3, 4, 8, 10		2, 4, 5, 6

PRETEST

Answer the following questions to test your initial understanding of the material in this chapter:

1. How is export demand tied to the national income of the U.S. and other countries?

2. Why will the multiplier be lower when a model of the economy includes automatic stabilizers?

3. Explain why expansionary fiscal policy will increase the federal deficit.

4. Why are federal budget deficits expected to increase when the U.S. economy experiences a recession?

5. Explain the difference between the structural deficit and the actual deficit.

6. Explain the relationship between unemployment and the cyclical deficit.

7. Explain the relationship between import demand and national income.

8. What factors account for the dramatic increases in the federal deficit during the 1980s?

9. What are the costs to society of running large budget deficits year after year?

10. When can structural deficits be justified?

TRUE/FALSE PRACTICE QUESTIONS

1. The spending multiplier in the U.S. is higher due to imports.   T   F
2. Income taxes are an example of an automatic stabilizer.   T   F
3. Imports act as an automatic stabilizer.   T   F
4. A decrease in the structural deficit means that fiscal policy has been expansionary.   T   F
5. During the Reagan era the national debt grew faster than GDP.   T   F
6. External debt is owed to U.S. and foreign citizens.   T   F
7. Transfer payments are contractionary during recessions.   T   F
8. The cyclical deficit is likely to increase during a recession.   T   F
9. President Clinton supports a balanced budget amendment.   T   F
10. Increases in income in the U.S. are likely to increase import demand.   T   F

MULTIPLE CHOICE QUESTIONS

Choose the best option for the following questions.

1. An increase in the value of the dollar will
    a. shift the import demand curve up.
    b. shift the import demand curve down.
    c. move the economy up along the import demand curve.
    d. not affect the import demand curve.

2. The demand for U.S. exports will
    a. increase with U.S. national income.
    b. decrease with an increase in U.S. national income.
    c. increase with an increase in the national incomes of other countries.
    d. decrease with an increase in the national incomes of other countries.

3. An increase in the structural deficit is indicative of
   a. a contractionary fiscal policy.
   b. an expansionary fiscal policy.
   c. a decrease in government spending.
   d. an increase in taxes.

4. The cyclical deficit is the
   a. difference between the actual and potential deficit.
   b. ratio of the actual and structural deficit.
   c. difference between the actual and structural deficit.
   d. actual deficit divided by national income.

5. When national income rises
   a. transfer payments decline, disposable income declines, and consumption demand declines.
   b. transfer payments increase, disposable income increases, and consumption demand increases.
   c. transfer payments decline, disposable income increases, and consumption demand increases.
   d. transfer payments increase, disposable income declines, and consumption demand declines.

6. Which of the following will not affect the value of the spending multiplier?
   a. transfer payments
   b. taxes
   c. national income
   d. import demand

7. Import demand increases when
   a. national income falls.
   b. national income rises.
   c. exports rise.
   d. the value of the dollar falls.

8. Crowding out is likely to occur when
   a. the cyclical deficit increases.
   b. the structural deficit increases.
   c. the actual deficit increases.
   d. there is a balanced budget.

9. The cyclical deficit is zero when
   a. unemployment is less than the natural rate.
   b. national income rises.
   c. unemployment is equal to the natural rate.
   d. tax increases equal government expenditures increases.

SHORT ANSWER QUESTIONS

Fill in the blanks in the following statements.

1. The four principal automatic stabilizers in the U.S. economy are _____, _____, _____ and _____.

2. Tax revenues _____ when national income _____ and _____ when national income _____.

3. The _____ is the change in import demand to the change in _____.

4. The slope of the ADE line for a simple closed economy is _____ than the line for an economy that includes the foreign sector.

5. An appreciation of the dollar will increase _____ and _____ the level of national income.

PROBLEMS

1. Explain why the increase in the value of the dollar exerted a significant drag on aggregate demand during the 1980s.

2. Why did the structural deficit increase following the 1982-83 recession and what was the effect on the economy?

3. Explain why automatic stabilizers will reduce the impact of fiscal policies designed to correct problems in the economy.

4. Explain why the structural deficit increased dramatically during the Reagan era in spite of his position of fiscal conservatism.

5. Both Presidents Reagan and Bush supported a balanced budget amendment. Why would requiring the federal government to balance its actual budget result in procyclical fiscal policy? (i.e. contractionary during recessions and expansionary during inflationary periods)

6. How can President Clinton justify structural deficits in the 1990s in order to "grow the economy?"

Use the following table for questions 7-9:

Import Demand	National Income
1,500	10,000
2,500	20,000
3,500	30,000
4,500	40,000

7. What is the marginal propensity to import?

8. Draw a graph to show import demand.

9. What will happen to import demand if the value of the dollar increases? Show your answer graphically.

10. Use graphs to explain the effect of an increase in import demand on the equilibrium level of national income.

POST-TEST

Answer the following questions to determine how well you have learned the material in the chapter and to determine those areas where you need to focus your studies.

1. What is likely to happen to the cyclical and structural deficits of a country during a severe recession?

2. How will changes in import demand have a "automatic" stabilizing effect on the economy?

3. Why is it possible to have a zero structural deficit and still have a positive cyclical deficit?

4. How do changes in income tax rates affect the spending multiplier?

Use the following table for questions 5-7:

Import Demand	National Income
3,500	50,000
6,000	100,000
8,500	150,000
11,000	200,000

5. What is the marginal propensity to import?

6. Draw a graph of the import demand function.

7. Graphically show the effects of a decrease in the value of the dollar on import demand.

8. What impact do automatic stabilizers have on fiscal policy?

9. What are the effects on the equilibrium level of national income when the value of the dollar decreases?

10. How will reductions in transfer payments affect the spending multiplier?

Chapter 13

Business Cycles: The Multiplier-Accelerator Model and the Real Business Cycle

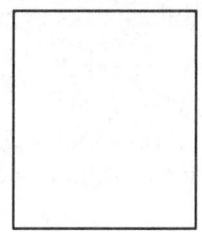

LEARNING OBJECTIVES

CONCEPTS TO LEARN

The business cycle	Indexes of cyclical indicators
Multiplier-accelerator model	Real business cycle model

CONCEPTS TO RECALL

Laws of supply and demand	Gross domestic product
Aggregate Demand and Aggregate Supply	Equilibrium level of national income
Investment demand	Life-Cycle Hypothesis

CHAPTER REVIEW

Chapter 13 focuses on business cycles in the macroeconomy. The first section describes how business cycles are tracked in the U.S. and the remainder of the chapter is devoted to a discussion of the current debate in the economics profession regarding the causes of the observed business cycles. New

Keynesians use the Multiplier-Accelerator model and the New Classical economists use Real Business Cycle theory to explain the observed fluctuations in the macroeconomy.

1. U.S. business cycles are tracked by the National Bureau of Economic Research (NBER) which has been the leading research center on business cycles since it was founded in 1920 by Wesley C. Mitchell. According to the NBER traditional view, the macroeconomy experiences a reoccurring series of expansions and contractions that move around a permanent trend rate of growth in real GDP. The production possibilities frontier shifts out according to the permanent trend rate of growth.

2. Cyclical indicators are analyzed by the NBER to monitor economic performance. Cyclical indicators are required to be reliable, currently available, economically significant, and reflective of the timing of the business cycle. Output, income, employment, and trade are the factors that are traditionally monitored by the NBER.

3. The Department of Commerce publishes three indexes that are composites of NBER cyclical indicators: The Index of Leading Indicators which are used to forecast troughs and peaks in the business cycle; the Index of Coincident Indicators are expected to be consistent with the peaks and troughs of the business cycle while they are occurring; and the Index of Lagging Indicators are used to confirm the existence of troughs and peaks in the business cycle after they occur.

4. The Business Cycle Dating Committee identifies the peaks and troughs in the business cycle data reported by the NBER. Normative judgements are used to determine which indicators should be used and exactly when the upswings or downward trends in the economy occur. Since WWII the Business Cycle Dating Committee has identified nine peaks and eight troughs or eight complete business cycles.

5. Victor Zarnovitz's study on business cycles from 1945 to 1982 versus cycles form 1912 to 1945 concluded that they are much less severe in the more recent period due to the increase in automatic stabilizers in the economy. Zarnovitz also found that expansion phases last relatively longer than contraction phases. While there is a lot of variation in length and severity, the average cycles in both time periods were 45 months.

6. The multiplier-accelerator model introduced by Paul Samuelson examines how internal mechanisms within the economy generate business cycles.

7. Investment demand is volatile because of the stock-flow relationship of capital and investment. Small changes in demand for capital lead to even larger changes in the demand for investment. Investment demand is a function of replacement as well as new capital demands.

8. Both the demand and supply side of the economy affect investment demand. Investment demand is a component of aggregate demand and a constant level of investment is consistent with a constant level of national income and a single equilibrium in the economy. The supply side of the economy will also affect investment demand because as the economy grows firms will need to increase their stocks of capital to maintain a constant capital-output ratio in production. Since the demand side requires a constant level of investment and the supply side of the economy requires an increase when national income increases, the economy reacts to this internal inconsistency by moving in business cycles over time.

9. The two main implications of the multiplier-accelerator model are that the expansion phase can only continue if consumption demand increases at an increasing rate. Once the economy reaches its production possibilities frontier, consumption demand can not continue to increase at an increasing rate. If investment demand levels off the economy will reach a peak, and the expansionary period will stop. The contraction or recession stage is dependent on the durability of capital. Depreciated capital will eventually be replaced resulting in an increase in investment demand and an end of the recessionary period.

10. New Keynesians generally accept the multiplier-accelerator model as an important explanation for the existence of business cycles in the U.S.

11. New Classical theorists generally accept real business cycle theory as an explanation for the troughs and peaks in the economy. A major underlying assumption of the model is that the economy is generally consistent with a competitive model based on the laws of supply and demand. The Real Business Cycle theory stresses the role of outside shocks to the real structure of the economy as the major cause of economic instability. The real structure consists of preferences, resources, and production technologies. Recent models have focused on productivity shocks caused by technological change.

12. According to the Real Business Cycle, temporary technical changes push out the production possibilities frontier and increase the real wage. Since households are Life-Cycle consumers they will save most of any temporary wage increase which will lead to an overall increase in investment in the economy. Increases in the real wage will also increase labor supply and employment which in turn will increase the economy's output. These characteristics of the model are consistent with data on the U.S. which show that output, consumption, investment, and employment all tend to increase (and decrease) simultaneously, and real wages are pro-cyclical.

13. According to Real Business Cycle advocates there is no permanent trend growth rate, only random shocks which cause the economy to move from the output level consistent with the production possibilities frontier. Since markets are competitive the laws of supply and demand will ensure that the economy will naturally move towards an efficient output level that fully employs resources.

14. Observed economic fluctuations are responses to the random shocks in the economy according to the Real Business Cycle advocates. Since their reactions are assumed to be efficient, fiscal and monetary policy are not effective in improving economic performance in the short run.

15. New Keynesians challenge Real Business Cycle theorists based on their beliefs that wages and prices are sticky and a large percentage of unemployment is involuntary. Changes in involuntary unemployment explain why real economic variables move in the same direction and swings in labor productivity can be traced to labor hoarding, not technical change. New Keynesians discount the New Classical argument that economic downturns are efficient responses to economic shocks. They also believe that corrective fiscal and monetary policies are useful economic stabilization tools.

16. New Classical economists counterattack the New Keynesians on their assumption that wages and prices are sticky. They argue that wage and price stickiness is inconsistent with rational agents solving their economic problems through exchange.

A FEW HELPFUL TIPS

While you may be more persuaded by one of the theories currently used to explain business cycles, the economics profession is still divided on the issue. It is important to understand both the New Keynesian and the Real Business Cycle approach in order to defend either one.

QUICK STUDY GUIDE

	T/F	Mult. Choice	Short Answer	Problems
Economic Indicators	5	2, 3		7
The Business Cycle	1, 2, 3	1, 4, 5	1, 3	2
Multiplier-Accelerator Theory	6, 10	6	3, 5	1, 4, 6, 10
Real Business Cycle Theory	6, 7, 8, 9	7, 8, 9, 10	2, 5	3, 4, 5, 8, 9

PRETEST

Answer the following questions to test your initial understanding of the material in this chapter:

1. How are expansionary and contractionary periods defined in the U.S.?
2. What are the economic indicators used to track business cycles in the U.S.?
3. How do pre-WWII business cycles differ from post war cycles?
4. What are the internal contradictions in the economy that account for economic instability according to the multiplier-accelerator theory?
5. Why is investment demand inherently unstable according to the multiplier-accelerator theory?
6. Which business cycle theory is generally supported by New Keynesians? Why?
7. Which business cycle theory is generally supported by New Classical economists? Why?
8. Explain the importance of the Life-Cycle theory in the Real Business Cycle theory.
9. How do Real Business Cycle advocates explain movements away from the production possibilities frontier?
10. What position do Real Business Cycle theorists take on fiscal and monetary policy in the short run? Why?

TRUE/FALSE PRACTICE QUESTIONS

1. Economic troughs appear to last longer than peaks.   T   F
2. A complete business cycle is the period from one economic peak to another.   T   F
3. When GDP declines in two consecutive quarters, the economy is generally considered to be in a recession.   T   F

4. Automatic stabilizers can explain the decreases in stability in the economy since WWII.   T   F

5. The Index of Leading Indicators is a good economic forecasting tool.   T   F

6. A volatile investment demand leads to the inherent instability of the economy according to the Real Business Cycle theorists.   T   F

7. Real Business Cycle Theorists assume that markets are generally competitive in the U.S.   T   F

8. Demand and Supply shocks move the economy towards full employment.   T   F

9. Fiscal and monetary policy are useful stabilizing tools according to the advocates of Real Business Cycle theory.   T   F

10. New Keynesians believe that wages and prices are sticky.   T   F

MULTIPLE CHOICE QUESTIONS

Choose the best option for the following questions.

1. An economic expansion continues until the economy
   a. reaches a trough.
   b. reaches a peak.
   c. has two periods of lower growth rates.
   d. decreases its rate of growth.

2. Cyclical data must meet all of the following criteria except for
   a. economic significance.
   b. current availability.
   c. simplicity.
   d. reliability.

3. Which of the following is NOT one of the three major indexes of cyclical indicators?
   a. The Index of Leading Indicators
   b. The Index of Macroeconomic performance
   c. The Index of Coincident Indicators
   d. The Index of Lagging Indicators

4. A general rule of thumb is that an economy is in a recession when
   a. your neighbor is unemployed.
   b. you are unemployed.
   c. the GDP declines in two consecutive quarters.
   d. the GDP declines in three consecutive quarters.

5. Since WWII there is evidence that the economy is
   a. more stable because of fiscal policy.
   b. more stable because of automatic stabilizers.
   c. less stable because of fiscal policy.
   d. more stable because of fiscal policy.

6. According to the multiplier-accelerator model
   a. investment demand is inherently stable and counteracts market forces in the economy.
   b. investment demand is inherently stable and leads to economic instability.
   c. investment demand is inherently unstable and counteracts any destabilizing forces in the economy.
   d. investment demand is inherently unstable and leads to further economic instability.

7. According to the Real Business Cycle theory
   a. wages and prices are sticky.
   b. wages are sticky but prices are flexible.
   c. wages and prices are both flexible.
   d. wages are flexible but prices are sticky.

8. Which of the following is inconsistent with the Real Business Cycle theory?
   a. markets are competitive
   b. random shocks explain economic instability
   c. economic growth follows a long-term upward trend
   d. fiscal and monetary policy will not increase economic stability

9. According to Real Business Cycle theory, productivity shocks are a result of
   a. changes in consumption.
   b. technological change.
   c. the volatility of investment demand.
   d. competitive markets.

10. New Classical economists are more likely to support
    a. Real Business Cycle theory.
    b. multiplier-accelerator theory.
    c. fiscal policies during recessions.
    d. monetary policies during recessions.

SHORT ANSWER QUESTIONS

Fill in the blanks in the following statements.

1. A _____ is when the expansion phase of a business cycle ends and the _____ phase begins.

2. _____ and _____ policies are ineffective in stabilizing the economy according the Real Business Cycle theorists.

3. The economy has been _____ stable in the post WWII period than in the pre-war period.

4. The multiplier-accelerator theory is based on the assumption that _____ demand is highly volatile.

5. New Keynesians are more likely to support _____ theory and New Classical economists are more likely to support _____ theory.

PROBLEMS

1. Why will investment grow at an increasing rate during expansionary periods according to the multiplier-accelerator theory?

2. How have automatic stabilizers affected economic stability in the 20th Century?

3. Why won't an increase in Aggregate Demand affect output in the Real Business Cycle model of the economy?

4. How does Real Business Cycle and the multiplier-accelerator theory differ with regard to labor market outcomes?

5. What types of policy options would you expect from a New Classical economist following a supply shock due to oil price increases?

6. What types of policy options would you expect from a New Keynesian economist following a supply shock due to oil price increases?

7. How does the NBER monitor the overall performance of the economy?

8. Why won't temporary increases in wages affect Aggregate Demand or output according to the Real Business Cycle Theory?

9. Why does the economy tend to grow over time according to the Real Business Cycle theory?

10. Explain why output increases more rapidly than employment during recoveries according to the New Keynesians?

POST-TEST

Answer the following questions to determine how well you have learned the material in the chapter and to determine those areas where you need to focus your studies.

1. Why will an increase in consumption demand increase the level of investment demand according to the multiplier-accelerator theory?

2. Why will the economy always return to full employment according to the New Classical economists?

3. How is the Life-Cycle theory incorporated into the Real Business Cycle Theory?

4. Why does labor hoarding affect changes in employment levels during economic expansions and contractions?

5. What is the likely policy response of a New Classical economist to a recession? Why?

6. What is the likely policy response of a New Keynesian economist to a recession? Why?

7. What are the major criticisms of the Real Business Cycle theory?

8. What are the major criticisms of the New Keynesian theories?

9. Explain the differences between the three economic indicators compiled by the Department of Commerce.

10. Why is investment demand likely to expand at an accelerating rate during an expansion according to the multiplier-accelerator model?

Part III–Sample Test
National Income Determination, Fiscal Policy, and Unemployment

1. The aggregate desired expenditures line relates
   a. planned aggregate consumption and income.
   b. planned total spending in the economy and income.
   c. planned aggregate consumption and prices.
   d. planned total spending in the economy and prices.

2. The consumption function most directly relates
   a. changes in consumption and change income.
   b. the average consumption divided by average income.
   c. total consumption and total disposable income.
   d. total consumption and the price level.

3. If income is $1,200 when consumption is $800, and income is $1,300 when consumption is $875 then the marginal propensity to consume is
   a. 2/3 or .67
   b. 3/4 or .75
   c. $67
   d. $75

4. When the aggregate desired expenditures line crosses the 45 degree line
   a. the economy is at full employment.
   b. the unemployment is at the natural rate.
   c. the economy is at the break even level.
   d. the economy is in an equilibrium.
   e. all of the above

5. The life-cycle hypothesis theory explains
   a. the growth and death of the typical business firm.
   b. the patterns of national economic growth.
   c. the pattern of consumer spending over his/her life.
   d. why the defeated World War II countries of Germany and Japan now grow so fast.

6. The balanced budget multiplier is
   a. the multiplier required to obtain full employment.
   b. the effect of equal changes in government purchases and taxes on income.
   c. the result of tax increases to balance the budget.
   d. the result of government spending cuts to balance the budget.
   e. all of the above

7. The time required for policy makers to realize that the economy is in trouble and needs a dose of counter-cyclical policy is called the
   a. decision lag.
   b. recognition lag.
   c. expenditure lag.
   d. outside lag.

8. If government purchases increase by $100 and the marginal propensity to consumer is 0.8, then national income increases
   a. 100
   b. 100.8
   c. 100/.8 or 125
   d. 500
   e. none of the above

9. If the marginal propensity to consume is 0.8, then the marginal propensity to save is
   a. 0.2
   b. -0.8
   c. $1/.8 = 1.25$
   d. 0.8

10. The Balanced Budget Multiplier equals
    a. 1/marginal propensity to consume.
    b. 1/marginal propensity to save.
    c. 1.
    d. zero.
    e. none of the above or insufficient information

11. The government purchases multiplier is
    a. one greater than the transfer multiplier.
    b. one less than the transfer multiplier.
    c. equal to the transfer multiplier.
    d. equal to the tax multiplier.

12. The aggregate desired expenditures line becomes steeper when
    a. government purchases increase.
    b. taxes increases $10 billion at all income levels.
    c. the marginal propensity to consumer increases.
    d. transfer payments increase $10 billion at all income levels.

13. The differences between government spending and taxes at full employment is
    a. the structural deficit.
    b. the actual deficit.
    c. the cyclical deficit.
    d. the cash deficit.

14. A government policy that lowers the size of the multiplier is
    a. a discretionary policy.
    b. an automatic stabilizer.
    c. a pro cyclical policy.
    d. a deficit increasing policy in times of prosperity.

15. The external debt is the part of the government debt held by
    a. government agencies other than the Social Security System.
    b. the Federal Reserve System.
    c. private American citizens and American businesses.
    d. foreigners.

16. Which of the following is(are) automatic stabilizer(s)?
    a. personal income tax
    b. corporate income tax
    c. social security tax
    d. unemployment insurance tax
    e. all of the above

17. Depreciation of the dollar tends to
    a. increase both exports and imports.
    b. decrease both exports and imports.
    c. increase exports and decrease imports.
    d. decrease exports and increase imports.

18. The chief burden of the government debt is that it
    a. must be paid for by our grandchildren.
    b. it reduces the rate of private capital formation.
    c. it immediately causes high rates of inflation.
    d. it makes people feel uncomfortable.

19. The proportion of the individual cyclical indicators within each index of the business cycle that are rising or falling
    a. diffusion index
    b. duration index
    c. amplitude index
    d. refraction index

20. The National Bureau of Economic Research classifies indicators as
    a. leading.
    b. coincident.
    c. lagging.
    d. all of the above

21. Which of the following is an internal theory of the business cycle?
    a. herds on innovation in investment
    b. Federal Reserve misconduct of monetary policy
    c. Multiplier-Accelerator model
    d. foreign supply shock theory

22. The U.S. political business cycle associates business cycles most closely with
    a. pork barrel legislation.
    b. reapportionment of Congress.
    c. Congressional elections.
    d. Presidential elections.

23. Which theory of the business cycle associates cycles with fluctuations in the productivity of the economy
    a. the Monetary business cycle.
    b. the Political business cycle.
    c. the Real business cycle.
    d. none of the above.

24. The father of modern business cycle research is
    a. Paul Samuelson.
    b. Milton Friedman.
    c. Wesley C. Mitchell.
    d. Stanley Jevons.

25. New Keynesians contend that pro cyclical changes in real wages are caused by
    a. the real business cycle.
    b. labor hoarding.
    c. the multiplier-accelerator.
    d. interest rate changes.

Chapter 14
The Nature of Money and Banking: First Principles

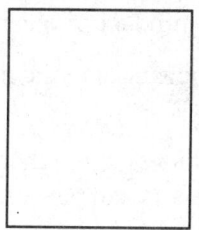

LEARNING OBJECTIVES

CONCEPTS TO LEARN

U.S. money supply	Balance sheet, assets, and liabilities
Demand for money	Velocity of circulation
The equation of exchange	The properties of money
The Fed	Commercial banks (depository institutions)
Open market operation	

CONCEPTS TO RECALL

Circular flow of economic activity	Hyperinflation

CHAPTER REVIEW

Chapter 14 focuses on how money is defined in the U.S. economy. The chapter explores the importance of money as a means of exchange and how changes in the money supply can affect output, inflation, and employment. The second half of the chapter goes into depth about the nature of money and ends with a description of common balance sheet transactions.

1. The money supply in the U.S. is most commonly defined as the sum of currency, checking account balances (with unlimited checking privileges), and travelers' checks. Currency consists of coins and dollar bills (Federal Reserve Notes).

2. The major components of the U.S. money supply include paper currency and checking accounts. Most developed countries have the same major components.

3. The circular flow of economic activity in terms of money is the equation of exchange, $M*V = P*Q$. Where M is the money supply and V is the velocity of circulation, the number of times money turns over during the course of a year. Prices are P and Q represents the national output or income in the economy.

4. Velocity changes very slowly over time and is a function of institutional factors including the form of payment consumers use in transactions (i.e. credit cards versus currency) and the length of pay periods.

5. Demand for money is the amount individuals want to hold at one point in time. The ratio of the overall demand for money to national product or income is the inverse of the velocity.

6. The equation of exchange shows how changes in the money supply will affect inflation rates, output growth and unemployment.

7. Many substances have been used for money throughout history. Various metals, beads, paper currencies, and checking accounts are all examples of money.

8. Money has three functions: a medium of exchange; a unit of account; and a store of value. Money must be routinely accepted in exchange for goods and services. A unit of account is the universal standard which is used to define the value of money in exchange for goods and services. Money serves as a store of value that enables individuals to save for future consumption.

9. Three different measures of money are reported by the U.S. government, M1, M2, and M3. M1 is a narrow definition of currency, checking account balances, and travelers' checks. M2 is equal to M1 plus numerous highly liquid short-term financial securities including money market deposits, mutual funds, and small savings and time deposits less than $100,000. M3 includes M2 plus savings and time deposits in excess of $100,000 and some other securities.

10. Balance sheets list assets, liabilities, and net worth.

11. Assets include property and other forms of wealth that are owned and liabilities are those that are owed. Net worth or wealth is the difference between assets and liabilities.

12. The exchange of assets and loans are important balance sheet transactions that affect the amount of money banks issue.

13. Open Market exchanges of Treasury securities in the secondary market allows the Federal Reserve Bank to change the supply of money or Federal Reserve Notes, FRN, in the system. When the Fed buys securities the supply of FRN increases and when the Fed sells securities the supply of FRN decreases. Most of these exchanges are done with a few large securities dealers.

14. Bank loans will create new currency when the loan proceeds are eventually deposited in a checking account. When banks call in loans or decrease the number of loans through attrition, checking account balances decline. In the absence of a secondary market in government securities

the borrower-lender transactions are the primary means of changing the currency in a country. (note: the large national debt in the U.S. allows for a huge secondary market in securities)

15. Money is an asset to the individual who owns it and a liability to the bank that issues it.

A FEW HELPFUL TIPS

It's usually a surprise to some beginning economics students that there is nothing backing the U.S. dollar except for good faith. No, there's not enough gold in Fort Knox for everyone to exchange their little green bills for but, they are an accepted means of exchange anywhere in the world. Those who have traveled around the world are very aware of the value of a dollar.

QUICK STUDY GUIDE

	T/F	Mult. Choice	Short Answer	Problems
U.S. Money Supply	1, 3, 4, 7	1, 2, 4, 7		5
Equation of Exchange	5, 6	5	3	
Velocity	2	6		1, 3
Open Market Operations	8	8, 9		8, 9

PRETEST

Answer the following questions to test your initial understanding of the material in this chapter:

1. Why is a FRN accepted as a means of exchange while a note with President Clinton's picture on it isn't worth much in our economy?

2. What is the difference between M1, M2, and M3?

3. What are some of the examples of items that have been used as money in the past?

4. Given the equation of exchange, explain what will happen to the price level when the economy is already at full employment and the money supply increases.

5. What is likely to happen to the nation's output if the velocity of circulation increases according to the equation of exchange?

6. What are the three functions of money?

7. Use a balance sheet to show how the assets, liabilities, and net worth of a college student changes after the receipt of a $3000 bank loan intended to cover expenses during the academic year.

8. How can the Fed decrease the supply of currency in the economic system?

9. How can the Fed increase the supply of currency in the economic system?

10. Why will bank loans change the amount of currency in the economy?

TRUE/FALSE PRACTICE QUESTIONS

1. All money in the U.S. is backed by gold supplies.   T   F
2. The velocity of circulation changes slowly in the U.S.   T   F
3. Checking accounts are not included in M1.   T   F
4. Currency includes coins and dollar bills or FRNs.   T   F
5. The equation of exchange is MV = PQ.   T   F
6. Given the equation of exchange an increase in M will increase V.   T   F
7. Credit card accounts are included in M1.   T   F
8. When the Fed sells securities the amount of currency in the country increases.   T   F
9. Loans are assets of commercial banks.   T   F
10. Net worth increases when liabilities decrease.   T   F

MULTIPLE CHOICE QUESTIONS

Choose the best option for the following questions.

1. The common definition of money supply includes
    a. currency and checking accounts.
    b. currency, checking accounts, and credit card accounts.
    c. currency, checking accounts, and travelers' checks.
    d. only currency.

2. The common definition of money is the same as
    a. M1.
    b. M2.
    c. M3.
    d. M4

3. Melting coins and selling the metal makes sense when the currency has been
    a. inflated.
    b. debased.
    c. devalued.
    d. declared insolvent.

4. Which of the following is not considered money?
    a. checking accounts
    b. travelers' checks
    c. NOW accounts
    d. credit cards

5. When velocity of circulation increases and output is at full employment the equation of exchange would predict
    a. a decline in output.

b. an increase in output.
   c. inflation.
   d. deflation.

6. When the personal velocity for money increases an individual is likely to
   a. increase the amount of money held.
   b. decrease the amount of money held.
   c. either increase or decrease the amount of money held.
   d. not change the amount of money held.

7. A national paper currency has
   a. always been the norm in the U.S.
   b. been a post WWII phenomenon.
   c. its roots in the mid 1860s.
   d. its roots during the War of 1812.

8. When the Fed sells securities the money in circulation
   a. increases.
   b. decreases.
   c. increases or decreases.
   d. remains the same.

9. When the Fed buys securities the money in circulation
   a. increases.
   b. decreases.
   c. increases or decreases.
   d. remains the same.

10. When a bank issues a loan the money in circulation will
    a. increase.
    b. decrease.
    c. increase or decrease.
    d. remain the same.

SHORT ANSWER QUESTIONS

Fill in the blanks in the following statements.

1. A NOW account differs from a regular checking account because it _____ and _____ can not hold these types of accounts.

2. A balance _____ would list a car loan as a _____ and a savings account as an _____.

3. The equation of exchange is _____.

4. _____ assets are those that can be easily converted to money.

5. _____ is the difference between assets and liabilities.

PROBLEMS

1. How do you suppose credit cards and ATM machines have affected the velocity of circulation?

2. Explain the difference between NOW accounts and traditional checking accounts. And explain which sectors of the economy own the majority of both types of accounts.

3. Suppose the money supply was $850 billion and national income was $4500. Solve for the velocity of circulation.

4. How is an individual's demand for money likely to change when their income rises?

5. Explain why silver dollars were often melted down in the "Old West."

6. Use a balance sheet to explain an individual's net worth when there is $1000 in a checking account, $100 in a savings account, $5000 in student loans, and a $4000 loan on a car worth $5600.

7. Explain why money is created when a bank loans an individual $150,000 to build a new home.

8. What will happen to the supply of money if the Fed purchases securities in the secondary market?

9. What will happen to the supply of money if the Fed sells securities in the secondary market?

10. Why will "calling in loans" decrease the amount of currency in the system?

POST-TEST

Answer the following questions to determine how well you have learned the material in the chapter and to determine those areas where you need to focus your studies.

1. Why is money a stock variable and income a flow variable?

2. How will an individual's personal demand for money change when their personal velocity decreases?

3. Why is the velocity of circulation in the U.S. relatively stable?

4. Describe the roots of paper currency in the U.S.

5. Explain when a loan is an asset and when it is a liability.

6. How can the banking industry's reluctance to make loans affect the amount of currency in circulation?

7. How can the Fed change the amount of money in circulation?

8. What is the velocity of money when the real national income equals $360 billion and the money supply equals $120 billion?

9. What gives money value in the U.S.?

10. What effect will a $100 million dollar loan to a corporation have on the amount of currency in the U.S. economy?

Chapter 15
The Monetary System of the U.S.

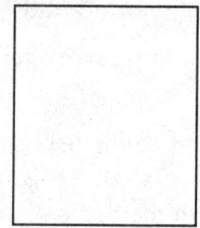

LEARNING OBJECTIVES

CONCEPTS TO LEARN

Federal reserve banking system	Reserves
The reserve requirement	Money multiplier
Savings and loan associations	

CONCEPTS TO RECALL

U.S. money supply	The Fed
Commercial banks (depository institutions)	Open market operation
Balance sheet, assets, and liabilities	

CHAPTER REVIEW

Chapter 15 is an overview of the monetary system in the U.S. The three key players in the monetary system; the Federal Reserve Banking System, Commercial Banks and other depository institutions, and the non-bank public, are described in the chapter. The chapter concludes with a discussion of the money multiplier and explanation of how money is created within the system.

1. The Federal Reserve Banking System was established by Congress in 1913. The Fed was designed as an independent, non-profit government agency that could be a lender of last resort for banks.

2. The main responsibilities of the Fed are: conducting monetary policy for the U.S.; acting as fiscal agent for the U.S. government; and overseeing the operation of commercial banks and other depository institutions.

3. The vast majority of all checking accounts are held by commercial banks.

4. Households, business firms, and government agencies hold the money supply and use it in the exchange of goods and services.

5. Commercial banks and other depository institutions are required to hold onto cash reserve accounts at the Fed. The Fed can limit the financial institutions' ability to make loans and increase checking account reserves by changing reserve requirements.

6. The current reserve ratio for checking account balances is 10% of deposits. Banks must hold onto a minimum of 10% of their deposits in reserves at the Fed but may choose to hold extra reserves.

7. Extra reserves are equal to the amount in reserves held by an institution in excess of the required reserve ratio.

8. Banks can increase their reserves by attracting deposits of Federal Reserve Notes or an Open Market operation where the proceeds of a sale of securities to the Fed are deposited in their bank. They can also borrow reserves through the Fed's discount window.

9. Checks drawn on one bank and deposited in another result in transfers of reserves from one financial institution to another.

10. The money multiplier measures the effect on the money supply of an Open Market purchase or sale by the Fed.

11. When the Fed buys securities through an open market transaction new FRNs are deposited in a bank's account that are from outside the current monetary supply. The portion of these deposits that are in excess of the required reserve ratio will be loaned out and create new reserves. The excess of these reserves can then be lent out and the multiplier process continues as it expands the supply of money. An Open Market sale of securities will shrink the money supply as each bank reduces its loan portfolio in order to meet required reserve ratios after the withdrawal of FRNs.

12. The simple money multiplier is equal to $1/r$ where r is the required reserve ratio. The multiplier assumes that no one wants to hold onto FRNs and banks never want to hold onto excess reserves.

13. Banks profit from loans and will change their actual reserve balances with shifts in the overall performance of the economy. During high growth periods, banks will compete to attract deposits with higher interest rates and other perks so that they can make more loans. During bad times, they will not be as anxious to attract deposits and issue new loans. As a result, the money multiplier is subject to frequent changes and the Fed finds it extremely difficult to control the money supply.

A FEW HELPFUL TIPS

Remember, an open market purchase is going to increase the money supply and an open market sale will decrease the money supply.

	QUICK STUDY GUIDE			
	T/F	Mult. Choice	Short Answer	Problems
The Federal Reserve Banking System	2	1, 2, 3	3	6
Reserves	1, 9	5	4	
Money Multiplier	4, 5		5	1, 2, 3, 4
The Reserve Requirement	3, 10	6, 10		10

PRETEST

Answer the following questions to test your initial understanding of the material in this chapter:

1. When and why was the Federal Reserve System established?
2. Describe the major responsibilities of the Fed.
3. What is the purpose of the Fed establishing a reserve requirement?
4. What is the difference between required and excess reserves?
5. Suppose banks hold onto exactly the required amount of reserves and individuals do not want to hold onto FRNs. If the required reserve ratio is 10%, what will happen to the money supply if the Fed buys $250,000 in government securities on the open market?
6. Suppose banks hold onto exactly the required amount of reserves and individuals do not want to hold onto FRNs. If the required reserve ratio is 5%, what will happen to the money supply if the Fed buys $100,000 in securities on the open market.
7. How will increasing the reserve ratio affect the money supply?
8. Describe the membership of the Federal Open Market Committee and the role they play in U.S. monetary policy.
9. What is the role of the Federal Deposit Insurance Corporation?
10. What will happen to the money multiplier if banks hold onto excess reserves?

TRUE/FALSE PRACTICE QUESTIONS

1. Required reserves for savings accounts are currently zero. T F
2. The head of the N.Y. Fed always serves on the Federal Open Market Operations Committee. T F
3. An increase in the reserve ratio will decrease the money supply. T F
4. The multiplier increases when the Fed makes an open market purchase. T F
5. The multiplier increases when the reserve ratio declines. T F

6. Individual savings accounts are insured up to $100,000.   T   F

7. The discount rate is the interest banks charge each other to borrow funds.   T   F

8. Open market operations are the most common method used by the Fed to control the money supply.   T   F

9. Banks are more likely to hold onto excess reserves during boom periods.   T   F

10. Changes in the reserve ratio will have very little effect on the money supply.   T   F

MULTIPLE CHOICE QUESTIONS

Choose the best option for the following questions.

1. The Federal Reserve System is
   a. in the Executive Branch of the federal government.
   b. under the direct supervision of Congress.
   c. a separate non-profit independent institution.
   d. a separate for-profit independent institution.

2. The Board of Governors are appointed to
   a. four year terms coinciding with each presidential term.
   b. four year terms that stagger each presidential term.
   c. two year terms.
   d. fourteen year terms that are staggered.

3. Which of the following is not a Fed function?
   a. issuing paper currency
   b. lender of last resort
   c. monetary policy
   d. fiscal policy

4. If the Fed wants to increase the money supply which of the following options would conflict with their goals?
   a. decreasing the reserve ratio on checking accounts
   b. increasing the discount rate
   c. buying government securities
   d. decreasing the reserve ratio on NOW accounts

5. Required Reserves are equal to
   a. Actual reserves.
   b. Excess reserves minus actual reserves.
   c. Actual reserves minus excess reserves.
   d. FRNs.

6. An increase in the required reserve ratio will
   a. expand the money supply.
   b. increase the multiplier.

c. decrease the multiplier.
   d. decrease the discount rate.

7. The rate the Fed charges to lend funds to banks is the
   a. discount rate.
   b. the reserve rate.
   c. federal funds rate.
   d. prime rate.

8. When the Fed makes an open market purchase
   a. the money supply will increase.
   b. the money supply will decrease.
   c. the money supply will either increase or decrease.
   d. the money supply will remain unaffected.

9. When the Fed makes an open market sale
   a. the money supply will increase.
   b. the money supply will decrease.
   c. the money supply will either increase or decrease.
   d. the money supply will remain unaffected.

10. A $100,000 open market purchase will increase the money supply by $1 million when
    a. the multiplier equals .10.
    b. the required reserve ratio equals 10
    c. the multiplier equals 10
    d. the required reserve ration equals .20

SHORT ANSWER QUESTIONS

Fill in the blanks in the following statements.

1. The _____ is the interest the Fed charges banks to borrow funds.

2. The _____ is the interest rate banks charge each other to borrow funds.

3. The _____ buys and sells treasury debt for the Fed.

4. _____ reserves are equal to the difference between required reserves and _____ reserves.

5. The multiplier _____ when the reserve ratio decreases.

PROBLEMS

1. Explain why the money multiplier is likely to be smaller during recessionary periods.

2. Why will the money multiplier increase when banks don't want to hold onto excess reserves?

3. What will happen to the money supply if the Fed makes an open market sale of $2 million in securities if the required reserve ratio equals 5%? (Assume that banks hold exactly the required reserve amounts and that individuals do not want to hold onto FRNs).

4. Explain the effect of an open market purchase of $5 million in securities if the required reserve ratio is 10%? (Assume that banks hold exactly the required reserve amounts and that individuals do not want to hold onto FRNs.)

5. Why will changes in the discount rate have an effect on the money supply?

6. Who is responsible for monetary policy in the U.S. and what tools can they use to change the stock of money?

7. Use a Balance Sheet Account to explain why a Fed open market purchase will increase the money supply.

8. Use a Balance Sheet Account to explain why a Fed open market sale will decrease the money supply.

9. Describe why it is difficult for the Fed to control the growth in the money supply.

10. Why doesn't the Fed get rid of the reserve requirement for all types of accounts?

POST-TEST

Answer the following questions to determine how well you have learned the material in the chapter and to determine those areas where you need to focus your studies.

1. Explain the role of the Federal Open Market Committee in monetary policy.

2. What does it mean to say that a bank is "fully loaned up?"

3. How does the Fed serve as the central bank of the U.S.?

4. Explain why the amount of excess reserves are likely to be linked to the business cycles in the economy.

5. How will the money supply be affected by a $3 million open market purchase if the multiplier is equal to 5?

6. How will the money supply be affected by a $8 million open market sale if the multiplier is equal to 10?

7. What is likely to happen to the money supply if the required reserve ratio is increased?

8. Why would the Fed want to lower the discount rate?

9. Describe how the Federal Funds market operates.

10. Solve for the multiplier when the required reserve ratio is 10% and banks hold onto no excess reserves and no one wants to hold FRNs.

Chapter 16
Monetary Policy

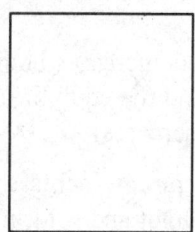

LEARNING OBJECTIVES

CONCEPTS TO LEARN

Transactions demand for money	Precautionary demand for money
Speculative demand for money	Loan markets
Practical limitations of U.S. monetary policy	Interest rates

CONCEPTS TO RECALL

Long-run economic growth	Laws of supply and demand
New Keynesian economics	Monetary policy
Equilibrium level of national income	Balance sheet, assets, and liabilities
Demand for money	Open market operation
Money multiplier	

CHAPTER REVIEW

Chapter 16 focuses on the economic effects of monetary policy in the U.S. in the short run in a new Keynesian policy environment. The first section explains how changes in the supply of money will affect the economy in an abstract sense and the last section focuses on the institutional details associated with monetary policy.

1. Household real assets include consumer durables, houses, and other types of real estate. Business real assets include their productive capital; plant, equipment, and inventories. Financial assets held by both households and businesses include money, deposit accounts, stocks, bonds, insurance, and business account receivables.

2. When the amount of money increases in the economy, the asset markets are temporarily out of equilibrium. Given the demand for money at the original interest rate, there is too much money relative to other assets.

3. After an increase in the money supply, households and businesses attempt to exchange the new excess money that they don't want to hold for other assets. The result is that the interest rate declines and the price of non-money assets increases until the markets find the new equilibrium. When the interest rates decline individuals and businesses will be willing to hold onto more money.

4. The increase in demand for other assets increases both consumption and investment demand, which increases Aggregate Demand and the equilibrium level of national income. (Note: There will be a multiplier effect when AD increases)

5. Any increase in national income will spur an increase in the transactions demand for money. Since more goods and services are bought and sold, more money is needed to complete these transactions. When national income increases by 1% the demand for money increases by approximately 6%.

6. Any increase in the price level will increase the transactions demand for money by the same amount because FRN and checking account balances are nominal values.

7. The interest rate and the price of stocks and bonds are inversely related. For example, when an "old" $10,000 bond pays 5% interest and "newer" bonds in the same denomination pay only 4%, the "older" bonds are worth more than $10,000.

8. Since the demand for money is inversely related to interest rates, an increase in the money supply will lower interest rates and individuals and firms will be willing to hold onto more money because the opportunity cost has declined.

9. The economy returns to an equilibrium when national income increases and interest rates decline to the point where the demand for money equals the new supply.

10. A contractionary monetary policy reduces the supply of money driving interest rates up, investment and consumer spending down, Aggregate Demand down, and the level of National Income down.

11. When the Fed buys Treasury securities through an open market purchase, the increase in the money supply increases excess reserves of banks. Banks then increase their loans to firms and consumers as interest rates decline. Interest rates will decline because of the increase in the money supply. Households and firms buy more consumer and investment goods which increases Aggregate Demand and real national income.

12. When the Fed sells Treasury Securities through an open market sale, the money supply decreases, interest rates increase, consumer demand declines, firm's investment demand declines, Aggregate Demand falls and national income falls.

13. The Fed can not fine tune the economy with monetary policy. Operational lags, the time line from the Open Market operation to a change in national income can be very long (i.e. more than one year) and is highly variable. The value of the money multiplier and uncertainties about the demand for money make the Fed's job even more difficult. Also, contractionary policy is more effective than expansionary policy.

14. The Fed looks at a wide range of financial indicators including broad money aggregates such as M2 and M3.

15. Benefits of low interest rates include increases in investment, long-term economic growth, increases in home ownership, and lower costs for debtors who may be among our poorest citizens.

16. The main benefit of high interest rates is the increase in value of the dollar against foreign currencies.

A FEW HELPFUL TIPS

Remember, interest rates and the price of bonds are inversely related. If there is more money in the system than people want to hold their demand for other financial assets will rise. When they bid up the price of these other financial assets the effective interest rate will decline.

QUICK STUDY GUIDE

	T/F	Mult. Choice	Short Answer	Problems
Money Demand	6, 7	5, 6		5
Assets Markets	1, 2	2, 4, 10	1, 5	9
Monetary Policy	3, 4, 5	1, 3, 8, 9	3, 4	1, 2, 3, 4, 7, 8
Lags	10		2	6, 10

PRETEST

Answer the following questions to test your initial understanding of the material in this chapter:

1. Describe the real and financial assets held by households.
2. Describe the real and financial assets held by firms.
3. How can households and firms have "too much money?"
4. How does the transactions demand for money change when national income rises?
5. What happens to the transactions demand for money during an inflationary period?
6. Why will individuals consume less when the money supply decreases?
7. How will an open market purchase by the Fed affect the overall investment levels in the economy?
8. How will an open market sale by the Fed affect national income?

9. What factors are likely to increase the time lags of monetary policy?
10. Who benefits from low interest rates in the economy?

TRUE/FALSE PRACTICE QUESTIONS

1. Investment will decrease when interest rates rise.   T   F
2. The price of a bond is positively related to the interest rates.   T   F
3. An open market purchase will increase the supply of money.   T   F
4. An open market sale will decrease interest rates in the economy.   T   F
5. When the money supply increases investment is likely to decrease.   T   F
6. The transactions demand for money will decrease with inflation.   T   F
7. The transactions demand for money will increase when national income increases.   T   F
8. Low interest rates encourage individuals to purchase homes.   T   F
9. Low interest rates will increase the value of the dollar relative to foreign currencies. T F
10. Monetary policy lags are usually less than one month.   T   F

MULTIPLE CHOICE QUESTIONS

Choose the best option for the following questions.

1. The short-run effects of an open market sale of government securities results in
   a. an increase in interest rates.
   b. a decrease in interest rates.
   c. either an increase or decrease in interest rates.
   d. no change in interest rates.

2. When there is "too much" money, bond prices are likely to
   a. rise and so will interest rates.
   b. rise and interest rates will fall.
   c. fall and interest rates will fall.
   d. fall and so will interest rates.

3. When the Fed buys securities interest rates will
   a. rise and so will national income.
   b. rise but national income will fall.
   c. fall and national income will rise.
   d. fall and so will national income.

4. Bond prices are
   a. positively related to interest rates.
   b. inversely related to interest rates.

c. affected positively in some cases and negatively in other cases when interest rates rise.
d. not related to interest rates at all.

5. When national income rises the transactions demand for money will
   a. fall.
   b. rise.
   c. rise or fall.
   d. not change.

6. An increase in the price level will _____ the transactions demand for money.
   a. increase
   b. decrease
   c. increase or decrease
   d. not affect

7. Which of the following is not an advantage of low interest rates?
   a. increased investment
   b. long-term economic growth
   c. a strong dollar relative to other currencies
   d. increases in home ownership

8. A contractionary monetary policy will
   a. increase interest rates and increase national income.
   b. increase interest rates and decrease national income.
   c. decrease interest rates and increase national income.
   d. decrease interest rates and decrease national income.

9. An expansionary monetary policy will
   a. decrease interest rates and investment demand.
   b. decrease interest rates and increase investment demand.
   c. increase interest rates and investment demand.
   d. increase interest rates and decrease investment demand.

10. Real household assets include all of the following except for
    a. houses.
    b. consumer durables.
    c. real estate.
    d. government securities.

SHORT ANSWER QUESTIONS

Fill in the blanks in the following statements.

1. _____ is the chair of the Federal Reserve.
2. _____ lags are the time required for the Federal Board of Governors to recognize the economy is in trouble.
3. _____ monetary policy will lower interest rates and _____ national income.

4. _____ monetary policy will increase interest rates and _____ national income.

5. Bond prices are _____ related to _____ rates.

PROBLEMS

1. What is money rain and how will it affect national income?

2. What were the effects of the contractionary monetary policy that Fed Chair Paul Volker implemented in the early 1980's? Explain your answer.

3. Why would the real estate industry be in favor of expansionary monetary policies?

4. How will the trade deficit be affected when the Fed decreases the money supply?

5. What's likely to happen to the demand for money during inflationary periods?

6. Why is monetary policy an ineffective method of fine tuning the economy?

7. What will happen to investment demand when the Fed implements a contractionary monetary policy?

8. What is likely to happen to national income levels if the Fed increases the money supply?

9. Why are bond markets affected by changes in the money supply?

10. Describe how lags affect monetary policy.

POST-TEST

Answer the following questions to determine how well you have learned the material in the chapter and to determine those areas where you need to focus your studies.

1. Why will the transactions demand for money decline when national income declines?

2. Why will the transactions demand for money decline when the price level declines?

3. How is consumption affected by a decline in interest rates?

4. How did Fed chair Alan Greenspan's expansionary monetary policy in the early 1990's affect national income and the economy?

5. Why will bond prices fall when the money supply decreases?

6. Suppose the Fed makes an open market purchase of securities. Explain the effects on national income, interest rates, and aggregate demand.

7. Why would someone want to hold onto less money?

8. How will the U.S. dollar be affected by an expansionary monetary policy?

9. What kinds of financial assets are held by firms and households?

10. Explain the effects of a contractionary monetary policy on national income, interest rates, and Aggregate Demand.

Chapter 17

Fiscal Policy, Monetary Policy, and the Macroeconomic Policy Goals

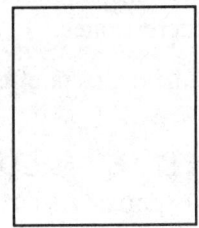

LEARNING OBJECTIVES

CONCEPTS TO LEARN

Crowding out: Changes in consumer durables and investment demand and net export demand

Okun's law

Short-run Phillips curve

CONCEPTS TO RECALL

Macroeconomic policy goals

Fiscal policy

Equilibrium level of national income

Spending multiplier

Equation of exchange

Interest rates

New Keynesian economics

Monetary policy

The macroeconomic policy problem

Multiplier-accelerator model

Balance sheet, assets, and liabilities

CHAPTER REVIEW

Chapter 17 incorporates the material covered in Chapters 29-35. The first section focuses on how changes in aggregate demand can affect interest rates and crowd out the economy. The second section focuses on how government can use fiscal and monetary policy to reach desired levels of national income and interest rates. The final section summarizes the relationship between the four macroeconomic policy goals and national income and interest rates.

1. Increases in consumption demand will mean an increase in the demand for money. Consumers will either sell other assets to get more money or borrow money. Either option will put upward pressure on interest rates.

2. Decreases in consumption will have the opposite effect, decreasing the demand for money and lowering interest rates.

3. Expansionary fiscal policies increase money demand because of increases in consumption and any deficit spending by the government. The consumption increases and the government's demand for funds will all put upward pressure on interest rates.

4. Contractionary fiscal policies will have the opposite effect of decreasing the demand for money and interest rates.

5. Changes in interest rates due to changes in Aggregate Demand will crowd out spending on consumer durables, investment and net exports. As a result, the spending multiplier is lower. The higher interest rates will discourage purchases of consumer durables and investments. Net exports will decline because the value of the dollar will increase when interest rates in the U.S. rise relative to other countries. A strong dollar means that American goods will become more expensive and foreign goods will be less expensive. Net exports will decline and Aggregate Demand will fall.

6. Initially, output will expand rapidly after an expansionary fiscal policy is implemented. But, once the level of income and interest rates start to rise, the crowding out effect will dampen the expansion. The hump-shaped pattern of the multiplier process can be explained by crowding out.

7. Both fiscal and monetary policies can be used by the government to reach national income and interest rate targets. Expansionary fiscal and monetary policy will increase national income levels. However, interest rates decline as a result of expansionary monetary policy and increase due to expansionary fiscal policies. Contractionary policies work in the symmetrical way.

8. Since fine-tuning of the economy is not possible the best the federal government can do is to influence the general direction of national income and interest rates.

9. Changes in national income will affect all four Macroeconomic policy goals. Increases in Aggregate Demand will increase national income, promote long run investment and growth, lower unemployment, increase inflation, and increase the trade deficit. Decreases in Aggregate Demand and national income will have the opposite effect.

10. The short-run Phillips curve demonstrates the trade-off between inflation and unemployment due to changes in Aggregate Demand. Increases in Aggregate Demand will increase national income, reduce unemployment and increase prices. Decreases work in just the opposite manner.

11. Okun's Law refers to the observed relationship between output growth and unemployment. For every 2.5% increase in output, unemployment decreases by 1%.

12. Changes in interest rates will affect long-term growth by altering investment levels in the economy. Interest rates will also affect the exchange rate for the dollar and foreign currencies. An increase in interest rates will attract foreign funds and increase the value of the dollar. Decreases in interest rates will have the opposite effect.

A FEW HELPFUL TIPS

Now that you have a basic understanding of fiscal and monetary policy don't get carried away with the idea that you know how to solve most macroeconomic problems. Remember, the theory works fine in a textbook but the same plan in the real world may lead to very different results due to institutional factors and unexpected shocks in the economy.

QUICK STUDY GUIDE

	T/F	Mult. Choice	Short Answer	Problems
Fiscal Policy	1, 5	1, 4	3	1, 5, 6
Crowding Out	3, 4, 9	3, 6	2, 5	3, 8
Phillips Curve	7	7		
Okun's Law	6	5	1	

PRETEST

Answer the following questions to test your initial understanding of the material in this chapter:

1. What is the effect of an expansionary fiscal policy on interest rates?

2. Why will the multiplier be smaller for a change in Aggregate Demand due to fiscal policy than one due to monetary policy?

3. What is the effect of a deficit financed fiscal expansion versus one that is financed by taxes?

4. Why is investment crowded out by an expansionary fiscal policy?

5. Why will net exports decline when an expansionary fiscal policy is implemented?

6. What type of fiscal policy could be used to decrease unemployment in the economy?

7. What type of monetary policy could be used to decrease unemployment in the economy?

8. What types of policies would allow the government to reduce unemployment and interest rates at the same time?

9. How much would the economy have to grow in order to reduce unemployment by 3%?

10. What are the trade-offs explained by the short-run Phillips curve?

TRUE/FALSE PRACTICE QUESTIONS

1. An expansionary fiscal policy is likely to decrease interest rates.   T   F
2. An expansionary monetary policy is likely to decrease interest rates.   T   F
3. Crowding out occurs when interest rates rise due to fiscal policies.   T   F
4. A contractionary fiscal policy will crowd out investment in the economy.   T   F
5. An expansionary fiscal policy is likely to decrease unemployment.   T   F
6. According to Okun's law when Q increases by 5%, unemployment should decrease by 2.5%.   T   F
7. The short-run Phillips curve shows the relationship between unemployment and inflation.   T   F
8. Net exports are likely to decline as a result of expansionary fiscal policy.   T   F
9. Crowding out effects lower the value of the spending multiplier.   T   F
10. A contractionary monetary policy will reduce output and interest rates.   T   F

MULTIPLE CHOICE QUESTIONS

Choose the best option for the following questions.

1. An expansionary fiscal policy will
   a. increase output and decrease interest rates.
   b. increase output and increase interest rates.
   c. decrease output and decrease interest rates.
   d. decrease output and increase interest rates.

2. A contractionary monetary policy will
   a. increase interest rates and output.
   b. decrease interest rates and output.
   c. increase interest rates and decrease output.
   d. decrease interest rates and increase output.

3. Crowding out occurs when consumer demand increases because
   a. interest rates rise.
   b. the increased demand drives prices up.
   c. the supply does not increase by as much as the demand.
   d. interest rates are likely to decline.

4. A contractionary fiscal policy is likely to
   a. decrease net exports.
   b. increase net exports.
   c. either increase or decrease net exports.
   d. not affect net exports.

5. According to Okun's law a 7.5% growth in output will decrease unemployment by
   a. 3.75%.
   b. 3%.
   c. 7.5%.
   d. 2.5%.

6. Crowding out will
   a. increase the value of the spending multiplier.
   b. decrease the value of the spending multiplier.
   c. either increase or decrease the value of the spending multiplier.
   d. have no effect on the spending multiplier.

7. According to the short-run Phillips curve an expansionary fiscal policy used to combat a high level of unemployment can
   a. reduce unemployment and inflation.
   b. reduce unemployment and only moderately increase the price level.
   c. reduce unemployment but will significantly increase the price level.
   d. reduce unemployment and have no effect on prices.

8. Which of the following policy options would not be appropriate during a recession?
   a. increases in government spending financed by debt
   b. increases in government spending financed by taxes
   c. increases in the money supply
   d. decreases in the money supply

9. Which of the following policy options will increase output and lower interest rates?
   a. increases in government spending financed by debt
   b. increases in government spending financed by taxes
   c. increases in the money supply
   d. decreases in the money supply

10. Expansionary monetary and fiscal policies are likely to
    a. decrease net exports.
    b. increase net exports.
    c. either increase or decrease net exports.
    d. have no effect on net exports.

SHORT ANSWER QUESTIONS

Fill in the blanks in the following statements.

1. Okun's law states that for every _____ change in output the _____ rate changes by _____.
2. The crowding out effect _____ the value of the spending multiplier.
3. Expansionary fiscal policy is likely to _____ interest rates.
4. Expansionary monetary policy is likely to _____ interest rates.

5. Net exports are likely to _____ when expansionary _____ and _____ policy are used.

PROBLEMS

1. Suppose the country is experiencing 10% unemployment. What fiscal policies would you recommend and describe the effects on output and interest rates?

2. Suppose the country is experiencing 10% unemployment. What monetary policies would you recommend and what are the effects on output and interest rates?

3. Explain why crowding out is a result of an expansionary fiscal policy but not an expansionary monetary policy.

4. What is likely to happen to the level of net exports when fiscal policy is expansionary?

5. President Clinton was faced with a sluggish economy in the early 1990's and a very high national debt. Discuss the fiscal and monetary policy options that could be used to improve economic conditions.

6. Suppose the economy has high inflation and low unemployment rates. What type of fiscal policy would you recommend?

7. Suppose the economy has high inflation and low unemployment rates. What type of monetary policy would you recommend?

8. Explain the effects of net export crowding out on slowing down an economic recovery.

POST-TEST

Answer the following questions to determine how well you have learned the material in the chapter and to determine those areas where you need to focus your studies.

1. Use the equation of exchange to explain the effects of crowding out when Aggregate Demand increases.

2. Why will interest rates increase when the government implements an expansionary fiscal policy?

3. Suppose the economy is experiencing high unemployment and high interest rates. What type of policy is likely to bring down both rates?

4. Suppose the economy is experiencing high inflation rates and unemployment is relatively low. What type of policy would you recommend?

5. How much will the economy have to grow in order to bring down unemployment rates by 3% according to Okun's law?

6. Why will the value of the dollar be affected by expansionary fiscal policies?

7. How will net exports be affected by a contractionary fiscal policy?

8. Why would an increase in consumption demand result in crowding out?

9. What types of policies will increase long-term investment and growth in the economy?

10. Why will an expansionary fiscal policy cause the economy to grow faster during the first rounds of the multiplier process than in the later rounds?

Part IV–Sample Test
Money and Monetary Policy

1. A stipulation in a loan contract that the lender has the right to demand immediate and full repayment of the loan at any time is a
   a. demand feature.
   b. right of recourse.
   c. call feature.
   d. time deposit.

2. Something that is owed; a claim against someone by some other person or institution is a(n)
   a. liability.
   b. loan.
   c. accounts payable.
   d. notes payable.

3. Anything that people are routinely willing to accept in exchange for goods and services (and factors of production) is a(n)
   a. medium of exchange.
   b. asset.
   c. current asset.
   d. primary asset.

4. A purchase or sale of Treasury debt by the Fed for the purpose of controlling the money supply is a(n)
   a. open market operation.
   b. primary market operation.
   c. secondary market operation.
   d. tertiary market operation.

5. A loan in which the lender can assume ownership of a particular asset stipulated in the loan contract if the borrower defaults on the loan is a
   a. secured loan.
   b. call loan.
   c. demand deposit.
   d. habeas corpus loan.

6. The velocity of circulation is
   a. the ratio of nominal national income to the money supply.
   b. how fast the typical dollar bill wears out.
   c. the ratio of trades to the number of stocks on the NY stock exchange.
   d. the rate of spending by the Federal government.

7. Banks generally create money by
   a. selling securities to the public.
   b. making loans.
   c. selling off their assets.
   d. receiving payment for loans outstanding.

8. The rate of interest that the Fed charges commercial banks for loans of reserves to help the banks meet their reserve requirements.
   a. Discount rate
   b. Prime rate
   c. T-bill rate
   d. LIBOR

9. What are a bank's excess reserves?
   a. The difference between a commercial bank's total reserves and its required reserves; the amount of reserves that a commercial bank can lend and satisfy the reserve requirement.
   b. The difference between a commercial bank's statutory reserves and its needed reserves.
   c. The difference between a commercial bank's total number of customers and the required number.
   d. The total of a commercial bank's total reserves and its excess reserves.

10. An act of Congress that established the Federal Reserve Banking System, the first true central bank in the United States.
    a. Federal Reserve Act of 1913
    b. National Banking Act of 1863
    c. National Banking Act of 1933
    d. Securities Act of 1933

11. What is the monetary base?
    a. all currency
    b. the sum of gold and silver reserves
    c. the sum of Federal Reserve Notes plus bank reserves
    d. the sum of Federal Reserve Notes plus fiat reserves

12. What is the money multiplier?
    a. The ratio that relates the money supply to the amount of Treasury debt that the Fed purchases or sells on the Open Market.
    b. The ratio that relates the reserve requirement to the money supply to the amount of Treasury debt that the Fed purchases or sells on the Open Market.
    c. The ratio that relates the total change in coins and currency to the amount of Treasury debt that the Fed purchases or sells on the Open Market.
    d. The ratio that relates the total change in the money supply to the amount of Treasury debt that the Fed purchases or sells on the Open Market.

13. The financial panic that brought about the creation of the Federal Reserve System was
    a. the Great Depression.
    b. the Depression of 1818-1820.
    c. the Panic of 1907.
    d. Mint Act of 1792.

14. The savings and loan industry is extremely vulnerable during periods of
    a. falling interest rates.
    b. rising interest rates.
    c. stable interest rates.
    d. declining prices.

15. The time required to change the course of monetary policy once the Board of Governors decides to do so.
    a. recognition lag
    b. legislative lag
    c. administrative lag
    d. outside lag

16. The motive for holding money based on expectations of future interest rates.
    a. asset demand
    b. transaction demand
    c. speculative demand
    d. expectations demand

17. A decrease in the money supply undertaken by the Fed for the purpose of decreasing aggregate demand; the Fed sells Treasury debt on the open Market.
    a. expansionary monetary policy
    b. discretionary monetary policy
    c. contractionary monetary policy
    d. inflationary monetary policy

18. The amount the borrower agrees to pay back to the lender on the date when the bond matures; the principal of the bond.
    a. coupon rate
    b. sinking fund
    c. face value
    d. call price

19. If the interest rate on a bond is 8%, and the nominal or current market rate of interest is 7%, one would expect the bond price to be
    a. above face value.
    b. below face value.
    c. equal to face value.
    d. none of the above.

20. A curve that shows how the rate of inflation and the unemployment rate respond to a change in aggregate demand in the short-run.
    a. short-run demand curve
    b. short-run Phillips Curve
    c. short-run supply curve
    d. Keynesian Cross model of income determination

21. By liquidating assets to finance increased consumption demand
    a. increases interest rates and price on the assets liquidated.
    b. increases the price on the assets liquidated.
    c. decreases interest rates and rates of return on the assets liquidated.
    d. increases interest rates and rates of return on the assets liquidated.

22. A decrease in consumption demand
    a. increases the employment rate.
    b. leaves interest rates unchanged.
    c. raises interest rates.
    d. lowers interest rates.

23. Financing a government expenditure with debt is
    a. highly contractionary.
    b. highly expansionary.
    c. highly deflationary.
    d. causes unemployment.

24. The equation of exchange is
    a. $V + Q = M * V$
    b. $V = M \div PQ$
    c. $M * V = P * Q$
    d. $C + I + G + (X - M) = GDP$

25. What would the government policy makers *not* do to increase national income and decrease interest rates?
    a. expand the money supply
    b. buy Treasury securities on the open market
    c. sell Treasury securities on the open market
    d. lower the discount rate

Chapter 18
Aggregate Supply and Aggregate Demand

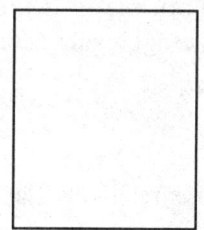

LEARNING OBJECTIVES

CONCEPTS TO LEARN

Aggregate demand curve

Long-run aggregate supply curve

Short-run aggregate supply curve

Stagflation

CONCEPTS TO RECALL

Laws of supply and demand

New Keynesian economics

Aggregate demand and aggregate supply shocks

Aggregate demand and supply

New Classical economics

Real business cycle model

CHAPTER REVIEW

Chapter 18 explores how changes in the price level can be incorporated into a macroeconomic model of the economy. An aggregate demand and aggregate supply model is used to analyze the equilibrium price and output levels. The final section of the chapter focuses on the differences between the New Keynesian and New Classical theories.

1. The quantity demanded by households, firms, government, and the foreign sector at each price level is represented by the aggregate demand curve.

2. The aggregate demand curve is negatively related to the price level. The inverse relationship can be explained by the change in the transactions demand for money when the price level changes. An increase in the price level will increase the transactions demand for money, increase interest rates and decrease consumer demand for durables, decrease investment by firms, decrease net exports and therefore decrease real national output. A decline in the price level will have just the opposite effect.

3. Aggregate supply curves show the relationship between output supplied and the overall price level.

4. Both New Keynesians and New Classical economists agree that the aggregate supply curve is vertical in the long-run. They agree that competition in the economy will mean that wages and prices will adjust to the full employment level of output corresponding with the production possibilities frontier. Real National Output is determined by the supply side and changes in aggregate demand can only affect the price level in the long-run. Prices adjust so that the economy reaches an equilibrium where aggregate demand is equal to the full employment level of output.

The New Keynesian View

5. The short-run aggregate supply curve is relatively flat at output levels that are significantly lower than the full employment level of output. At low levels of output any increases in real national income will be accompanied by small if any changes in the price level. As the economy expands to output levels closer to full employment there is upward pressure on prices and the aggregate supply curve becomes positively sloped. At output levels at or near full employment the aggregate supply curve becomes extremely steep. Therefore changes in aggregate demand in the short-run can have an effect on the equilibrium level of output.

6. The relatively flat portion of the aggregate supply curve can be explained by sticky prices and wages. Imperfections in the market result in slowly changing prices and wages. Sticky wages are a by-product of institutional factors such as long-term labor contracts, unions, and internal labor markets. Prices are also sticky because of a combination of menu costs and the size and complexity of final goods manufacturers. Firms and workers do behave rationally its just that the adjustments are made slowly in the markets.

7. The economy will eventually adjust to the long-run full employment level of output. Suppose the economy is at full employment and aggregate demand decreases. Initially, output and prices will decline as the short-run equilibrium level is reached. Over time, the excess capacity in the economy will put downward pressure on the costs of production shifting the short-run aggregate supply curve down to the right until the equilibrium is reached at the long-run full employment output level. An increase in aggregate demand will have just the opposite effect. Both cases explain the business cycle pattern of output.

8. Long-run adjustments are so slow that fiscal and monetary policy are needed to keep the economy at or near full employment levels of output.

9. Changes in the price level due to changes in aggregate demand imply that the spending multiplier has a lower value. For example, an increase in aggregate demand will increase output and the price level but the increase in prices will increase transactions money demand, increase interest rates and bring aggregate demand back down. The initial increase in AD will have a greater overall effect than the secondary decrease in AD. Decreases in aggregate demand will have the opposite effect.

10. Adverse supply shocks are a result of increases in the cost of production for all or most sectors of the economy. For example, an oil price increase will cause the aggregate supply curve to shift to the left raising both prices and unemployment. Positive supply shocks occur when costs of production decrease throughout the economy. A rightward shift of the aggregate supply curve will decrease both prices and unemployment. Adverse supply shocks will move the short-run Phillips curve to the right and positive shocks move the Phillips curve to the left.

The New Classical View

11. The economy is highly competitive and wages and prices are highly flexible. Therefore, the economy always operates at or close to its production possibilities frontier. There is very little difference between short-run and long-run aggregate supply curves. The government can not use fiscal or monetary policy to improve the performance of the economy. Real National Output is determined by the supply side of the economy and can only change if the production possibilities frontier itself changes. Real Business Cycle Theory is one of the leading theories of the New Classical school.

12. Changes in aggregate demand can only affect output levels if the nation's production possibilities frontier changes in response to the shift in demand.

13. Changes in aggregate demand will cause interest rates to change and will affect the supply of labor which in turn changes the production possibilities frontier according the New Classicalists. The labor supply increases when interest rates increase due to life-cycle consumption patterns. There is no empirical evidence to support a relationship between interest rates and labor supply. However, New Classical economists downplay the lack of evidence because they believe most changes in output are due to changes in productivity rather than aggregate demand.

14. Changes in the money supply have no effect on aggregate demand or output. When the money supply changes prices change by the same amount eliminating any real effects on the economy.

A FEW HELPFUL TIPS

Remember, the main distinction between the New Keynesian and New Classical arguments is whether or not the market operates efficiently in the short-run. New Keynesians point to market failures as justification for government intervention. The New Classical economists believe the markets are competitive and efficient in the short-run and that government intervention can only destabilize the economy.

QUICK STUDY GUIDE

	T/F	Mult. Choice	Short Answer	Problems
Aggregate Demand	2, 8, 9		4	
Aggregate Supply	4, 6, 7	4, 5	5	8
New Keynesian Theory	3	2, 8, 9	3	1, 2, 5, 7
New Classical Theory	3, 5	1, 3, 10	1	2, 4, 6, 7

PRETEST

Answer the following questions to test your initial understanding of the material in this chapter:

1. What is the relationship between interest rates and aggregate demand?

2. Why does the aggregate demand curve have a negative slope?

3. Describe the long-run aggregate supply curve and explain its relationship to the production possibilities frontier.

4. How will long-run aggregate supply be affected by a new technological breakthrough in solar energy that significantly reduces demand for oil?

5. Describe and draw a short-run aggregate supply curve according to New Keynesian assumptions about the macroeconomy.

6. Suppose aggregate demand increases due to an increase in government spending. Explain what will happen to prices and output according to the New Keynesian assumptions if the economy was at an output level below full employment.

7. What will happen to prices and output as a result of an adverse supply shock according to the New Keynesian model?

8. Why can't changes in aggregate demand affect output according to the New Classicalists?

TRUE/FALSE PRACTICE QUESTIONS

1. When the price level increases the transactions demand for money increases.   T   F

2. Changes in the price level will shift the ADE curve up or down.   T   F

3. Both New Keynesians and New Classical economists believe that wages and prices are flexible in the short-run.   T   F

4. The long-run aggregate supply curve is vertical.   T   F

5. New Classical economists believe output can increase in the short-run when government uses fiscal policy.   T   F

6. An adverse supply shock will lower output and prices.   T   F

7. At low levels of output the aggregate supply curve is almost horizontal.   T   F

8. At output levels beyond full employment any increases in aggregate demand will increase both output and prices.   T   F

9. Sticky wages and prices explain the vertical portion of the aggregate demand curve.   T   F

10. The spending multiplier becomes larger once changes in the price level are taken into account.   T   F

MULTIPLE CHOICE QUESTIONS

Choose the best option for the following questions.

1. New Classical economists believe that
   a. monetary policy is useful but fiscal policy is not in the short-run.
   b. fiscal policy is useful but monetary policy is not in the short-run.
   c. fiscal and monetary policy is useful in the short-run.
   d. neither fiscal or monetary policy is useful in the short-run.

2. New Keynesians believe that
   a. monetary policy is useful but fiscal policy is not in the short-run.
   b. fiscal policy is useful but monetary policy is not in the short-run.
   c. fiscal and monetary policy is useful in the short-run.
   d. neither fiscal or monetary policy is useful in the short-run.

3. According to New Classical economists an increase in interest rates
   a. increases labor supply and output.
   b. decreases labor supply and output.
   c. decreases output but has no effect on labor supply.
   d. has no effect on output or labor supply.

4. An increase in oil prices would
   a. shift the aggregate demand curve to the right.
   b. shift the aggregate demand curve to the left.
   c. shift the aggregate supply curve to the left.
   d. shift the aggregate supply curve to the right.

5. Stagflation occurs when
   a. prices and output rise.
   b. prices and output fall.
   c. prices fall and output rises.
   d. prices rise and output falls.

6. An increase in the price level will cause the ADE curve to
   a. shift up.
   b. shift down.

c. become steeper.
d. become flatter.

7. Price level increases
   a. decrease the value of the spending multiplier.
   b. increase the value of the spending multiplier.
   c. can either increase or decrease the spending multiplier.
   d. will not affect the value of the spending multiplier.

8. In the long-run, New Keynesians
   a. and New Classical economists believe the aggregate supply curve is upward sloping.
   b. believe the aggregate supply curve is upward sloping while the New Classicalists believe it is vertical.
   c. and New Classical economists believe the aggregate supply curve is vertical.
   d. believe the aggregate supply curve is vertical while the New Classicalists believe it is upward sloping.

9. Which of the following is inconsistent with the New Keynesian theory?
   a. vertical short-run aggregate supply curve
   b. fiscal policy
   c. monetary policy
   d. sticky wages and prices

10. Which of the following is inconsistent with the New Classical theory?
    a. a vertical short-run aggregate supply curve
    b. perfectly competitive markets
    c. monetary policy
    d. flexible wages

SHORT ANSWER QUESTIONS

Fill in the blanks in the following statements.

1. _____ rates and the labor supply are _____ related according to the New Classical economists.

2. An increase in the price level will cause the ADE curve to _____.

3. According to the New Keynesians, at low levels of output an increase in aggregate demand will cause the price level to _____ and the output level to _____.

4. At output levels close to full employment, an increase in aggregate demand will cause the price level to _____ and the output level to _____.

5. Stagflation occurs when _____ increase and output _____.

PROBLEMS

1. Suppose aggregate demand decreases due to a decrease in government spending. Explain what happens to prices and output according to the New Keynesian assumptions if the economy was at full employment.

2. What types of public policies do the New Keynesians and New Classical economists agree are beneficial to the economy?

3. How will the spending multiplier be affected when a model of the macro economy takes into account changes in the price level?

4. Explain the relationship between interest rates and labor supply according to the New Classical approach. What empirical evidence supports the theory?

5. In the 1990's President Clinton is faced with a high national debt and a sluggish economy. Inflation rates are relatively low and economic growth is low. What policy options would be appropriate if you were a new Keynesian?

6. Given the circumstances described in question 5, how would you respond to the situation if you were a New Classical economist?

7. How can long-term growth in the economy be stimulated according to both New Keynesians and New Classical economists?

8. Describe a scenario where the price level increases and output falls.

POST-TEST

Answer the following questions to determine how well you have learned the material in the chapter and to determine those areas where you need to focus your studies.

1. What types of government policies can effectively increase long-term economic growth?

2. Describe the differences between the short and long-run aggregate supply curves according to New Keynesians and New Classicalists.

3. What is the relationship between the price level and investment demand in the economy?

4. What factors make wages sticky?

5. What factors make prices sticky?

6. Why do Classical economists argue that labor supply is affected by interest rates?

7. Suppose the economy is operating at full employment and an adverse supply shock occurs. What types of policies might a New Keynesian recommend?

8. Suppose the economy is operating at an output level significantly below full employment and aggregate demand decreases. What will happen to prices and output?

Chapter 19
Controlling Inflation and Other Policy Issues

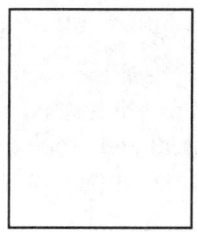

LEARNING OBJECTIVES

CONCEPTS TO LEARN

Rational expectations	Long-run Phillips curve
Supply-side economics	Policy credibility

CONCEPTS TO RECALL

Laws of supply and demand	Inflation
Fischer equation	New Keynesian economics
New Classical economics	Aggregate demand and aggregate supply
Aggregate supply shock	The equation of exchange
Short-run Phillips curve	

CHAPTER REVIEW

Chapter 19 focuses on the New Keynesian and New Classical views on inflation and macroeconomic policy. The long-run implications and causes of sustained inflation are analyzed. The chapter concludes with a discussion of Reaganomics and current policy options.

159

1. The four factors that determine inflation are: growth in nominal aggregate demand, the state of the economy, aggregate supply shocks, and expectations of future inflation.

2. Inflation is a long-run problem that is driven by growth in aggregate demand and expectations of inflation.

3. One-time changes in aggregate demand or one-time supply shocks will affect short-run inflation rate but can not sustain long-run inflation. Once the economy returns to the full employment long-run equilibrium the inflation will stop after a series of short-term adjustments.

4. The state of the economy will have an effect on short-run inflation as indicated by the short-run Phillips curve. The farther away from full employment at the production possibilities frontier the lower the rate of inflation. The state of the economy has almost no long-run effects on inflation.

5. Expectations of inflation drive up inflation through the supply-side of the economy. Inflation expectations increase wages and nominal interest rates which increase firms' capital costs. These increases in production costs will cause the aggregate supply to shift up and to the left continually over time. Therefore, expectations of inflation lead to a continual adverse aggregate supply shock.

6. Individuals have rational expectations about the future course of inflation according to most economists. These rational expectations are formed based on all available information including past inflation rates and government fiscal and monetary policies. According to the theory, individuals' rational expectations of inflation will be right over time on average.

7. Nominal aggregate demand also fuels inflation in the long-run. Prices can only rise if there is an increase in demand for products at the same time.

8. Government fiscal and monetary policies can be used to change nominal aggregate demand and inflation rates. The equation of exchange $MV = PY$ implies that controlling the money supply is the key to controlling inflation.

9. Inflation can be stopped by stopping the growth of the money supply but the policy often leads to high short-run costs. These costs include job losses, bankruptcies, and high government deficits due to declines in tax revenues. Instead, government can continue to fuel inflation by printing money to finance deficits. The dangers of printing money include the possibility of hyperinflation.

10. There is no long-run trade-off between unemployment and inflation. The long-run Phillips curve is vertical at the natural rate of unemployment, U_{NR}. Once expected inflation adjusts to actual inflation rates the economy will return to the natural rate of unemployment of the production possibilities frontier. Individual short-run Phillips curves relate to different expected rates of inflation.

11. In the long-run, the economy will be at the natural rate of unemployment at any rate of inflation. Any attempts to change the unemployment rate will affect the inflation rate once the economy is at the natural rate.

12. Government can eradicate inflation by using fiscal and/or monetary policy to create a recession and bring inflation expectations down to zero. The costs of these anti-inflationary policies are high in terms of unemployment.

13. Supply-side theories were designed to respond to the adverse conditions caused by OPEC related supply shocks in 1979. Reaganomics or supply-side economics was designed to lower prices and increase output by shifting the aggregate supply curve out and to the right. Lower taxes on individuals and firms were supposed to shift the aggregate supply curve outward according to the supply-side theory because of lower costs of production and increases in saving. The evidence on the 1981 supply-side inspired tax cuts do not support the theory. However the outcome is consistent with the Keynesian model, the short-run effects of the tax cuts led to an increase in aggregate demand.

14. In the long-run, tax policy can impact saving, investment, and economic growth. Replacing personal and corporate taxes with a consumption tax will promote saving, investment, and productivity by as much as 20% according to simple long-run models of the economy.

15. An emerging consensus among economists is that a consistent and credible government policy that removes uncertainty is the best course. A consistent policy can reduce the search component of unemployment, promote investment, and reduce the threat of inflation.

A FEW HELPFUL TIPS

It's important to remember that the full employment level of output or the natural rate of employment assumes that there will still be some people searching for jobs. The economy will get to the full employment output level on its own. The New Keynesians and New Classical economists just disagree about how long it takes to get to the full employment output level.

	QUICK STUDY GUIDE			
	T/F	Mult. Choice	Short Answer	Problems
Long-Run Inflation Factors	6	2, 3, 4	3	1, 3
Rational Expectations	8			
Long-Run Phillips Curve	1, 2	7		
Supply-Side Economics	5, 10	9, 10	5	8

PRETEST

Answer the following questions to test your initial understanding of the material in this chapter:

1. What are the four factors that determine inflation rates over time?
2. Why can't adverse supply shocks sustain prolonged inflation?
3. Why won't a one-time tax cut result in a sustained period of inflation?
4. What factors will cause a sustained prolonged inflation?
5. How do expectations of inflation affect long-run inflation rates?
6. What are rational expectations?

7. Explain why the long-run Phillips curve is vertical.
8. How can the government stop long-term inflation?

TRUE/FALSE PRACTICE QUESTIONS

1. The short-run Phillips curve is vertical. T F
2. Expectations of inflation will cause the Phillips curve to shift to the right. T F
3. Increases in inflation reduce the real rate of interest. T F
4. Monetary policy can be used to reduce the natural rate of unemployment. T F
5. Supply-side economics called for tax increases to balance the budget. T F
6. A one-time increase in government spending can fuel long-run inflation. T F
7. The economy can be in long-run equilibrium at any rate of inflation. T F
8. Rational expectations of inflation are equal to actual inflation in every time period. T F
9. Decreases in the money supply can eradicate inflation. T F
10. Reductions in corporate and individual taxes are likely to promote long-term economic growth. T F

MULTIPLE CHOICE QUESTIONS

Choose the best option for the following questions.

1. Which of the following will not affect the annual rate of inflation?
   a. nominal aggregate demand
   b. aggregate supply shocks
   c. expectations of inflation
   d. the real level of full employment output

2. The only two factors that can cause long-run inflation are
   a. positive supply shocks and increases in nominal aggregate demand.
   b. negative supply shocks and increases in nominal aggregate demand.
   c. expectations of inflation and negative supply shocks.
   d. expectations of inflation and continued growth in nominal aggregate demand.

3. A one-time aggregate supply shock will affect
   a. inflation in both the short and long-run.
   b. inflation in only the short-run.
   c. inflation in only the long-run.
   d. not affect inflation.

4. The long-run effects of an adverse supply shock are
   a. a decrease in the equilibrium output level and an increase in prices.
   b. increases in both the equilibrium output level and prices.

c. decreases in both the equilibrium output level and prices.
d. increases in prices and no effect on the equilibrium output level.

5. Expectations of inflation will cause the aggregate
   a. demand curve to shift up and to the right.
   b. demand curve to shift down and to the left.
   c. supply curve to shift down and to the right.
   d. supply curve to shift up and to the left.

6. Increases in expected inflation rates will cause interest rates to
   a. increase.
   b. decrease.
   c. either increase or decrease.
   d. stabilize.

7. The long-run Phillips curve is
   a. horizontal.
   b. vertical at the natural rate of unemployment.
   c. constantly changing.
   d. undefined.

8. Monetary policy designed to increase the full employment output level will
   a. increase output and prices.
   b. increase prices but not output.
   c. decrease output and prices.
   d. decrease output and increase prices.

9. According to supply-side theory a decrease in individual income and corporate taxes
   a. will shift aggregate demand to the right.
   b. will shift aggregate demand to the left.
   c. will shift aggregate supply to the right.
   d. will shift aggregate supply to the left.

10. Which of the following did not occur after President Reagan's supply-side tax cut in 1981?
    a. private savings decreased
    b. unemployment fell
    c. federal income tax revenues declined
    d. aggregate supply shifted to the right

SHORT ANSWER QUESTIONS

Fill in the blanks in the following statements.

1. The four factors affecting annual inflation are: _____, _____, _____ and _____.
2. The Phillips curve will be _____ as output levels approach full employment.
3. A one-time supply shock will affect inflation in the _____ but not the _____.

4. _____ inflation rate is consistent with a full employment level of output.

5. Supply-side economics assumes that income tax decreases will shift the _____ curve to the _____.

PROBLEMS

1. Use the short-run Phillips curve to explain why expectations of inflation are likely to raise the price level of the economy but have no effect on output in the long-run.

2. Explain why inflation and unemployment problems can not be solved simultaneously by fiscal or monetary policy.

3. Explain what will happen to prices and output in the long-run if the money supply is increased and the economy is already at full employment.

4. Suppose the economy is experiencing a period of sustained inflation and high unemployment. What are the policy options and the related costs of the options?

5. What are the costs of eradicating inflation by decreasing the money supply?

6. How do expectations of inflation affect the aggregate supply curve?

7. Explain why nominal aggregate demand growth is an essential ingredient in fueling inflation.

8. How was supply-side economics supposed to reduce inflation and unemployment at the same time?

9. Why do economists generally agree that tax policy should be changed infrequently?

POST-TEST

Answer the following questions to determine how well you have learned the material in the chapter and to determine those areas where you need to focus your studies.

1. Explain why there is no relationship between inflation and unemployment in the long-run.

2. What are the benefits of a stable tax policy on long-term growth in the economy?

3. Explain why shifts in the aggregate supply curve can't affect the natural rate of unemployment.

4. What are the long-run effects on price and output of an adverse supply shock caused by OPEC raising the price of oil?

5. Explain how prices and output will be affected in the short and long-run after a one-time increase in government spending.

6. Explain why a supply-side tax cut is supposed to reduce prices and raise output.

7. How will increases in the expected rates of inflation affect the price and output levels in the short and long-run?

8. Why will government be reluctant to decrease the money supply to stop an inflationary spiral?

Part V–Sample Test
The Role of Prices and the Problem of Inflation

1. The aggregate demand curve
   a. is vertical in the long run.
   b. shows the amount of aggregate desired expenditure at each price level.
   c. shows the amount of aggregate desired expenditure at each income level.
   d. is the same as the aggregate desired expenditure (ADE) line.

2. The aggregate supply curve
   a. is vertical in the long run.
   b. shifts upward or left when the level of technology increases.
   c. is more elastic in the long run than in the short run.
   d. shifts downward or to the right when wages increase.

3. A schedule that indicates the quantity of national output the four sectors of the economy are willing to purchase at each overall level of prices is the
   a. equation of exchange schedule.
   b. the purchasing schedule.
   c. price response schedule.
   d. aggregate demand schedule.

4. Menu costs are
   a. costs to producers of publishing new price catalogs and informing customers of price changes.
   b. the price that producers charge for their catalogs.
   c. the surcharge placed on diners at sophisticated restaurants.
   d. none of the above

5. Stagnation is
   a. any period in which economic growth slows.
   b. a period of falling or stagnant prices.
   c. a period of inflation with slowly growing or decreasing output.
   d. a period of ever accelerating inflation.

6. The downward slope of the aggregate demand curve results from
   a. the downward slope of the microeconomics demand curve.
   b. the law of demand.
   c. the relation between money wages and real wages.
   d. the relationship between the price level and the transactions demand for money.

7. Both New Keynesians and New Classicals agree that
   a. the long-run AS curve has a finite positive slope.
   b. the long-run AS curve is vertical.
   c. the long-run AS curve is horizontal.
   d. the two groups agree on nothing.

8. In the short run the level of output is determined
   a. only by aggregate demand.
   b. only by aggregate supply.
   c. by both aggregate demand and aggregate supply.
   d. by neither aggregate demand or aggregate supply.

9. The New Keynesian perspective on the short-run aggregate supply is
   a. that it has no characteristic shape.
   b. that it's relatively steep, but not vertical.
   c. that it's relative flat, but not horizontal.
   d. that it's horizontal.

10. The New Classical perspective on the short-run aggregate supply is
    a. that it has no characteristic shape.
    b. that it's relatively steep, but not vertical.
    c. that it's relative flat, but not horizontal.
    d. that it's vertical when price expectations are correct.

11. The inside-outside theory is emphasized by which group of economists?
    a. New Keynesians
    b. New Classicals
    c. Monetarists
    d. Classicals

12. The typical short-run aggregate supply curve
    a. increases at a constant rate with the level of output.
    b. increases at a decreasing rate with the level of output.
    c. increases at an increasing rate with the level of output.
    d. is vertical.

13. We can derive the aggregate demand curve from
    a. aggregate supply curve.
    b. the Phillips curve.
    c. the production function.
    d. the ADE–45 degree diagram.

14. The long-run Phillips curve has the property or properties that
    a. only one inflation rate is compatible with the natural unemployment rate.
    b. in the long run there is a small, but significant tradeoff between inflation and unemployment.
    c. stimulative fiscal policy has no long-run effect on unemployment.
    d. all of the above

15. As the unemployment fall below the natural rate, the short-run Phillips curve
    a. continues its constant slope.
    b. becomes steeper.
    c. becomes flatter.
    d. may become either steeper or flatter.

16. A key assumption of rational expectations is that
    a. inflation will not increase over time.
    b. economic agents make unbiased estimates of inflation.
    c. discretionary government fiscal policy can improve economic performance.
    d. people base their price expectations on past behavior of prices.

17. Empirical estimates on how people form inflation estimates supports
    a. the extrapolation theory.
    b. the rational expectations theory.
    c. the zero inflation theory.
    d. none of the above

18. What relates money interest rates to real interest rates?
    a. equation of exchange
    b. Phillips curve
    c. Okun's law
    d. Fisher equation

19. The percentage growth of prices plus the percentage growth of output equals
    a. the growth of nominal GDP.
    b. the growth of the standard of living.
    c. the growth of real GDP.
    d. the growth of velocity.

20. The best long-term way to control inflation in the long run is to
    a. control the growth of government purchases.
    b. control the growth of the money supply.
    c. control the growth of tax rates.
    d. control the growth of foreign trade.

21. After a period of price stability an expected increase in the growth of the money supply will
    a. reduce nominal and real interest rates the same amount.
    b. reduce nominal interest rates more than real rates.
    c. reduce real rates more than nominal rates.
    d. have no effect on the real interest rate.
    e. move the nominal rate upward and the real rate downward.

22. The supply-side tax theory is associated with what administration?
    a. Richard Nixon
    b. Bill Clinton
    c. Gerald Ford
    d. John Kennedy
    e. none of the above

23. The government's need for a reputation of consistency and creditability
    a. is favored only by New Classicals.
    b. is favored only by New Keynesians.
    c. is favored by both New Classicals and New Keynesians.
    d. is opposed by both New Classicals and New Keynesians.

24. A policy of long-term low tax rates and a balanced budget is favored by
    a. New Classical economists.
    b. New Keynesian economists.
    c. Supply-Side economists.
    d. all of the above

25. The Laffer curve relates
    a. unemployment and the inflation rate.
    b. tax rates and unemployment.
    c. tax rates and tax revenues.
    d. economic growth and unemployment.

Chapter 20
International Trade and Barriers to Trade

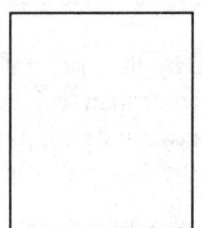

LEARNING OBJECTIVES

CONCEPTS TO LEARN

Ricardo's comparative advantage model	The factor endowment's model
Product differentiation, economies of scale model	Economic effects of tariffs, quotas, and other trade restrictions
North American Free Trade Agreement (NAFTA)	The European Community
GATT (General Agreement on Tariffs and Trade)	

CONCEPTS TO RECALL

Opportunity cost	Production possibilities frontier
Principle of comparative advantage	Laws of supply and demand

CHAPTER REVIEW

Chapter 20 is an overview of the three basic models of international trade used by economists: Ricardo's theory of comparative advantage, the factor endowments model, and the product differentiation/economies of scale model. The chapter includes a discussion of both the North American Free Trade Agreement (NAFTA) and the European Community. The final section focuses on trade barriers.

1. According to Ricardo's theory of comparative advantage, countries benefit from trade because of differences in the opportunity costs of production across countries. Countries will gain from trade when they specialize in the production of goods where they have a comparative advantage over other countries. A country will be able to consume beyond its production possibilities frontier by trade with other countries.

2. The Fundamental Principles of International Trade derived from Ricardo's model are:
   a. Countries gain more from specialization and trade the greater the price of export goods relative to the price of imports or the terms-of-trade. The relative demands for the goods determines the terms-of-trade.
   b. Over time the value of imports must equal the value of exports. Imbalances of trade may exist in the short run but in the long run trading partners will insist on receiving real goods in exchange for their own goods.
   c. Exchange rates will be determined by the price ratios of good exchanged between countries.
   d. Differences in opportunity costs rather than technology or wages are the key to the gains from trade between countries. Trade between developing and industrialized countries will be beneficial to both trading partners because of differences in opportunity costs.

3. The factor endowment model explains why increasing marginal costs and incomplete specialization will lead a country to both import and produce some goods. Countries will export those goods using inputs that are abundant in the economy and import those goods that use factors of production that are in short supply.

4. Trade will have distributional implications according to the factor endowment model. Those factors used in the production of export goods will increase in value and factors used in goods with a comparative disadvantage will decrease in value. In the U.S., products that use large amounts of capital, land and highly skilled labor will earn high returns and those that use large amounts of unskilled labor will have low returns.

5. Fears that NAFTA will hurt American workers is exaggerated because Mexico's economy is so much smaller, many Mexican workers already are working in the U.S., and many American companies are already taking advantage of low wages of unskilled workers in Mexico through the Maquiladora program.

6. Product differentiation and economies of scale explain the two-way trade between countries of highly similar products. Multinational companies compete internationally and often develop similar products that can be both imported and exported. The economies of scale enjoyed by these large multinational companies leads to research and development that results in the development of new products with distinct characteristics.

7. The major gains from the European Community are likely to be a result of eliminating local trade barriers which have prevented multinational corporations from markets in individual countries. The estimated potential gains from establishing the European Community are approximately equal to 1% of the European National Product. Most of the increase in trade will be two-way trade of similar products.

8. Trade barriers include tariffs, quotas and other restrictions. Tariffs are taxes on imported goods, quotas limit the quantity of imports and examples of other restrictions include product standard specifications or marketing regulations.

9. Tariffs raise prices for consumers of the taxed goods, benefit industries in the import-competing industries and raise revenues for the government. Quotas have the same effects except that the government revenues are instead collected by firms importing foreign goods. Trade restrictions are politically popular because those employed in the "protected" industry have a lot to gain and those consumers who lose do not directly perceive their losses. Gains from free trade to individual consumers are small and diverse while the losses are heavily concentrated among a small number of import-competing industries and their workers.

10. Losses due to trade restrictions far exceed any gains according to the overwhelming majority of economic studies.

11. The General Agreement on Tariffs and Trade, GATT, is an international agreement to reduce tariffs and trade restrictions. The original agreement was signed in 1947 by 23 nations. The agreement now covers 100 nations and has been most successful in reducing tariff rates but has not prevented quotas and other nontariff barriers from proliferating.

12. Strategic tariffs are often imposed by a large industrial nation when a new product is being developed. The barriers are justified as a means of protecting firms during the research and development stage of production. Recent examples include the European Airbus and Japan's microchip industry. Economic studies show that strategic barriers are not cost beneficial.

A FEW HELPFUL TIPS

It's very easy to get caught up in the "Buy American" campaigns financed by U.S. firms but remember that trade restrictions and barriers create more costs than benefits in the overall economy. Don't get confused between distributional effects and overall benefits. Free trade will create some losers but overall, society benefits.

	QUICK STUDY GUIDE			
	T/F	Mult. Choice	Short Answer	Problems
Ricardo	1	5		6
Law of Comparative	2, 3	3	2	
NAFTA	6			1
Quotas and Tariffs	7, 8, 9, 10	1	3, 4	3

PRETEST

Answer the following questions to test your initial understanding of the material in this chapter:

1. Explain Ricardo's theory of comparative advantage.

2. Why won't industrialized nations lose all their jobs to developing countries that have lower prevailing wage rates?

3. How will the price ratios of goods reflect the opportunity costs of production in two countries?

4. Why would a country want to both import and produce the same good within its own borders?

5. What is NAFTA?

6. What is GATT?

7. Explain why the European Community is likely to increase the standard of living in member countries.

8. Describe three trade barriers and explain who wins and who loses when they are imposed.

TRUE/FALSE PRACTICE QUESTIONS

1. The terms-of-trade will be determined by relative demands for goods in Ricardo's model. T F

2. It is likely that underdeveloped countries will not have any comparative advantage. T F

3. The Law of Comparative Advantage implies that specialization in production is likely to occur. T F

4. Countries rarely import and produce goods simultaneously. T F

5. The European Community was dissolved in 1992. T F

6. NAFTA will increase trade between the U.S. and Mexico. T F

7. Quotas have the same effects as tariffs on import goods. T F

8. Strategic tariffs are usually beneficial to an economy according to most recent economic studies. T F

9. GATT has resulted in a reduction of tariffs. T F

10. Tariffs and quotas are easily justified by current economic research. T F

MULTIPLE CHOICE QUESTIONS

Choose the best option for the following questions.

1. Which of the following is not an example of a trade restriction?
   a. an import quota
   b. a strategic tariff
   c. government subsidies for research and development
   d. quotas

2. Two countries will benefit from trade whenever
   a. opportunity costs are the same.

b. opportunity costs of production differ.
   c. there are differences in productivity.
   d. productivity rates are the same.

3. No country has a comparative advantage when
   a. opportunity costs are the same.
   b. opportunity costs of production differ.
   c. there are differences in productivity.
   d. productivity rates are the same.

4. Which of the following is not an example of an effort to increase free trade?
   a. NAFTA
   b. The European Community
   c. GATT
   d. "Buy American" campaigns

5. In Ricardo's model the value of exports
   a. must exceed imports.
   b. must be less than imports.
   c. must be the same as imports.
   d. can be more or less than imports.

6. The value of the currency in a country with a positive balance of trade is likely to
   a. increase.
   b. decrease.
   c. either increase or decrease.
   d. not change.

7. The factor endowment model predicts that unskilled laborers in the U.S. wages will be
   a. higher.
   b. lower.
   c. unpredictable.
   d. constant over time.

8. Since 1940 average tariff rates on manufactured goods for industrialized countries within GATT have
   a. increased.
   b. decreased.
   c. not changed.
   d. both increased and decreased.

SHORT ANSWER QUESTIONS

Fill in the blanks in the following statements.

1. The _____ principle states that any GATT reduction in tariffs or trade restrictions applies to trade between the two countries.

2. _____ principle states a country should specialize in the production of goods that can be produced at a lower _____ cost.

3. A government limit on imports is a _____.

4. Taxes on imports are _____.

5. When net exports are positive the value of a country's currency is likely to _____.

PROBLEMS

1. Discuss the benefits and costs of NAFTA.

2. Who is likely to win and lose as a result of a strong European Community?

3. Use graphs to explain how a tariff on imported cars is likely to affect the prices and quantities of both American and foreign imports.

4. Explain why a decrease in the value of the dollar is likely to help the trade deficit.

5. How can a currency be undervalued?

6. What are Ricardo's fundamental principles of foreign trade?

7. Explain the distributional implications raised by the factor endowment model.

8. How effective have the GATT agreements been in lowering tariffs over the last 50 years?

POST-TEST

Answer the following questions to determine how well you have learned the material in the chapter and to determine those areas where you need to focus your studies.

1. Why don't developing countries have to be concerned about the superior skills of workers in industrialized countries?

2. What groups and individuals are most likely to fight for tariffs and quotas on foreign cars?

3. What are strategic tariffs and what are they designed to accomplish?

4. The most favored nation status of China has been questioned by many Americans. What are the costs and benefits to Americans of this distinction?

5. Why will a country both import and export the same type of goods?

6. How can the factor endowment model be used to explain the differences in wages between skilled and unskilled workers in the U.S.?

7. Use the law of comparative advantage to explain why it makes more sense for U.S. farmers to grow rice than Japanese farmers.

8. What is likely to happen to the value of the dollar when the U.S. is running a trade deficit?

Chapter 21

International Finance

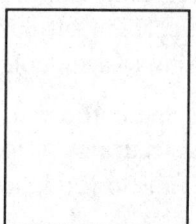

LEARNING OBJECTIVES

CONCEPTS TO LEARN

Balance of payments

Fixed exchange rates

Fiscal and monetary policies under flexible and fixed exchange rates

Flexible exchange rates

The Bretton Woods fixed exchange rate system

CONCEPTS TO RECALL

Laws of supply and demand

Monetary policy

Fiscal policy

CHAPTER REVIEW

Chapter 21 focuses on the balance of trade and the international transactions between countries. The second portion of the chapter includes an analysis of the benefits and costs of fixed versus variable exchange rates. Finally, the chapter ends with a discussion of the European Community.

1. The balance of payments must have a net zero value overall and is a double-entry accounting of international credits and debits. International credits accrue when the demand for dollars increases because of exports, capital inflows and sales of foreign currency by the Fed. International debits

accrue when the supply of dollars increases because of increases in the demand for foreign currency.

2. The balance of payment account is divided into three sub-accounts: the current account, the capital account, and the official settlements account.

3. The current account records the flow of exports and imports of goods and services, receipts and payments of factor incomes and net unilateral transfers. The difference between merchandise exports and imports is the balance of trade. The balance of trade plus exports minus imports of services plus receipts minus factor income payments is the balance of goods and services. The current account balance is the balance of goods and services minus net unilateral transfers.

4. If foreign residents and central banks are accumulating dollars and dollar assets the current account deficit will rise. When U.S. residents and the Fed accumulate foreign currencies the current account surplus rises. Current account surpluses and deficits must eventually balance out because trading partners will be unwilling to accumulate surpluses forever.

5. The difference between capital inflows and outflows is the capital account balance. Capital inflows are purchases of U.S. financial securities or loans to foreign interests. Capital outflows are purchases of foreign securities or loans to foreigners originating from Americans.

6. The difference between the purchase and sale of international reserves by the Fed is the official settlements balance. International reserves are foreign currencies, gold, and short-term financial securities held by central banks.

7. The U.S. has become the largest debtor nation in recent years because the country has had large current account deficits offset by large capital account and official settlement account surpluses. Americans have been exporting more than they import and foreigners are holding more U.S. assets.

8. The laws of supply and demand determine currency exchange rates under a flexible exchange rate system. Factors affecting supply and demand will include tastes for traded goods, worldwide productivity changes, the state of the economy, interest rates, and speculation based on expectations of future values of exchange rates.

9. Currencies can be kept in alignment with one another through arbitrage. The absolute value of exchange adjusting for inflation can be fixed by purchasing power parity fixes.

10. Since 1973 the dollar has been subject to a flexible exchange rate with brief interludes where the Fed or other central banks have intervened to stabilize the currency. Intervention by the banks is referred to as a dirty float in a flexible exchange system.

11. When exchange rates are fixed, the central banks must intervene in foreign exchange markets to maintain the agreed upon exchange rate.

12. The Bretton Woods Agreement in 1944 established worldwide fixed exchange rates. The dollar was pegged at $35 an ounce of gold and all other currencies were pegged to the dollar or the cost of gold. In 1973, President Nixon abandoned the agreement and the U.S. moved to a flexible exchange rate.

13. Fiscal policy is relatively ineffective and monetary policy is effective under a flexible exchange rate system. When exchange rates are fixed, fiscal policy is effective in the short run but monetary policy is not.

14. Flexible and pegged exchange rates are both used throughout the world. The Japanese yen and the U.S. dollar are subject to market forces while most European currencies are tied to the German mark.

A FEW HELPFUL TIPS

It is very easy to get turned around when analyzing the relationship between net exports and the value of a currency. Remember, if Americans are buying more imports, the dollars eventually have to be exchanged for foreign currencies to buy the goods. Then, the demand for foreign currency rises and the demand for dollars declines so that the relative value of the dollar is lower. The reverse logic works when Americans are selling more exports.

	QUICK STUDY GUIDE			
	T/F	Mult. Choice	Short Answer	Problems
Balance of Payments	1	1		
Fixed Exchange Rates	2, 3, 4			4, 7
Flexible Exchange Rates	5			4
European Community	4	4		8

PRETEST

Answer the following questions to test your initial understanding of the material in this chapter:

1. What are the three sub-accounts in the balance of trade payments?
2. What are the differences between fixed and floating exchange rates?
3. Why did the value of the dollar decrease when Americans became enamored with Japanese products?
4. What was the Bretton Woods agreement?
5. How will a flexible exchange rate affect a fiscal policy designed to increase aggregate demand?
6. What are the capital accounts?
7. Why did Europeans decide to fix their currencies to the German mark?
8. Why will increases in the interest rate in the U.S. affect the value of the dollar?

TRUE/FALSE PRACTICE QUESTIONS

1. Increases in net exports are likely to devalue the dollar.   T   F
2. The value of the dollar on world markets is fixed to the price of gold.   T   F
3. The U.S. has a fixed exchange rate.   T   F
4. Most European currencies are fixed to the German mark.   T   F
5. A dirty float is illegal.   T   F
6. Capital account balances are likely to rise when foreigners finance the U.S. national debt.   T   F
7. When the dollar appreciates exports become more costly.   T   F
8. The U.S. is a net lender nation.   T   F

MULTIPLE CHOICE QUESTIONS

Choose the best option for the following questions.

1. An increase in sales of U.S. produced computer software will increase
   a. capital accounts.
   b. the current account deficit.
   c. the balance of trade.
   d. the value of foreign currencies.

2. Which of the following options is NOT in place today?
   a. Compliance with Bretton Woods
   b. floating exchange rates
   c. GATT
   d. The U.S. is a debtor nation

3. When U.S. imports increase, the value of the dollar is likely to
   a. increase
   b. decrease
   c. either increase or decrease
   d. remain constant.

4. Most European currencies are pegged to the value of the
   a. U.S. dollar.
   b. yen.
   c. German mark.
   d. French franc.

5. A dirty float is designed to
   a. destabilize the value of a currency.
   b. stabilize the value of a currency.
   c. allow speculators to profit from fluctuating exchange values.
   d. none of the above.

6. An increase in interest rates in the U.S. will probably
   a. increase the value of the dollar.
   b. decrease the value of the dollar.
   c. either increase or decrease the value of the dollar.
   d. have no effect on the value of the dollar.

7. Purchase of foreign securities will
   a. increase the capital outflows account.
   b. decrease the capital outflows account.
   c. either increase or decrease the capital outflows account.
   d. not have any effect on the capital outflows account.

8. When Americans' demand for Japanese cars increases, the value of the yen will
   a. increase.
   b. decrease.
   c. either increase or decrease.
   d. not be affected.

SHORT ANSWER QUESTIONS

Fill in the blanks in the following statements.

1. A sale of foreign currency by the Fed in exchange for dollars is a _____ in the U.S. _____ of payments.

2. An increase in the demand for American made blue jeans is likely to _____ the value of the dollar.

3. American capital accounts are likely to _____ when interest rates are higher in the U.S.

4. Dollar denominated accounts in foreign banks are called _____.

5. The U.S. balance of payments have been _____ since 1986 with the exception of 1991.

PROBLEMS

1. What is likely to happen to the value of the dollar when inflation rates are higher in this country relative to the rest of the world?

2. Why do smaller nations have to maintain a near-equality between exports and imports?

3. Why do you suppose the U.S. has managed to continue to be a debtor nation over the last decade without upsetting world currency markets?

4. What are the benefits of a flexible versus fixed exchange rate?

5. Explain what will happen to the value of the yen if Americans stop buying Japanese automobiles.

6. Suppose the NAFTA agreement is in effect and as a result Mexicans buy more U.S. products. What will happen to the value of the dollar and the peso?

7. Why is fiscal policy useless when exchange rates are flexible?

8. Describe exchange rates within the European Community.

POST-TEST

Answer the following questions to determine how well you have learned the material in the chapter and to determine those areas where you need to focus your studies.

1. How did OPEC oil price increases in the seventies affect world currencies?

2. Why is there a limit on the amount of time a country can continue to be a debtor nation?

3. What will happen to the value of the British pound when interest rates are higher in Great Britain than elsewhere?

4. What are the downsides of a fixed exchange rate and why did the U.S. abandon the Bretton Woods agreement?

5. When might a central bank want to have a "dirty float"?

6. How will inflation rates affect currency exchange rates?

7. Who benefits from arbitrage in world money markets?

8. Generally describe the U.S. balance of payments position over the last 10 years.

Chapter 22
Developing Nations

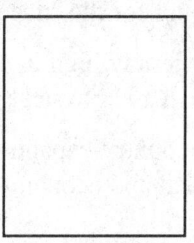

LEARNING OBJECTIVES

CONCEPTS TO LEARN

Developing countries	The determinants of long-run economic growth in developing countries
The relationship between income distribution and economic development	The supply of and the demand for children
Outward-oriented versus inward-oriented strategies for economic development	

CONCEPTS TO RECALL

Opportunity cost	Long-run economic growth
The laws of supply and demand	

CHAPTER REVIEW

The economic conditions of the world's peoples in developing nations are described in Chapter 22. The chapter begins with an examination of the standards of living in developing countries. Then, the chapter evaluates the key determinants of economic growth in developing countries: labor force participation rates, savings and productive investment, choice of production technologies, and the population growth rate. The chapter also evaluates the relationship between income distribution and economic development and concludes with a comparison of the outward-oriented and inward-oriented strategies for development.

1. Four fifths of the world population live in developing countries in Latin America, Africa, and Asia.

2. The sub-Saharan African, Southeast Asian, and Central Asian countries are the poorest in the world and are primarily agriculturally based.

3. Comparisons using GDP figures are difficult due to differences in measurement and problems in adjusting for the relative values of the currencies. Comparisons based on purchasing power parities are more accurate but are still subject to error.

4. Economic development occurs over time and it is difficult at best to single out those economic policies and institutions that can account for the success or failure of a particular country.

5. Labor force participation rates are generally high in developing countries. However, labor is not very productive due to a lack of human and physical capital.

6. Increases in savings rates will help a country expand its economy. But, in many developing nations the culture and existing political and economic institutions stand in the way of productive investment.

7. Direct foreign investments, loans, and grants can increase a country's savings and promote growth.

8. The choice of technology and capital should reflect the factor prices of labor and capital. Developing countries often invest in high technology that is too capital-intensive given the low cost of labor. These inappropriate capital investments drain money from other areas and can hinder growth.

9. Population growth rates are much higher in developing countries. Both the supply and demand for children exceed the levels in the developed countries. High population growth rates further strain these developing countries.

10. Simon Kuznets found that income distributions in the poorest countries and the richest countries were most equal. Those countries in the middle tend to have the most unequal income distributions.

11. The Asian Newly Industrializing Countries, (NICS) followed a labor-intensive outward-oriented export strategy for development. By using their comparative advantage in labor and producing goods desired in the developed nations the NICS were able to dramatically improve their economic status.

12. Latin American countries followed an inward-oriented, import-substituting industrialization strategy and were not successful. They chose to produce goods for internal consumption that had previously been imported from abroad. The high costs of this strategy include high inflation, large budget deficits, trade deficits, and enormous foreign debt.

A FEW HELPFUL TIPS

Don't confuse per capita wealth and income distribution. A country like Saudi Arabia has a high per capita wealth but the majority of the citizens have very little and a small percentage of the population (i.e. the royal family) owns most of the wealth.

QUICK STUDY GUIDE

	T/F	Mult. Choice	Short Answer	Problems
GDP Growth	1, 2, 8	3, 5	4, 5	4, 5, 7
Income Distribution vs. Economic Development	4, 6		2	
Outward vs. Inward-Oriented Strategies	5			

PRETEST

Answer the following questions to test your initial understanding of the material in this chapter:

1. Why is per capita GDP a bad measure of the economic development of a country?
2. What are the four key determinants of economic growth in developing countries?
3. Why are low savings rates in developing countries a problem?
4. In what case would a state-of-the-art tractor be a bad investment in a country?
5. Compare and contrast population growth rates in the less developed countries to the developed countries.
6. Describe outward-oriented export strategies.
7. Describe inward-oriented import substituting industrialization strategies.
8. What is petrodollar recycling?

TRUE/FALSE PRACTICE QUESTIONS

1. Per capita incomes in LDCs are significantly lower than in the rest of the world. T F
2. Methods of calculating GDP are standardized throughout the world. T F
3. Capital flight occurs because of the comparative advantage of labor in LDCs. T F
4. The Kuznets curve shows the relationship between investment and growth. T F
5. The outward-oriented export strategy in Hong Kong has been successful. T F
6. Income Distributions are most equal in middle income nations. T F

7. Population growth rates are highest in developing countries.   T   F

8. In 1990, the country with the highest per capita GDP was Kuwait.   T   F

MULTIPLE CHOICE QUESTIONS

Choose the best option for the following questions.

1. Developed countries account for
   a. over half of the world's population.
   b. over 90% of the world's population.
   c. two-thirds of the world's population.
   d. less than 15 percent of the world's population.

2. Which of the following is not a NIC?
   a. New Zealand
   b. Hong Kong
   c. Taiwan
   d. Singapore

3. The statistic obtained by dividing GDP by the population is
   a. real GDP.
   b. nominal GDP.
   c. per capita GDP.
   d. NNP.

4. Which of the following countries could not be considered a developed country?
   a. U.S.
   b. Saudi Arabia
   c. Australia
   d. Sweden

5. Which of the following countries has the lowest per capital GDP?
   a. Mozambique
   b. Kuwait
   c. Libya
   d. Mexico

6. High inflation rates are likely to
   a. increase capital flight.
   b. decrease capital flight.
   c. either increase or decrease capital flight.
   d. have no effect on capital flight.

7. Unemployment rates in developing countries
   a. are higher than in industrialized countries.
   b. are lower than in industrialized countries.
   c. can be lower or higher than in industrialized countries.
   d. are the same as in industrialized countries.

8. The highest population growth rates are found in
   a. the richest countries.
   b. the poorest countries.
   c. the middle income countries.
   d. countries at all income levels.

SHORT ANSWER QUESTIONS

Fill in the blanks in the following statements.

1. _____ occurs when individuals in less developed countries invest their foreign currencies abroad.
2. The _____ curve shows the relationship between income distribution and per capita income.
3. Labor force participation rates in developing countries tend to be _____.
4. Less developed countries are those with a 1992 per capita income below _____.
5. Kuwait has a _____ per capita income than the U.S.

PROBLEMS

1. Where are the highest concentrations of world poverty located?
2. What are the economic growth trends in mainland China?
3. Explain why a developing country might purposefully overvalue its currency.
4. Explain why even though the per capita GDP of Japan exceeds the U.S. amount, Americans are able to enjoy a higher standard of living.
5. What measures other than GDP are useful measures of the state of development of a country?
6. Why might weather conditions affect labor participation rates of a country?
7. Describe some of the cultural traits that discourage development in many North African and Middle Eastern countries.
8. Why do many wealthy citizens of less developed countries put their savings into American and European financial institutions?

POST-TEST

Answer the following questions to determine how well you have learned the material in the chapter and to determine those areas where you need to focus your studies.

1. Explain the role of direct foreign investment in economic development.
2. How do distorted capital prices lead to inefficient production in many developing countries?

3. Explain why unemployment rates in developing countries are often higher than in industrialized countries.

4. Explain the Kuznets curve and its implications.

5. Why are population growth rates a significant factor in economic development?

6. Why are the demand and supply of children expected to be higher in less developed countries?

7. Describe the economic development strategy that has been so successful for the Asian newly industrializing countries (NIC).

8. What development strategies did the Latin American countries follow in the latter half of this century and why didn't they work?

Part VI–Sample Test
International Economics Issues

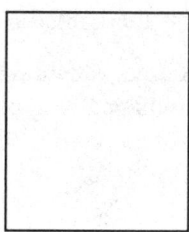

1. The definition of currency appreciation is when
   a. a country's inflation rate falls.
   b. a country's price level falls.
   c. a country's currency is redenominated.
   d. a country's currency rises in value relative to other nations.

2. A beggar-thy-neighbor policy occurs when a country
   a. cuts its welfare payments.
   b. borrows from another nation.
   c. attempts to export it unemployment by means of trade restrictions.
   d. defaults on its foreign debt.

3. If a country takes more resources to produce each of its products than another country it will likely have
   a. a comparative advantage.
   b. no basis for trade.
   c. an absolute advantage.
   d. none of the above

4. The factor endowments model was constructed to explain
   a. why different countries produce the same product differently.
   b. the pattern of economic specialization in international trade.

c. the Ricardian theory of international trade.
   d. why resources migrate from one country to another.

5. Economists call the amount that a nation gains through international trade relative to producing itself all the goods and services that it consumes are the
   a. rate of imperialism.
   b. exploitation rate.
   c. absolute advantage.
   d. gains from trade.
   e. the reciprocal advantage ratio.

6. The GATT agreement
   a. set up the International monetary fund.
   b. fixed the exchange rate among the nations of the world.
   c. seeks to promote barrier free international trade.
   d. sets up the financing mechanism for the United Nations.

7. A fundamental principle that states that any reduction in tariffs or other trade restrictions that is negotiated between any two nations automatically applies to all nations is the
   a. the Golden Rule.
   b. tit-for-tat policy.
   c. Slutsky effect.
   d. most-favored-nation principle.
   e. Downer's principle.

8. A tax on a good or service entering a country is a(n)
   a. quota.
   b. tariff.
   c. ad valorem tax.
   d. unit tax.

9. A per unit tariff on a good will make the supply curve of the imported goods
   a. disappear.
   b. move to the right.
   c. move upward by the amount of the tariff.
   d. none of the above

10. The buying and selling of commodities whose prices are out of line in such a way as to guarantee a profit is
    a. impossible.
    b. arbitrage.
    c. business as usual.
    d. hedging.

11. Which of the following is not one of the three major parts of the Balance of Payments?
    a. current accounts
    b. long run accounts
    c. capital accounts
    d. official settlements accounts

12. The current exchange rate system in the world economy is best described as
    a. fixed exchange rates.
    b. the gold standard.
    c. flexible exchange rates.
    d. the floating peg.

13. If the U.S. buys automobiles from Japan this will appear in the Balance of Payments as
    a. a credit on the capital account.
    b. a debit on the capital account.
    c. a credit on the current account.
    d. a debit on the current account.

14. Purchases of foreign financial securities or loans to foreign residents by domestic residents are
    a. net capital flows.
    b. capital outflows.
    c. external balance.
    d. official settlements balance.
    e. capital inflows.

15. The purchase of domestic stock or other assets by foreign residents that give them a controlling interest in a domestic firm is
    a. indirect foreign investment.
    b. direct foreign investment.
    c. external investment.
    d. stock accumulation.

16. Eurodollars consist of
    a. any dollar-denominated account in a foreign bank.
    b. U.S. currency that American travelers take to Europe.
    c. U.S. currency that American travelers take anywhere abroad.
    d. Earning of American corporations on the investments abroad.

17. The exchange Rate Mechanism (ERM) is most closely associated with
    a. flexible exchange rates.
    b. SDR accounts.
    c. the Bretton Woods System.
    d. the European Monetary System (EMS).

18. The IMF is an international agency that
    a. helps to resolve exchange rate and balance of payments problems.
    b. only makes foreign loans to developing countries.
    c. coordinates international trade policy.
    d. studies multi factor productivity among nations.
    e. assists in setting labor standards.

19. Countries that range from the nearly developed to the very poor, with a per capita income of less than $7050 (as of 1992) are
    a. underdeveloped countries.
    b. developed countries.

c. second world countries.
d. developing countries.

20. Export-enclave production occurs when
    a. resource-using firms in the developing countries export to the First World.
    a. government controls, but does not own, the production plant.
    b. government controls and owns the production plant.
    c. there is a beggar thy neighbor strategy.
    d. diversification strategy.

21. The Kuznetz curve shows the relationship between
    a. export growth and per capita income growth.
    b. the income distribution and per capita income for different countries.
    a. the currency value and the balance of trade.
    b. economic growth and government ownership of economic enterprises.

22. Interest rate ceilings are described as
    a. a bonus to the poor.
    b. necessary to prevent speculative excesses.
    c. necessary to stimulate economic investment.
    d. financial repression.

23. Countries which have recently achieved sustained growth have
    a. a market system to generate prices.
    b. a high degree of savings.
    c. international trade based on comparative advantage.
    d. all of the above

24. To successfully break out of poverty a nation should
    a. increase its employment in agriculture.
    b. increase the size of government.
    c. reduce its dependence on international trade.
    d. reduce its average propensity to consume.

25. The newly industrialized countries of the Pacific rim
    a. pursued export oriented growth policies.
    b. had high consumption rates.
    c. depended primarily on import substitution.
    d. all of the above

Chapter 23

The Role of Government in the U.S. Economy and Government Expenditures

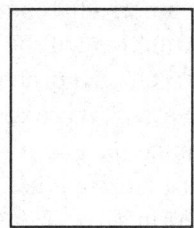

LEARNING OBJECTIVES

CONCEPTS TO LEARN

Vertical equity	The economics of information
The principal-agent problem	Adverse selection
Moral hazard	Externalities
Non-exclusive public goods	

CONCEPTS TO RECALL

Equality of opportunity	Horizontal equity
Distribution question	Economies of scale
Oligopoly	Natural monopoly

CHAPTER REVIEW

Chapter 23 focuses on the role of government in a capitalist economy. The first section focuses on the need for government intervention in a market economy and the second section focuses on actual government expenditures in the U.S. The role of government is viewed as a response to market failure.

1. Society's twin goals of efficiency and equity are results of perfectly competitive markets. Perfectly competitive markets allow individuals to have the freedom to do as they wish, bring order to the process of exchange, and are responsive to the needs of consumers.

2. Perfectly competitive markets result in allocational and production efficiency. Output will maximize the net value of consuming and producing goods and services because of efficiency gains. In a perfectly competitive market the economy will be operating on its production possibilities frontier and the goods and services will be produced at the least cost with the minimum amount of society's scarce resources.

3. Competitive markets promote horizontal equity by insuring the equal treatment of equals. However, vertical equity is not a natural outcome of the market system.

4. Distributional market failure occurs in a perfectly competitive economy because there is no guarantee that the resulting wealth distribution will be satisfactory from society's point of view. When markets are not competitive distributional problems are likely to increase. Those who start with more resources are likely to end up with more resources in a market based economy. Since everyone starts from an unequal beginning the end result will also be unequal. Government intervention is warranted to correct for perceived distributional imbalances. The tax system and government transfer programs are the primary tools used to correct for distributional deficiencies.

5. Allocational market failures occur when inefficiencies arise and the government can take a role in correcting the problems.

6. Economies of scale exist for many goods leading to markets dominated by a few large firms with monopoly power. Also, in the case of natural monopolies, it is more efficient to have one large firm produce a good. Public utilities and highways are examples of natural monopolies. Government can correct for the inefficiencies that occur due to monopolization of the market through windfall profits taxes, regulation, government provision of services, and antitrust legislation.

7. Imperfect information can lead to market failures that can be corrected by government. When individuals have unequal access to information the results of a market transaction can be inefficient. Examples of government intervention to correct for imperfect information include: government agencies that test and monitor products; the need for government to establish the rules of exchange; and OSHA which promotes safety in the workplace.

8. Incomplete insurance markets are also an example of market failure. The principal agent problem occurs when the insurer can not obtain all of the necessary information needed to determine the appropriate rates for an individual. Moral hazard occurs when an individual has an incentive to take an action which will increase the costs to the insurer. For example, a policy offering unlimited stress therapy sessions might encourage people to attend more sessions than they actually need or could benefit from. Adverse Selection occurs when those individuals with the highest

likelihood of having the insured characteristics purchase coverage. These high risk individuals drive average costs up. Then, those with lower risks are likely to drop out of the insurance pool and create their own plan at a lower cost. The original insurer is left with a pool of high risk individuals. Medical insurance and old age insurance are examples of government programs designed to correct for market failures in the insurance markets.

9. Technological externalities occur when third parties are affected by a market transaction. The market does not take into account the social or external costs of an action and the market fails. Industrial pollution is an example of a technological externality. A firm that pollutes the air when it is producing a good does not have to take into account the costs of air pollution to society. Government can correct for negative externalities by regulation and taxation that brings social and private costs into line. Education is an example of a positive externality where the individual benefits both themselves and society as a whole when investing in human capital.

10. Non-exclusive goods are ones that everyone consumes regardless of whether or not they paid for the good or wanted the good. National defense is an example of a non-exclusive good. The free rider problem occurs because individuals have an incentive to undervalue non-exclusive goods because they know they can benefit regardless of what they pay. Government provision of non-exclusive or public goods is the only possible option.

11. Macroeconomic stabilization is a role for government when the market outcome does not achieve goals of full employment, price stability, long-run economic growth, and stability in a country's economic relations with foreign countries.

12. Federal government spending falls into three main categories: defense, redistribution, and the provision of public pensions and insurance. State and local governments are primarily responsible for allocational problems caused by externalities and economies of scale. State and local governments are responsible for education, highways, aid to the poor, and hospital care.

13. Recent changes in government expenditures have primarily occurred at the Federal level. The large defense increases of the 1980's have been followed by large cuts in the nineties, interest payments on the national debt have exploded due to the large increase in the Federal debt in the Reagan and Bush era, large expenditures were necessary for the federal bailout of depositors in failed financial institutions, and health care expenditures have risen dramatically.

A FEW HELPFUL TIPS

Remember, textbook models of perfectly competitive markets are just that, models. The real world diverges from the perfectly competitive ideal and that is the justification for government intervention.

	QUICK STUDY GUIDE			
	T/F	Mult. Choice	Short Answer	Problems
Market Failure	2, 3, 5, 7, 8, 9	1, 2, 5	2, 3	2, 3, 5, 6, 9
Government Expenditures	4, 10	3, 4, 9, 10	5	7, 10

PRETEST

Answer the following questions to test your initial understanding of the material in this chapter:

1. What are the three broad categories of market failure?
2. Why will perfectly competitive markets result in horizontal equity but not vertical equity?
3. How might economies of scale lead to market failure?
4. Explain why moral hazard may increase insurance rates for everyone.
5. How will adverse selection affect insurance rates and why?
6. Why will firms ignore pollution costs when determining output levels and choosing production methods in an unregulated market?
7. Why should government produce non-exclusive goods in a market based economy?
8. Why does the Federal government have to take a role in macroeconomic stabilization?
9. Which are the three main areas of Federal government expenditures?
10. Which are the main areas of state and local government expenditures?

TRUE/FALSE PRACTICE QUESTIONS

1. Horizontal and vertical equity are natural outcomes of competitive markets.   T   F
2. Adverse selection occurs when insurers can not separate high risk and low risk individuals.   T   F
3. A streetlight is an example of a non-exclusive good.   T   F
4. Presidents Reagan and Bush lowered overall government spending during their presidencies.   T   F
5. Pecuniary externalities are a rationale for government intervention in the market.   T   F
6. Health care for the poor is an example of a merit good.   T   F
7. A bank robber is an example of a free rider.   T   F
8. Economies of scale can increase monopoly power.   T   F
9. Air is a common use resource.   T   F
10. Education is mainly a function of the Federal government.   T   F

MULTIPLE CHOICE QUESTIONS

Choose the best option for the following questions.

1. Which of the following is an example of a non-exclusive good?
   a. a can of processed meat
   b. national defense

c. aspirin
   d. a bus trip

2. Which of the following will create a negative technological externality?
   a. higher education
   b. pre-school programs
   c. prisons
   d. driving an automobile

3. Defense spending in the 1990s
   a. has increased.
   b. decreased.
   c. not changed.
   d. increased in 91-92 and then decreased.

4. Which of the following is an example of moral hazard?
   a. robbing a convenience store
   b. embezzling money from your employer
   c. robbing a home
   d. smokers enrolled in a private health insurance plan

5. Vertical equity will be a likely result
   a. regardless of whether or not the market is perfectly competitive.
   b. only when the market is perfectly competitive.
   c. only when the market is imperfectly competitive.
   d. in only a few rare cases in a market economy.

6. Distributional problems can be corrected by
   a. allowing the market to operate independently of government.
   b. tax and transfer program policy.
   c. government regulation alone.
   d. clear private property rights.

7. Government can curb monopoly power by all of the following methods *except*
   a. windfall profits taxes.
   b. antitrust regulation.
   c. deregulation of the private sector.
   d. government provision of the services.

8. Which of the following is an example of a free rider?
   a. a neighbor who refuses to contribute to a fund to buy trees for the publicly owned median strip located in the middle of the street.
   b. a friend who always shows up at 6:00 p.m.
   c. a friend who never repays borrowed money.
   d. a student who does not repay a student loan.

9. Technological externalities occur because firms
   a. do not take into account the private costs of their actions.
   b. underestimate social costs.

c. do not properly estimate private costs.
d. do not pay social costs.

SHORT ANSWER QUESTIONS

Fill in the blanks in the following statements.

1. Water is an example of a _____ resource.

2. Moral Hazard and _____ are examples of the _____ agent problem.

3. Exhaust from private automobiles is an example of a technological _____.

4. Universal health coverage is an example of a _____.

5. Federal government expenditures are concentrated in three areas: _____, _____, _____.

PROBLEMS

1. Why would you expect the income distribution to be more equal in a socialist country than in a more free market orientated country?

2. When will a market economy result in allocational inefficiencies?

3. In the Los Angeles metropolitan area air pollution levels are among the worst in the world. Why do Southern Californians continue to drive private automobiles when most know they are contributing to this major health threat?

4. Name three examples of exclusive and non-exclusive goods.

5. President Clinton's health care reform is designed to provide universal coverage for all Americans. Why might critics of the reform be concerned about moral hazard? Why might supporters discount the moral hazard problem with regard to health services?

6. What kind of market failure might occur when you go shopping for a used car? Explain why.

7. Publicly funded higher education has been subject to a number of budget cuts during the 1990s. Discuss the private and social costs of the cutbacks.

8. The Insurance Commissioner of California is proposing a new state regulation that would lower car insurance rates for young men and women under 25 years to the same level as those in other age groups. What economic principles would you expect the insurance companies to use in their lobbying efforts against this proposal?

9. Suppose students in a college dormitory are taking up a collection from residents to buy a new microwave for the commons area. Assuming everyone can use the microwave and the contributions are voluntary why might the money be hard to raise?

10. Social insurance programs take the largest share of public dollars in the U.S. Who benefits most from these programs the poor or the non-poor? Explain why.

POST-TEST

Answer the following questions to determine how well you have learned the material in the chapter and to determine those areas where you need to focus your studies.

1. How do perfectly competitive models perform with respect to horizontal versus vertical equity?
2. What are the major causes of allocational inefficiency in a market economy?
3. Why will imperfect information lead to market failure?
4. Why is health care considered a merit good?
5. In a market economy what role does government have in macroeconomic stabilization?
6. What category of individuals would you expect to purchase nursing home insurance? What economic principle explains why you would you expect rates to be high for this type of insurance?
7. Russian fur traders came to Northern California in the 1800s to hunt for sea otters. In less than 30 years the traders moved on because the otters had disappeared from the coastal waters. Explain why this is an example of market failure.
8. What are non-exclusive goods and why are they usually provided by the public sector?
9. How does a pollution tax correct for market failure and what criteria should be used when determining the amount of the tax?
10. In the U.S. which expenditure categories account for the largest share of the federal government's budget?

Chapter 24

Government Revenues, the Principles of Taxations, and the Economics of Democracy

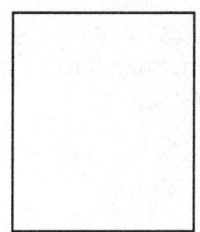

LEARNING OBJECTIVES

CONCEPTS TO LEARN

The five major U.S. taxes	Debt financing
The normative criteria for tax design	Progressive, proportional, and regressive taxes
The theory of public choice	Arrow's Impossibility Theorem
Special-interest lobbying	

CONCEPTS TO RECALL

Horizontal equity	The economic effects of taxation
Vertical equity	

CHAPTER REVIEW

Chapter 24 focuses on the different methods of government revenue collection. An analysis of federal, state, and local taxes is followed by a discussion of efficiency in a representative democracy. Finally, the chapter concludes with a look at the conservative debate regarding the efficacy of government with respect to improving efficiency and equity in the economy.

1. Taxes and debt are the two primary sources of government funding. The largest federal revenue sources are the personal income tax and the Social Security payroll tax.

2. State governments receive revenue from personal income taxes, sales taxes, grants-in-aid from the federal government, and user charges. Personal income taxes and general sales taxes produce the largest share of state revenues.

3. Local property taxes, grants-in-aid from state and federal governments, and direct user charges account for the main revenues of local government.

4. Direct user charges based on a benefit principle are assessed by state and local governments. Paying directly for a benefit received is generally accepted by taxpayers. User charges are not possible options for those goods that are non-exclusionary. For example, a direct user fee for national defense is unworkable.

5. The five economic norms applied to general taxes are: ease of administration; simplicity; flexibility; efficiency; and equity.

6. The taxpayer's ability to pay is the equity criteria applied to general taxation. Horizontal equity implies equals should be treated equally and vertical equity implies that unequals may be treated unequally.

7. Income or consumption can be used as a measure of an individual's ability to pay a tax. In the U.S., the tax base has been based on income.

8. Income subject to taxation should be broadly defined to include all forms regardless of the source. A Comprehensive Tax Base, CTB, including income from supplying factors of production, private or public transfer income, and capital gains, is considered the best measure of ability to pay.

9. Average tax burdens in the U.S. rise slightly as income rises.

10. At all but the lowest income levels the U.S. tax system is roughly proportional. Taxes are mildly progressive at low income levels. Federal and state personal and corporate income taxes are viewed as progressive taxes by economists. General sales and excise taxes are proportional to mildly regressive and the Social Security payroll tax is highly regressive. There is no consensus on property tax incidence. The new view of property tax has produced evidence to support the hypothesis that property owners bear the tax and it is progressive. However, many economists still believe the tax is passed on to renters and is regressive.

11. The Tax Reform Act of 1986 (TRA86) eliminated preferential tax treatment for capital gains and reduced the number of tax brackets or rates applied to different income levels. The highest tax bracket was lowered to 33 percent. The rate was later raised in 1993 to 36%. Reducing the number of tax brackets and lowering the overall rates was designed to reduce inefficiencies in the tax system. Low income individuals received tax relief in 1986 and also benefited from the increase in the Earned Income Tax Credit in 1993.

12. Public Choice Theory assumes that individuals act in their own best interest in political affairs rather than out of social responsibility or community spirit.

Government Revenues, the Principles of Taxations, and the Economics of Democracy

13. Majority votes are not necessarily consistent with economic efficiency. Any decision by a simple majority or a super majority will produce costs for some individuals that are not necessarily consistent with economic efficiency.

14. Kenneth Arrow's Impossibility Theorem demonstrates the majority voting rules do not necessarily produce a consistent set of social preferences based on citizens' preferences. Social policies aimed at redistributing income are particularly subject to social inconsistencies.

15. Economic inefficiency can be a direct result of representative government. Lobbying allows representatives of a group of voters to have undue influence on issues that are of particular interest to a small minority. Individual voters do not receive enough benefits given the costs relative to lobbyists who represent blocks of voters.

16. The self-interest of bureaucrats may not be consistent with the public interest. They are generally insulated from competitive market pressures and have an informational advantage over the legislators who are responsible for monitoring their behavior.

17. Public agencies are not always inefficient and public officials have often demonstrated that they are acting in behalf of the public good. While those supporters of public choice doubt the wisdom of any government intervention in the economy there is ample evidence that in many cases government improves conditions in society.

A FEW HELPFUL TIPS

While most of the text has stressed the efficiency of the market it is not a blanket argument against the public sector. Not all government is bad. Remember, government action is an appropriate response to market failure.

QUICK STUDY GUIDE

	T/F	Mult. Choice	Short Answer	Problems
Tax Equity	6, 7	5	2	1, 3, 4, 8
Federal Taxes	1, 2, 5, 9	6, 7	3, 4	2, 9
State Taxes			5	5
Public Choice	8, 10	8, 9		

PRETEST

Answer the following questions to test your initial understanding of the material in this chapter:

1. Which types of taxes are levied by the Federal Government and which two produce the most revenue?

2. Which types of taxes are levied by state and local governments?

3. How did the method that the federal government finances its expenditures change after Ronald Reagan became president?

4. Explain the difference between a progressive, regressive and proportional tax.

5. Why is the Social Security payroll tax considered to be an example of a regressive tax?

6. Describe the major changes in the income tax structure that occurred as a result of the 1986 Tax Reform Act.

7. Why won't majority voting insure economically efficient outcomes?

8. How were the needs of baby boomers met by the 1983 amendments to the Social Security Act?

9. What characteristics of many public programs preclude funding by means of a user tax?

10. What are the widely accepted criteria for "Good Taxes"?

TRUE/FALSE PRACTICE QUESTIONS

1. Corporate dividends are taxed twice.   T   F
2. Private sector debt financing is rare.   T   F
3. Social Security taxes are progressive.   T   F
4. The federal debt decreased as a result of President Reagan's get "government off our backs" philosophy.   T   F
5. Capital gains are subject to the same tax rate as other types of income.   T   F
6. Vertical equity is not a criteria used to judge taxes.   T   F
7. The U.S. tax system is almost proportional except for some progressiveness at the lowest income levels.   T   F
8. Public Choice theory is a justification for government intervention.   T   F
9. The top income tax rate as of 1993 is 36%.   T   F
10. Logrolling occurs when legislators trade votes in return for favors.   T   F

MULTIPLE CHOICE QUESTIONS

Choose the best option for the following questions.

1. According to Arrow's Impossibility Theorem
   a. government intervention is not necessary in the market.
   b. majority voting can't be expected to solve the distribution problem.
   c. income taxes are always progressive.
   d. government is inherently inefficient.

2. Federal government expenditures are financed by all of the following methods *except*
   a. grants-in-aid.

b. payroll taxes.
c. corporate income taxes.
d. personal income taxes.

3. The primary source of local tax revenue is derived from
   a. income taxes.
   b. payroll taxes.
   c. sales taxes.
   d. property taxes.

4. During the Reagan-Bush era the federal debt
   a. decreased.
   b. increased during the Reagan years and decreased in the Bush term.
   c. increased.
   d. did not change.

5. Taxes that increase as income levels increase are
   a. regressive.
   b. progressive.
   c. inefficient.
   d. uncommon.

6. The Social Security payroll tax is
   a. regressive.
   b. progressive.
   c. a good example of vertical equity.
   d. proportional.

7. Which of the following did *not* occur as a result of the Tax Reform Act of 1986?
   a. increases in taxes on capital gains
   b. reduction in the top tax rate from 50% to 33%
   c. elimination of the double taxation of corporate dividends
   d. reduction in the number of tax brackets from 11 to 4

8. When legislators trade votes for favors from their colleagues they are
   a. violating the law.
   b. logrolling.
   c. demonstrating Arrow's Impossibility Theorem.
   d. lobbying.

9. Majority voting rules are susceptible to all of the following except
   a. Arrow's Impossibility Theorem.
   b. lobbying.
   c. logrolling.
   d. universally efficient outcomes.

10. Direct user charges are
    a. equivalent to logrolling.
    b. consistent with the benefits received principle.

c. considered unfair by most economists.
d. are rarely used by state and local governments.

SHORT ANSWER QUESTIONS

Fill in the blanks in the following statements.

1. A _____ occurs when government's expenditures exceed revenues.
2. A tax is _____ if an individual pays more as _____ rises.
3. Capital gains are taxed at the _____ rate as income derived from working.
4. As income rises the federal marginal tax rate _____.
5. Economists are divided about whether or not property taxes are _____ or _____.

PROBLEMS

1. The majority of individual voters throughout the country are not in favor of federal tobacco subsidies. However, the American Tobacco Institute, which represents a much smaller number of individuals, spends millions on lobbying for the continuation of the subsidies. How can you explain why the majority have lost year after year on this issue?

2. In what major way was the Tax Reform Act of 1986 a move towards a more Comprehensive Tax Base?

3. President Clinton has proposed increases in cigarette and alcohol taxes to fund health care reform. Evaluate his proposal based on the five economic norms for general taxes.

4. Explain what criteria for a "good" tax many states are applying when food is exempted from state sales taxes.

5. Proposition 13 in California was the beginning of the conservative tax revolt in the late 1970s. Property taxes were drastically cut by the proposition. Supporters argued that property taxes unfairly taxed low income people more than the rich forcing many out of their homes. Explain how this position does and does not coincide with those of economists.

6. What steps has the federal government taken to insure the solvency of the Social Security fund when "baby boomers" begin to retire within the next 20 years?

7. How did the Reagan administration finance the defense buildup of the 1980s?

8. What are the equity issues raised by the Clinton Administration's decision to raise the marginal income taxes on families earning in excess of $200,000?

9. The 1993 changes in the Earned Income Tax Credit will in effect lower the tax liability for all families of four earning less than $30,000. Evaluate this change in the tax code on equity grounds.

10. Explain the implications of Arrow's Impossibility Theorem.

POST-TEST

Answer the following questions to determine how well you have learned the material in the chapter and to determine those areas where you need to focus your studies.

1. How does a consumption tax differ from an income tax?

2. List the different types of revenue generating sources for state government and state whether they are progressive, regressive, or proportional taxes.

3. Proponents of reductions in capital gains taxes argue that the change will encourage investment in the economy. Opponents argue that there is no guarantee of increases in investment and criticize the proposal on equity grounds. What are the equity issues?

4. Which tax affects low income workers the most? Why?

5. Explain why developing countries are more likely to use sales taxes than personal income taxes.

6. How are corporate profits subject to double taxation?

7. Explain why the Social Security System was not a true pension plan prior to 1983.

8. What are the major principles of a Comprehensive Tax Base?

9. State an example of a progressive, regressive, and proportional tax.

10. The honey bee subsidy is a favorite target of those pointing out "pork barrel" government programs. What features of our political system favor the needs of the small numbers of beekeepers over the needs of the majority of the citizens?

Part VII–Sample Test
Government in the U.S. Economy

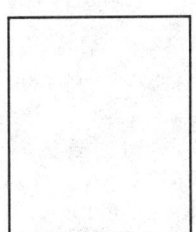

1. Government economic policies that respond to market failures relating to the goal of achieving an efficient use of society's scarce resources are
   a. distribution policies.
   b. stabilization policies.
   c. allocations policies.
   d. equity policies.

2. In the context of insurance, arises when individuals who are being insured can influence the probability of the event being insured, unbeknownst to the insurer is
   a. random hazard.
   b. stochastic hazard.
   c. moral hazard.
   d. elemental hazard.

3. A third-party effect of a transaction that directly affects either consumers' satisfaction or firms' production possibilities is a(n)
   a. pecuniary externality.
   b. conspicuous consumption.
   c. technological externality.
   d. inferior good.

4. What is an exclusive good?
   a. a good whose benefits are received only by the person who consumes it
   b. a good whose benefits are received by everyone
   c. a good which provides no benefits
   d. a good whose benefits are received only by the government

5. What are technological externalities?
   a. a third-party effect of a transaction that directly affects productivity
   b. the effect of a transaction that directly affects the government's level of taxation
   c. the effect business has on a transaction that indirectly affects either the government satisfaction or competitors' production possibilities
   d. a third-party effect of a transaction that directly affects either consumers' satisfaction or firms' production possibilities

6. Government intervention in economic affairs is only justified on the basis of
   a. guaranteed level of income.
   b. imposing excise taxes.
   c. the redistribution of income.
   d. market failure.

7. If left to its own devices, a market economy
   a. completely determines the distribution of income.
   b. completely undermines the fair distribution of factor incomes.
   c. redistributed income form the haves to the have-nots.
   d. needs government intervention.

8. Which is *not* a characteristic of a highway?
   a. if a nation wants a highway network the government must complete it.
   b. the private sector is willing to provide highways.
   c. the construction costs are a high percentage of the total costs.
   d. the average cost of construction declines as cost are spread over an ever larger number of vehicles.

9. The Occupational Safety and Health Administration is a response to
   a. a perfectly competitive labor market.
   b. health care funding by the federal government.
   c. innovation in the market place.
   d. the lack of information workers have about hazards in the work place.

10. Which situation best describes adverse selection?
    a. the individual can influence the outcome of the event being insured
    b. having complete information so profitable insurance policies can be written
    c. charging one premium to everyone despite the differences in risk
    d. a person's behavior can influence the outcome

11. Which is *not* an example of an externality of production?
    a. pollution caused by a paper manufacturing plant
    b. the benefits a public library brings to a community

c. the smoke from a refining process
d. the affluent from a city sewage plant

12. The principle that the taxes and other means of payment for public services are fair if they bear a direct relationship to the benefits people receive from the public services is the
    a. allocational principal.
    b. benefits received principal of taxation.
    c. proportional benefits principal.
    d. efficient allocational principal.

13. A promissory note issued by a government that pays the bondholder (the lender) an amount equal to the principal or, face value, of a bond at a specified future date is a(n)
    a. collateralized mortgage obligation.
    b. first mortgage bonds.
    c. government bond.
    d. revenue bond.

14. A tax for which the average tax burden declines as the taxpayer's income increases is a(n)
    a. progressive tax.
    b. marginal tax.
    c. regressive tax.
    d. proportional tax.

15. A theory of the government based on the premise that people behave in the same self-interested manner in the political arena as they do in the economic arena is the
    a. theory of benefits receives.
    b. theory of large numbers.
    c. theory of public choice.
    d. theory of personal choice.

16. When is there a budget surplus?
    a. exists when a government's expenditures are greater than grants-in-aid exceed its revenues
    b. cannot exist with a government's budget
    c. exists when a government's revenues from taxes, direct user charges, and grants-in-aid exceed its expenditures
    d. exists when a government's expenditures exceed its revenues from taxes, direct user charges and grants-in-aid

17. What are full faith and credit bonds?
    a. Municipal bonds issued to finance capital projects that are not expected to bring in revenues.
    b. Corporate bonds issued to finance capital projects that are not expected to bring in revenues; the bonds are backed by the corporation's general assets.
    c. Municipal bonds issued to finance capital projects that are not expected to bring in revenues; the bonds are backed by the revenue of the project.
    d. Government bonds issued to finance capital projects that are not expected to bring in revenues; the bonds are backed by the government's power to tax.

18. What is a graduated tax rate?
    a. marginal tax rates that decrease as a taxpayer's income increases

b. marginal tax rates that increase then decrease as a taxpayer's income increases
c. marginal tax rates that increase as a taxpayer's income increases
d. marginal tax rates that decrease then increase as a taxpayer's income increases

19. What are revenue bonds?
    a. government bonds that are used to pay for social services
    b. government bonds that are used to pay for self-financing capital projects
    c. government bonds that are used to pay for defense spending
    d. government bonds that are used to pay for unemployment benefits

20. What is taxable income?
    a. the income subject to tax under a personal income tax
    b. the income subject to tax because of personal consumption
    c. property subject to tax under a personal income tax
    d. property subject to tax under a corporate tax rate

21. Which is *not* a source of government's revenue?
    a. taxes
    b. direct charges to users of public services
    c. dividends
    d. debt

22. Which are the two primary sources of revenue for the federal government?
    a. taxes and debt
    b. state corporate income taxes and property taxes
    c. general sales and excise taxes
    d. state personal income taxes and federal payroll tax for Social Security

23. What kind of variable is the national debt?
    a. flow variable
    b. stock variable
    c. static variable
    d. minimum variable

24. U.S. Treasury debt maturing in 5 years would be classified as
    a. a Treasury bill.
    b. a Treasury certificate of deposit.
    c. a Treasury note.
    d. a Treasury bond.

25. The formula for the average tax burden (ATB) is
    a. tax payment by the family ÷ the family's income.
    b. the family's income ÷ tax payment by the family.
    c. the average monthly tax payment by the family ÷ the family's income.
    d. the average monthly tax payment by the family ÷ tax payment by the family.

Answer Key

Chapter 1

Pretest

1. Objective = maximizing satisfaction, alternatives = movie or studying, constraint = 3 hours
2. Objective = provide best university, alternatives = raise tuition or fire faculty, constraint = budget
3. You could use all of the necessary resources to achieve your objectives.
4. Faculty, students, buildings, equipment, etc.
5. Foregone wages
6. Lost advertising revenues
7. The owner is probably an imaginative risk taker.
8. No scarcity
9. Value of the satisfaction foregone at the movies
10. Government is a producer of education, defense, health services; government is a consumer of paper, telephone services, and computers.

T/F		Multiple Choice		Short Answer
1. F	6. F	1. c	6. c	1. Objectives, alternatives, and constraints
2. T	7. F	2. b	7. c	2. Opportunity
3. T	8. T	3. c	8. c	3. Interdependence
4. F	9. F	4. b	9. b	4. Scarce resources, exchange
5. T	10. F	5. c	10. b	5. Labor, machinery

Problems

1. 16,100
2. The price of water does not reflect the scarcity.
3. Student opportunity costs are the foregone wages for the two year period after graduation and the government opportunity costs are the next best govt. program that could be funded with the same dollars
4. Both solve their economic problems (i.e. consumer and producer).
5. No, the cost to the father and son is $1200.
6. It changes objectives and alternatives of the problem due to considerations of the trade-offs between present and future consumption.
7. Market share, sales growth, and community goodwill
8. Congestion and pollution
9. Objective = maximize your personal satisfaction, alternatives = studying, constraints = time
10. Giving up conveniences (i.e. personal automobiles, disposable products, energy conservation, etc.)

Post-Test

1. Without interdependence there would not be any foregone benefit or opportunity cost.
2. The first two are economic problems but the last example is not because there is no scarcity.
3. 1) the value of the time involved; 2) value of time it would take to cook at home; 3) the value of the book
4. Producer = health care, consumer = paper etc.
5. The value of the extra time it takes to drive versus fly
6. The fast-food owner is an entrepreneur.
7. No opportunity cost
8. Income and time
9. Additional revenues are $2500/wk so a physician's asst. will be hired as long as the pay is less than the additional revenues.
10. Ignores opportunity costs

Chapter 2

Pretest

1. a. yes b. yes c. no
2. Affirmative action programs are designed to correct for past or present discrimination or process equity concerns in the past. The end result is intended to correct for past or present discrimination.
3. a. meets equity criteria b. violates horizontal equity because customers are treated unequally c. violates horizontal equity because those renters with the same income are taxed at a different rate.
4. Compare the costs of employees versus computer program over time
5. a. microeconomics b. macroeconomics c. microeconomics
6. a. normative b. positive c. normative
7. ATMs are more efficient.

8. The benefits of redistribution outweigh costs due to inefficiencies.
9. Cash payments are consistent with the principle of consumer sovereignty.
10. The tax system meets horizontal equity criteria since those at the same income level are taxed at the same rate.

T/F		Multiple Choice		Short Answer
1. T	6. F	1. b	6. b	1. End-results equity, equals
2. F	7. T	2. c	7. c	2. Substitution, closer
3. F	8. F	3. d	8. c	3. Consumer sovereignty, own
4. F	9. T	4. a	9. a	4. Microeconomics
5. F	10. F	5. b	10. b	5. Outcomes, rules

Problems

1. BTU tax is paid on a broad range of goods while a gas tax will have a greater effect on those who spend a greater percentage of their income on gas.
2. Wealthy individuals are more likely to receive capital gains income and are more likely to benefit.
3. Efficiency gains include cost savings due to preventative care and equity gains include all individuals should have access to basic health care regardless of income.
4. Frictional unemployment due to job seeking plus those not in the labor force
5. a. micro b. macro c. macro
6. a. normative b. positive c. normative
7. There is a horizontal equity problem because owners of properties of equal value are taxed at very different rates.
8. Individuals with the same total income are taxed at different rates violating horizontal equity criteria
9. The Law of Substitution holds: a solution is efficient if moving closer to one objective requires moving away from another objective.
10. Vertical equity concerns

Post-Test

1. Full employment is above zero since it allows for frictional unemployment of those seeking jobs.
2. A solution is efficient if moving closer to one objective requires moving farther from the other objective according to the Law of Substitution.
3. Ignores equity issues
4. a. normative b. positive c. positive
5. a. micro b. macro c. micro
6. Equal treatment of equals criteria
7. Individuals who have equal access to opportunity and are then free to make their own choices which lead to different outcomes.
8. Food stamps, car insurance requirements, speed limits, etc.
9. a. does not b. does not c. does
10. End-results equity is a criteria for judging final outcomes while process equity judges whether the rules of the economy are fair.

Chapter 3

Pretest

1. The what or output question, the how or input question, the for whom or distribution question and the now versus the future question.
2. Under capitalism output is determined by the market, inputs are determined by individual consumers and firms, and the distribution and now versus future questions are determined by the market. Under planned socialism output, inputs, distribution and the now versus future questions are answered according to a national plan by the centralized decision making authority designated by the government.
3. Who receives the benefits of the goods and services produced by an economy
4. The incomes received reflect the scarcity of resources and the relative demand for them.
5. Draw a frontier and show a movement along the frontier away from defense towards other goods.
6. Draw the original frontier and show how the entire curve shifts in towards the origin.
7. Draw the original frontier and one that shifts outward away from the origin due to productivity increases attributable to education.
8. Decentralized economic decisions by individual consumers and firms, a market price system, private ownership of land and capital
9. Centralized decision making authority, national plan to process and coordinate economic info., public ownership of land and capital
10. Savings will increase leading to investment that can increase future growth rates.

T/F		Multiple Choice		Short Answer
1. F	6. T	1. d.	6. b.	1. Production possibilities, producing less
2. T	7. T	2. b.	7. c.	2. Outward, goods and services
3. T	8. T	3. c.	8. a.	3. Efficiency and equity
4. F	9. F	4. c	9. c.	4. Frontier, inefficiently
5. T	10. F	5. a.	10. b.	5. Capital, outward

Problems

1. The frontier will shift outward away from the origin.

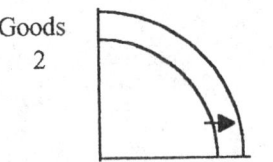

2. a. a point on the exterior or beyond the frontier

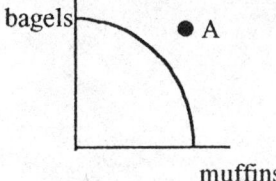

b. a point in the interior or inside the frontier

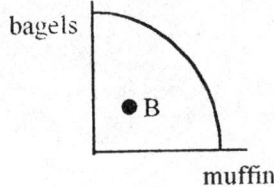

c. move along the frontier towards more bagels and less muffins

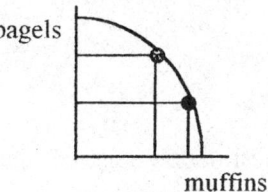

d. increases in resources will shift the curve outward

3. In the eighties the output as represented by a point on the frontier was closer to defense. The opportunity cost was the value of the non-defense goods not produced. In the nineties, the output point on the frontier moved towards non-defense goods and the opportunity cost is foregone defense production.

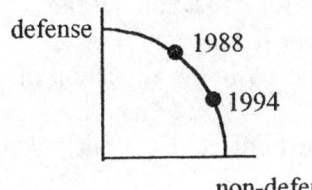

4. In capitalism, distribution is determined by the market while in socialism the central planning authority determines distribution. The central planning authority takes into account moral as well as material objectives.
5. A negative relationship since lower consumption now means increases in savings, investment and future growth.
6. 30-40 percent of their companies were not competitive and the transition will take at least 15 years

7. Immigration pushes the frontier outward

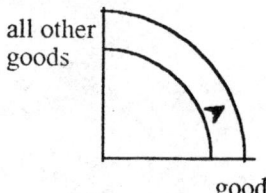

8. Increases in human capital push the frontier outward.

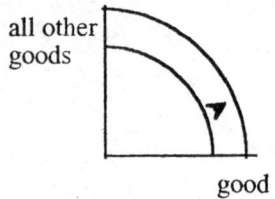

9. Increases in production can be made without decreasing production in other sectors of the economy.
10. Japan should have higher long-term growth rates.

Post-Test

1. Equity focuses on equal treatment while efficiency focuses on the best possible use of scarce resources as related to the four questions.
2. Long-term growth will slow down.
3. The production possibilities frontier will shift downward.
4. Show a movement along the curve toward defense where the opportunity cost is the amount of non-defense goods that are given up.
5. Shift the production possibilities curve out by investment or increases in technology.
6. Initially, the change would require a movement along the curve towards education but the investment in human capital will cause the curve to shift outward over time.
7. Individual freedom, responsiveness to consumer's desires, and efficiency in the allocation of scarce resources are benefits.
8. Principal strengths include the ability to formulate and pursue national objectives, a fairly equal income distribution, and a full employment guarantee.
9. Foregone current consumption

Chapter 4

Pretest

1. Product, geographic, factors of production, institutional settings
2. Specialization of labor allows the producers to take advantage of economies of scale.
3. Law of comparative advantage
4. Draw the diagram showing household, business, government and rest of the world sectors.
5. Sell labor and consumer goods and services.

6. Sell goods and services and buy labor.
7. Liability versus tax advantages
8. High growth in government and the rest of the world sectors, consumption doubled, high turnover of businesses, baby boomers changed age demographics, increases in the labor force participation of women, rise in single parent households, increase in urbanization
9. Whites have higher median incomes, smaller percentage of whites live in poverty, white unemployment rate is lower, higher percentage of whites own homes, whites are more likely to live in two parent families
10. Women have increasingly entered the labor force but continue to earn significantly less than men and are more likely to live in poverty.

T/F		Multiple Choice		Short Answer
1. T	6. T	1. c	6. a	1. Factor, National product
2. T	7. T	2. b	7. c	2. Durable goods
3. F	8. F	3. b	8. c	3. Tax revenues, government expenditures
4. T	9. T	4. c	9. a	4. Economies of scale, increases
5. F	10. T	5. b	10. c	5. Consumers, labor

Problems

1. If you fish all day and your friend carves coconuts total production of the island will increase to 16 fish and 24 coconuts.
2. $65,000 is the median which is slightly lower than the average income of $65,400.
3. Durables include cars, refrigerators, TV's, washing machines; non-durables include magazines, candy, soda, and bagels.
4. Highly specialized production, market exchanges do not occur in isolation, the size of the market
5. Automobile assembly lines
6. Federal income taxes, state income and sales taxes, local property and sales taxes
7. Social security, health care, welfare, grants-in-aid to local government, interest payments on the debt
8. The annual deficit is still positive and will increase the national debt.
9. Lower wages for jobs requiring the same level of human capital
10. The corporation is a distinct legal entity separate from the owners, owners have the right to exchange shares of stock, stockholders may delegate authority and responsibility to managers, the corporation has an unlimited life, corporations enjoy limited liability for business losses to the assets of the corporation.

Post-Test

1. Less liability versus double taxation
2. The deficit is the difference between government expenditures and revenues on an annual basis while the national debt is an accumulation of the annual deficits.
3. Government and rest of the world sectors
4. a. durable b. non-durable c. non-durable d. non-durable e. durable
5. Purchasers and producers of final goods and services
6. $11,000

7. In 1990, women earned approximately two-thirds of men, the average earnings of female college graduates are less than average male graduates, women have the majority of household responsibilities and are segregated into specific occupations. Differences in job experience and education can only partially explain wage differences and the evidence points to discrimination in labor markets.
8. The U.S. has an absolute advantage but because the opportunity costs of production differ in both countries trade can be advantageous.
9. National income measures the flow through the factor markets while national product measures the flow through product markets.
10. Transfers to individuals, interest payments on the debt, grants in aid

Chapter 5

Pretest

1. Shifts the demand curve out to the right
2. Market Demand Schedule

P	Q
3	2
2.5	5
2.0	8
1.5	11

   Katie has the more elastic demand
3. Draw positively sloped curve showing that the quantity supplied increases as price increases.
4. 1.11
5. a. supply curve shifts to the left b. a movement up along the supply curve due to an upward shift in demand c. supply curve shifts to the left d. supply curve shifts down to the right
6. Demand shifts down to the left and the equilibrium price and quantity decline.
7. Bread supply shifts up to the left driving price up and quantity down.
8. Draw upward sloping supply and downward sloping demand curves.
9. At a price of $20.00 supply exceeds demand creating an excess supply which will lead firms to decrease price until supply equals demand at $15.00.
10. Clothing demand is more elastic.

T/F		Multiple Choice		Short Answer
1. F	6. T	1. b	6. c	1. Price, elastic
2. T	7. F	2. c	7. b	2. Horizontal, individual firm
3. T	8. T	3. c	8. a	3. Curve, left
4. T	9. F	4. a	9. c	4. Increase, increase
5. T	10. T	5. b	10. c	5. Equals, demanded
				6. Inflation

Problems

1. a. draw curve b. 2.33, 1.0, 0.43, 0.18 c. 40,000, 60,000, 60,000, 40,000, 22,500 d. total revenue increases by $20,000 when the price is decreased from $200 to $150 because demand is elastic and decreases by $20,000 when price drops from $100 to $50 because demand becomes inelastic

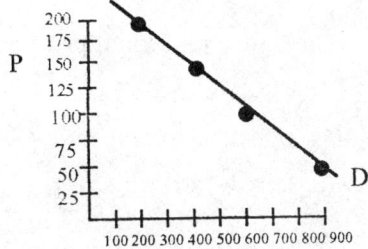

2. a. movement up along the curve b. a shift to the right c. a shift to the left d. a shift to the right
3. a. supply curve shifts to the left   b. supply curve shifts to the right

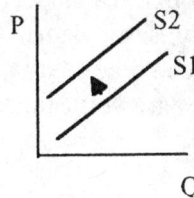   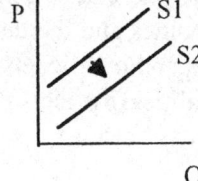

c. supply curve shifts to the left

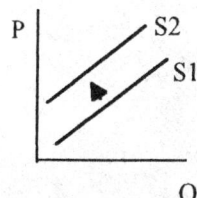

4. Increase output
5. The supply of stores shifts to the left and drives prices up and quantity down.

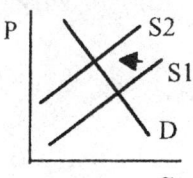

6. Draw an upward sloping supply and downward sloping demand curve intersecting where p = $3.00 and q = 3,500.

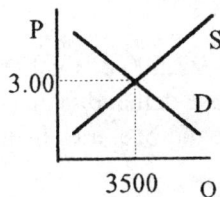

7. The demand curve shifts to the left by 500 units at each price. The new equilibrium price and quantity will be lower.

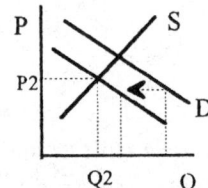

8. Elastic goods include luxuries and elastic demand curves should be drawn with a flat slope. Inelastic goods include necessities and the demand curves are steep; perfectly elastic demand curves are horizontal and Super Bowl tickets are an example of a good that could be sold in infinite quantity at the official ticket price. Perfectly inelastic demand curves are vertical and include addictive goods such as heroin.

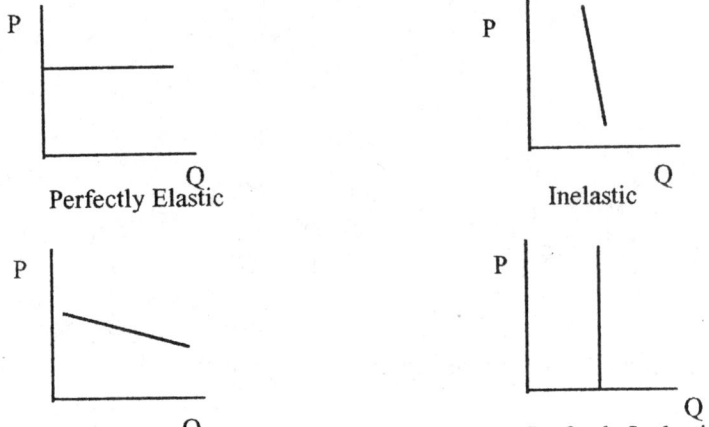

9. Less elastic demand
10. Demand is less elastic in the short run than in the long run.

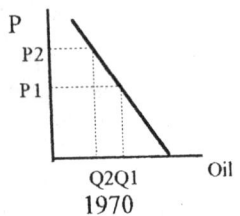 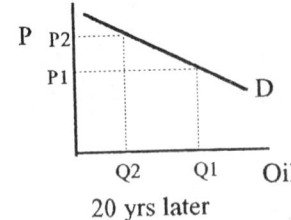

Post-Test

1. a. demand curve shifts to the left b. movement down and to the right along the demand curve c. demand curve shifts upward to the right d. demand curve shifts down to the left
2. Market Demand Schedule

P	Q
2.00	38
1.50	41
1.00	44
.50	47

3. .26, .18, .10
4. Shifts supply to the right
5. Shifts supply to the left
6. Firms will reduce price when excess supplies exist until the price where the quantity demanded equals the quantity supplied.
7. Demand shifts to the left and supply shifts to the right resulting in a decrease in price and an indeterminate effect on output.
8. Supply shifts to the right bringing price down and output up.
9. The demand for apartment rentals will shift to the right driving prices and quantity up.
10. a. inelastic b. inelastic c. elastic d. elastic

Chapter 6

Pretest

1. Those actively seeking work in the labor force
2. Good is over 3 and bad is under 3 and 3% is fair
3. 36 years using the rule of 72; divide 72 by the growth rate to determine then number of years it will take to double
4. High from 1950-74 and declining since 1974
5. 4.8%
6. Downturns in the economy decrease labor demand but wages remain high because of sticky wages.
7. Structural unemployment occurs when workers with specific skills or in specific geographic areas are no longer needed so that when the economy grows these people are still unemployable.
8. Institutional factors including insider/outsider theory, internal labor markets, preservation of the hierarchical wage structure
9. Frictional unemployment occurs due to lack of information regarding job opportunities when individuals change jobs.
10. Structural unemployment plus frictional unemployment

T/F		Multiple Choice		Short Answer
1. F	6. F	1. b	6. c	1. Lower
2. F	7. T	2. b	7. a	2. Frictional, structural
3. T	8. F	3. c	8. d	3. Discouraged workers
4. F	9. F	4. c	9. b	4. Sticky
5. T	10. F	5. a	10. d	5. Double, 36

Problems

1. Reduced search costs in two income families raises frictional unemployment initially, but the stabilization of female labor participation rates will neutralize any effects on the natural rate.
2. Structural unemployment that can not be solved by policies solely aimed at cyclical unemployment
3. Increased labor participation rates of women, movement from rural agricultural and manufacturing jobs to service industries, etc.
4. Declines because of decline in teenage unemployment, stabilization of women in the labor force, decrease in transfer payments that support increases in job search; increases because of technological change and internationalization of the economy
5. Women in the labor force, increases in search time, etc.
6. Declines in teenage unemployment and stabilization of women in labor force
7. Does not count discouraged workers or those working part time who wish to work full time
8. 12 years
9. Those with seniority want to preserve high wages because they know that the last hired will be fired and they can keep their high wage jobs.
10. Downturns in the economy, increases in social programs for the unemployed

Post-Test

1. Includes those who are not really seeking employment or stretching out their search time
2. Unemployed aerospace workers, unemployed civilian employees after base closures, elevator operators
3. College student seeking first professional job, entry of a homemaker into the labor market, individual seeking employment in a new city after a family move
4. Declines in teenage unemployment and stabilization of women in the labor force
5. Technological change and internationalization of the market
6. Firms keep wages high to improve worker morale, loyalty, and productivity
7. High unemployment
8. Tenured professors have job security and are not likely to be laid off
9. 5%
10. Cyclical unemployment and search unemployment

Chapter 7

Pretest

1. Inflation implies small to medium increases in the price level while hyperinflation implies large changes in the price level in a short time period
2. CPI = Price Index for Consumer Goods, PPI = Price Index for Producer Inputs and finished products sold wholesale, GDP deflator = Price Index for all goods in the economy
3. Year 1 CPI = 100   Year 2 CPI = 110.4
4. Blue jean and milk consumers
5. Distorts relative prices and consumer choice
6. Those on fixed incomes lose, relative to those with incomes adjusted for inflation
7. 8.89%
8. Brings it down
9. Imports exceed exports and the demand for dollars to purchase the imports increases while fewer imports means a decrease in supply. These shifts in demand increase the value of the dollar.
10. Other countries are unwilling to hold onto their currency

T/F		Multiple Choice		Short Answer
1. F	6. T	1. b	6. b	1. Continuously
2. F	7. F	2. c	7. c	2. Food, Shelter, Energy
3. T	8. F	3. a	8. b	3. Hyperinflation
4. F	9. T	4. d	9. a	4. Unbalanced
5. T	10. F	5. d	10. b	5. Menu

Problems

1. CPI may decrease
2. Borrowers, property owners
3. Those on fixed incomes, lenders
4. Family incomes may be changing at a different rate.
5. Unanticipated inflation
6. Wages, etc., are adjusted along with prices
7. Wages will decrease in real terms unless the labor contract includes adjustments for inflation.
8. Car buyers
9. CPI = 100   CPI = 110.15
10. Those buying imported goods and foreign producers selling imports

Post-Test

1. Lucas argues the economy adjusts rapidly and costs are minimal while Fisher believes high costs are incurred due to institutional factors
2. Consumers of imports and producers of imported goods
3. Winners – borrowers, property owners. Losers = lenders, those on fixed incomes

4. 47.73%
5. Subtract the inflation rate from the nominal rate to get the real rate of interest.
6. Positively rated, i.e. if the trade balance is positive and the value of the dollar increases
7. Tax rates are not fully indexed for inflation and capital gains taxes do not adjust for inflation.
8. Borrowers repay lenders with currency that has a lower value.
9. Welfare payments usually do not keep up with inflation.
10. Time lags for the cost of living adjustments.

Chapter 8

Pretest

1. Foreign saving increase
2. Changes in DI affect savings and consumption of households, which determines the amount available for investment
3. Consumption
4. 1600
5. CPI only evaluates household consumer goods while the GDP deflation tracks the prices of all goods in the economy
6. Inflation, pollution, no investment in the future, etc.
7. Illegal activities include cash transactions to avoid taxes
8. Increases GDP even though social welfare is lower
9. a.) Intermediate
   b.) Final
   c.) Intermediate
   d.) Final
10. Capital is existing stock, whereas investment includes new expenditures

T/F		Multiple Choice		Short Answer
1. F	6. F	1. c	6. b	1. GDP
2. F	7. T	2. d	7. b	2. Investment Government spending, Net Exports
3. F	8. F	3. b	8. a	3. Capital consumption allowance
4. T	9. T	4. b	9. c	4. Consumed
5. T	10. T	5. b	10. c	5. Increase

Problems

1. Shows increases in the value of goods and services produced
2. Does not take into account income distribution, pollution, social issues, etc.
3. GNP includes production of U.S. citizens regardless of where they live
4. It depends on the value of net exports; a larger increase in exports and imports will increase GDP
5. Increase
6. Increase productivity and GDP

7. To avoid double counting
8. Replacement expenditures boost GDP figures
9. None; transfer payments are not included
10. 1709.68

Post-Test

1. Not included
2. Decreases GDP
3. Must be equal
4. Intermediate goods are used in the production of final goods.
5. Increase GDP
6. 244.44
7. Decrease GDP
8. May affect only a small % of the population (i.e., increases are not shared by the entire population)
9. The increased costs of health care, pollution abatement increases GDP while the standard of living actually declines
10. Housework, caring for children in the home, caring for elderly parents

Chapter 9

Pretest

1. Stabilize the economy when there is high unemployment or inflation by affecting the circular flow of the economy
2. Same as #1
3. $Y = C^d + I^d + G^d + (Ex^d - Im^d)$, Y = national income, C^d = consumption demand, I^d = investment demand, G^d = government demand, $Ex^d - Im^d$ = net demand of the foreign sector
4. Full employment at the production possibilities frontier
5. Competitive factor markets, flexible wages and prices, real domestic product and the production possibilities frontier are determined by the supply side, changes in aggregate demand affect prices but not output as the economy will shortly return to the production possibilities frontier, fiscal and monetary policy are destabilizing
6. Wages and prices are sticky, economy responds to changes in aggregate demand and the supply side is passive, high levels of cyclical unemployment and/or inflation can persist over time, fiscal and monetary policy can be used to stabilize the economy
7. Both groups agree that aggregate supply is vertical in the long run and that the new classical approach is appropriate for long run policy.
8. Short-run predictions appear to be in error in light of long periods of high unemployment and inflation that have been observed; the long run analysis is fairly consistent with evidence of economic performance.
9. Keynesian analysis does a better job of explaining short-run cyclical unemployment and inflation.
10. New Keynesians believe fiscal and monetary policy is useful, while the New Classical economists believe it is destabilizing.

Answer Key

T/F		Multiple Choice		Short Answer
1. T	6. T	1. d	6. b	1. Adverse supply
2. T	7. T	2. c	7. b	2. Federal Reserve Bank
3. T	8. T	3. c	8. b	3. Monetary, fiscal
4. F	9. T	4. d	9. a	4. Production possibilities frontier
5. F	10. F	5. d	10. a	5. Sticky, short

Problems

1. Labor markets don't get to a market equilibrium and unemployment persists in the short run
2. Draw a vertical aggregate supply curve and then have the downward sloping aggregate demand curve shift to the right. Prices increase and output remains constant.

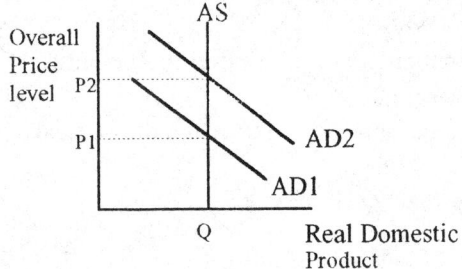

3. Draw an aggregate supply curve that is upward sloping to show that a rightward shift of AD will cause output to increase along with a rise in the price level.

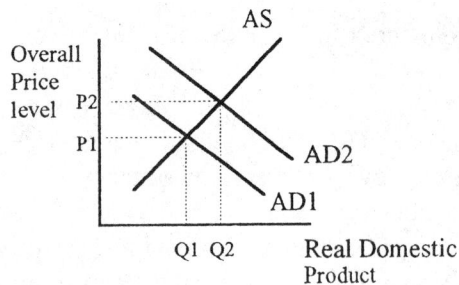

4. Draw a vertical AS curve and show the AD curve shifting down to the left so prices decrease and output does not change

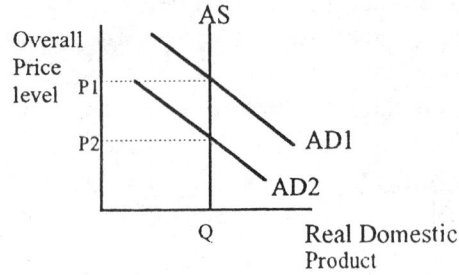

Answer Key

5. When AD shifts down output and prices come down.

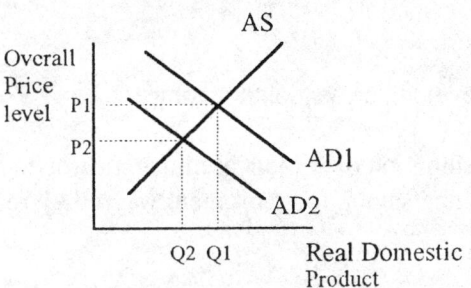

6. Believe it is destabilizing and the economy will shortly return to the production possibilities frontier due to market forces
7. Long periods of unemployment and inflation
8. Supply shocks when the economy experiences high inflation and high unemployment at the same time

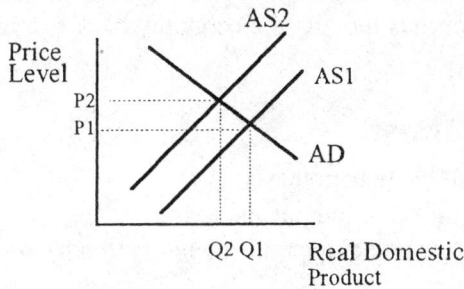

9. AS curve shifts to the left driving up prices and output down
10. Below potential output

Post-Test

1. U.S. has had a number of periods of sustained high unemployment and inflation which are inconsistent with the New Classical model
2. Existence of high unemployment and inflation concurrently
3. Prices rise and output does not change because of the vertical AS
4. Prices decrease but output does not change because of the vertical AS
5. New Classical = no change in policy, New Keynesian = fiscal or monetary policy to expand AD
6. Wages and prices remain high so the economy will not reach an equilibrium
7. Fiscal = Congress and Executive, monetary = Federal Reserve Bank
8. AS shifts to left bringing output down and prices up
9. Downward shifts
10. Bush/Reagan advisors more closely aligned with New Classicalists, and Clinton advisors are New Keynesians for the most part

Chapter 10

Pretest

1. Positively related with a minimum subsistence level at zero national income
2. Not related
3. Individuals want to have a constant level of consumption over their lifetimes, borrowing when they first enter the labor market and paying off debts and saving for retirement when they reach peak income years.
4. Pro-growth policies over the long run
5. .8
6. 1.2, 1, .93, .9
7. .2
8. Break-even = $2000, positive savings at DI over $2000 and negative savings at DI below $2000
9. Draw graph showing the ADE intersecting the 45 degree line at the equilibrium income level
10. At income levels beyond the equilibrium, output exceeds ADE and inventories will be above desired levels, so firms will cut back on production, thus moving the economy back towards the equilibrium

T/F

1. F   6. F
2. T   7. F
3. F   8. T
4. F   9. T
5. T   10. T

Multiple Choice

1. b   6. b
2. b   7. d
3. a   8. c
4. a   9. a
5. a   10. b

Short Answer

1. Life-cycle hypothesis
2. Equilibrium output, increase
3. Plant and equipment, inventory, housing
4. Up
5. Depleted, rise

Problems

1. Consumption does not change with changes in DI in the short run, according to the life-cycle theory.
2. Consumption decreases
3. Shifts ADE up and the equilibrium output level increases
4. .8
5. 1.2, 1, .93, .9
6. 10,000 where the level of consumption equals DI

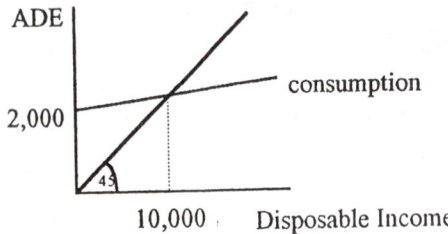

7. 5000

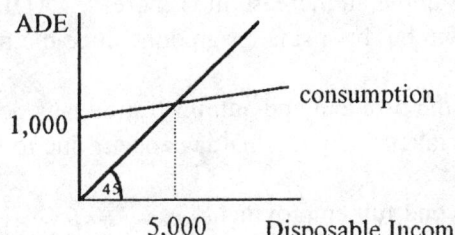

8. 15,000
9. ADE is less than output so inventories are above desired levels and firms reduce output

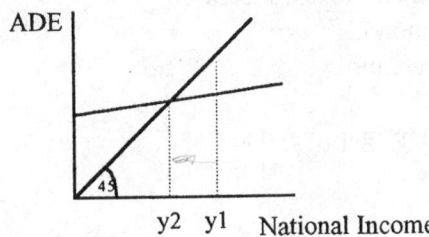

10. Consumption increases and ADE shifts up in both the short and long run

Post-Test

1. Consumption and savings both rise with DI
2. Only permanent changes in income will increase consumption
3. Savings decrease, consumption increases, and the break-even point increases
4. Firms want to hold onto less inventory
5. Investment and autonomous consumption
6. mpc = .9, mps = .1
7. 1.1, 1, .97, .95
8. 40,000
9. 60,000
10. Inventories are below desired levels so firms increase production

Chapter 11

Pretest

1. Decrease taxes or raise government spending
2. Increases DI and consumption raising ADE and the equilibrium output level
3. Multiplier is higher because more of each dollar will be consumed
4. Decrease G by 20 billion or increase taxes by 4 billion
5. Increase G by 40 or decrease taxes by 44.44

6. Increase G or taxes by 400 billion
7. Any change in G will be offset by a change in T, for example an increase in G increases ADE. But if taxes rise by the same amount ADE will shift down but by a smaller amount since the tax multiplier is smaller.
8. Recognition lags occur when it takes time to recognize the problem and administrative lags occur between the time the problem is identified and action is taken. Operational lags occur due to the time it takes to actually implement the policy.
9. ADE intersects the 45 degree line at an output level beyond full employment
10. ADE intersects the 45 degree line at an output level below full employment

T/F		Multiple Choice		Short Answer
1. F	6. T	1. c	6. c	1. Requirement, taxes, increased
2. F	7. F	2. a	7. b	2. Recognition lag
3. T	8. F	3. b	8. d	3. Decreases, mps
4. F	9. T	4. b	9. a	4. Lower
5. T	10. T	5. c	10. c	5. Inflationary gap, beyond

Problems

1. Increase govt. spending and lower taxes
2. 400, 1300, 2200, 3100, 4000, 4900
3. 4000

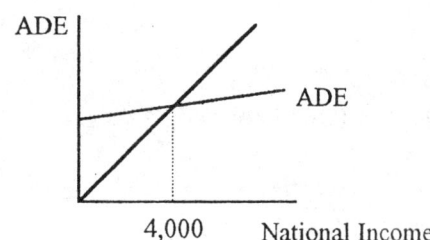

4. 10
5. 9
6. Raise taxes or lower govt. spending
7. Lower taxes or raise govt. spending
8. $500 billion decrease
9. $10 billion increase
10. Administrative lags occur between the time the problems are identified and legislative action is taken, while operational lags occur because once the policy has been approved it takes time to change government spending.

Post-Test

1. Lower government spending or increase taxes
2. Decreases the effectiveness
3. Permanent income hypothesis explains that individuals don't change consumption patterns when transitory income changes.

4. Economy will be $500 billion over full employment output, and the government could reduce spending or raise taxes.
5. Increase G by $10 billion or decrease taxes by $5.56 billion
6. Cut G or increase T by $200 billion
7. Decreases
8. Decreases the power of tax changes that are transitory
9. Tax increases offset the effects of the increase in government spending.
10. ADE shifts up and the equilibrium level of income increases

Chapter 12

Pretest

1. Increase in national income increases the demand for imports and brings ADE down
2. Income taxes, business savings and import demand are positively related to income and will push ADE in the opposite direction
3. Increases in G or lowering T increase the deficit
4. See #3
5. Structural deficit is the level assuming the economy is at full employment while actual includes the cyclical deficit.
6. A high cyclical deficit implies high unemployment.
7. When income rises the demand for imports increases, lowering ADE.
8. Lowering taxes and defense spending increases
9. Crowding out of private investment
10. To finance education, research, productive investment

T/F		Multiple Choice		Short Answer
1. F	6. F	1. a	6. c	1. Income taxes, import demand, transfer payments, and business savings
2. T	7. F	2. c	7. b	2. Increase, increases, decrease, decrease
3. T	8. T	3. b	8. c	3. Marginal propensity to import, national income
4. F	9. F	4. c	9. c	4. Steeper
5. T	10. T	5. a		5. Import demand, increase

Problems

1. Import demand increased while exports declined, reducing ADE at each income level.
2. Structural unemployment rose
3. Auto stabilizers have the opposite effects as fiscal policies on ADE.
4. Tax cuts and defense spending increases
5. Dampens the power of fiscal policy... for example, when expansionary policy was needed the government would be constrained by a balanced budget and any increase in G would require a tax increase that would slow down the economy

6. Long-term investments in education, research or productive investment
7. .10
8. Draw graph showing positive relationship between national income and import demand

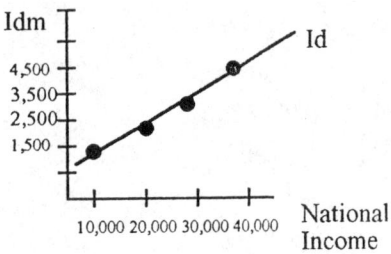

9. Shifts up

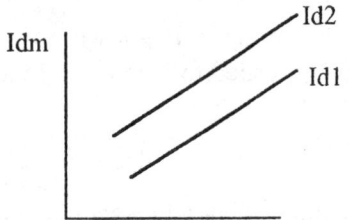

10. ADE curve shifts down and the equilibrium income level decreases

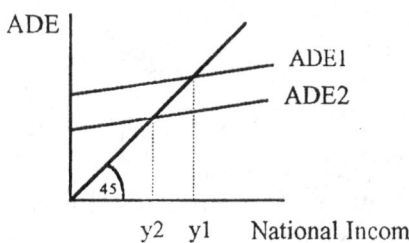

Post-Test

1. No change in the structural deficit and an increase in the cyclical deficit
2. When national income rises, import demand rises, shifting ADE down.
3. Budget may be balanced if everyone was employed, paying taxes, and collecting less unemployment and welfare benefits
4. Increases in tax rates lower the multiplier and vice versa
5. .05
6. Draw import demand positively related to national income
7. Shifts import demand down
8. Dampens the power of fiscal policy
9. Import demand shifts down and ADE shifts up increasing the equilibrium income level

Chapter 13

Pretest

1. Contractions are those time periods when economic activity is declining, and expansions are those periods when economic activity is increasing, these changes are tracked by the NBER.
2. Output income, employment, and trade data
3. Pre WWII cycles were more severe and longer
4. Once an economy reaches a peak at the production possibilities frontier, expansion stops and the contraction of the economy begins.
5. At some level of investment firms decide that the level of investment is sufficient and investment demand will stop increasing as will aggregate demand.
6. Multiplier-accelerator, can be away from a full employment equilibrium for long time periods due to expansion and contractions that are inherent to the economy
7. Real Business Cycle- assumes markets operate competitively and movements away from equilibrium are a result of random shocks
8. Smooth consumption patterns mean that economic policies designed to affect AD will be useless because individuals will not change their consumption patterns.
9. Random shocks
10. Against using fiscal and monetary policy

T/F
1. T   6. F
2. T   7. T
3. T   8. F
4. F   9. F
5. T   10. T

Multiple Choice
1. c   6. a
2. b   7. c
3. b   8. c
4. c   9. b
5. b   10. a

Short Answer
1. Peak, contraction
2. Fiscal, monetary
3. More
4. Investment
5. The multiplier-accelerator, Real Business Cycle

Problems

1. Both the demand and supply side of the economy affect investment demand; when the economy grows firms will need to increase their stocks of capital to maintain a constant capital-output ratio in production and the demand side will require a constant level of investment.
2. Since WWII auto stabilizers have smoothed out the business cycles
3. Economy will be at the production possibilities frontier and movements away can only occur due to random shocks and then will move back to the equilibrium
4. Multiplier-accelerator theorists accept sticky wages, while Real Business Cycle theorists argue that wage stickiness is inconsistent with rational behavior.
5. Steady course, i.e. no fiscal or monetary policy
6. If lowering unemployment is the goal, they will recommend an expansionary fiscal or monetary policy while contractionary policies will be advised if anti-inflation measures are desired.
7. NBER tracks business cycles using cyclical indicators to monitor economic performance
8. Economy will return to the full employment equilibrium level on its own

9. Technological changes push out the frontier and increase real wages which increase savings according to the Life-Cycle theory, and thus overall investment and increase the economy's output.
10. Labor hoarding during recessions

Post-Test

1. When consumption demand increases firms will increase investment to increase their stock of capital.
2. Movements away from equilibrium are explained by random shocks and will not affect the long-term growth rates of the economy which can only be affected by technological change.
3. Consumers follow the Life-Cycle theory and will save any temporary wage increase, which will lead to increases in investment.
4. Firms layoff fewer workers during a recession and hire fewer workers during a recovery.
5. Nothing; they believe using fiscal or monetary policy is destabilizing
6. Expansionary fiscal and monetary policy, believe they are useful stabilization methods
7. Critics point to sticky wages and imperfectly competitive labor markets, do not accept that changes in involuntary unemployment explain why real economic variables move in the same direction, argue that swings in labor productivity can be traced to labor hoarding not technical change, and do not accept that economic downturns are efficient responses to supply shocks
8. New Classical economists attack the New Keynesians on their assumption that wages and prices are sticky. They argue that wage and price stickiness is inconsistent with rational economic agents.
9. Index of leading indicators, index of coincident indicators, index of lagging indicators
10. Increases in demand due to consumption increases cause firms to increase their stock of capital, which leads to further increases in AD and propels the economy to an even higher multiplier level of national income; the increase in investment demand is accelerating in the multiplier process, started by an increase in consumption.

Chapter 14

Pretest

1. Fiat currency, i.e. backed by the U.S. govt. as an accepted means of exchange
2. M1 = currency, transactions deposits, travelers checks, M2 = M1 plus money market deposits, savings deposits below $100,000, certificates of deposit, M3 = M2 plus large deposits exceeding $100,000
3. Metals, beads, paper, etc.
4. Prices rise
5. Increase
6. Means of exchange, store of value, unit of account
   Assets   Liabilities
   D.D. $3,000 $3,000
   No change in net worth

8. Sell securities
9. Buy securities
10. The $1000 loan will be deposited in a bank, then a portion will be loaned out, the loan proceeds are deposited in another bank, and the process continues.

T/F		Multiple Choice		Short Answer
1. F	6. F	1. c	6. b	1. Earns interest, businesses
2. T	7. F	2. a	7. c	2. Sheet, liability, asset
3. F	8. F	3. b	8. b	3. MV = PQ
4. T	9. T	4. d	9. a	4. Liquid
5. T	10. T	5. c	10. a	5. Net Worth

Problems

1. Demand for money declines and velocity increases
2. Now accounts pay interest and can not be held by firms
3. 52.9
4. Increase
5. Debasing, silver content was more valuable than the currency
6. Assets   Liabilities
   D.D. $1000   car loan $4000   Net Worth = -$1300
   savings $100
   car equity $1,600
7. The proceeds of the loan will be deposited in a bank which will hold onto a portion in reserves and loan out the rest. The proceeds of those loans will be deposited and the process continues to repeat itself.
8. Increases
9. Decreases
10. multiplier effect in reverse, the loan money will be paid back from the reserves in other banks which will have to call in their loans

Post-Test

1. There is a finite amount of money in the system at a point in time while income is changing over time.
2. Money demand increases
3. Determined by institutional factors which change slowly
4. Banking Act of 1863
5. Loan is an asset for the lender and a liability for the loanee
6. Decreases currency
7. Buying and selling securities
8. 3
9. Faith in the system
10. When the money is deposited, a portion will be loaned out again and the process keeps repeating.

Chapter 15

Pretest

1. 1913, Fed was designed as an independent, non-profit government agency that was a lender of last resort
2. Monetary policy, fiscal agent for U.S > government, overseeing the operation of commercial banks and other depository institutions
3. Limiting financial institutions loans to deposits
4. Excess reserves are those held by the institutions in addition to the required reserves
5. Increase in M = $2,500,000
6. Increase in M = $2,000,000
7. Decreases the money supply
8. Seven members of the Fed Board of Governors plus five presidents of Federal Reserve Banks including the president of the N.Y. Fed
9. To guarantee deposits for individuals
10. Shrinks

T/F		Multiple Choice		Short Answer
1. F	6. T	1. c	6. c	1. Discount rate
2. T	7. F	2. d	7. a	2. Federal funds rate
3. T	8. T	3. d	8. a	3. Securities dealer
4. F	9. F	4. b	9. b	4. Excess, actual
5. T	10. F	5. c	10. c	5. Increases

Problems

1. Excess reserves increase
2. When reserves decline the multiplier increases
3. Money supply decreases by $40 million
4. Money supply increases by $50 million
5. Banks will be willing to hold onto less reserves and the multiplier will increase
6. Fed, buy and sell securities through open market transactions, change the reserve ratio, change the discount rate
7. Draw balance sheets showing how funds from the open market purchase are deposited into a demand deposit creating excess reserves which can be loaned out
   Assets
   Reserves: Increase by the amount of the open market purchase creating excess reserves to be loaned out.
   Liabilities
   Checking Account: Increase by the open market purchase.
8. Draw balance sheets to demonstrate that money will be taken out of demand deposits, lowering bank reserves which means banks will be forced to call in loans and the money supply will decrease

Assets
Reserves: decrease by the amount of the open market purchase so the bank is short of reserves and must decrease loans.
Liabilities
Checking Accounts: decrease by the open market purchase.
9. Velocity changes
10. Wants to ensure that bank reserves can meet depositors' demand

Post-Test

1. Buying and selling securities to change the money supply
2. Reserves = required reserves
3. Responsible for U.S > monetary system
4. During downturns banks are likely to hold onto excess reserves, and during boom years they are likely to want to hold fewer reserves.
5. M increases by $15 million
6. M decreases by $80 million
7. Decreases as banks call in loans
8. Increase the money supply
9. Financial institutions make short-term loans
10. 10

Chapter 16

Pretest

1. Consume durables, houses, real estate
2. Productive capital: plant, equipment, and inventories
3. At the market interest rate money supply exceeds money demand and they would prefer to hold onto other assets
4. Increases
5. Increases
6. Interest rates rise, decreasing investment and consumption demand, lowering national income and consumption
7. Interest rates fall and investment increases
8. Interest rates rise, investment demand decreases, and national income falls
9. Operational lags, recognition lags, and administrative lags are all affected by uncertainty.
10. Investors, consumers, loanees

T/F		Multiple Choice		Short Answer
1. T	6. F	1. a	6. a	1. Alan Greenspan as of 1994
2. F	7. T	2. b	7. c	2. Recognition
3. T	8. T	3. c	8. b	3. Expansionary, increase
4. F	9. F	4. b	9. b	4. Contractionary, decrease
5. F	10. F	5. b	10. d	5. Inversely, interest

Problems

1. Abstract device to represent an increase in the money supply from outside the system
2. High real interest rates led to a major recession which did bring down the price level.
3. Lower interest rates increase real estate sales.
4. Higher interest rates increase the value of the dollar which increases demand for imports, which in turn increases the trade deficit.
5. Increase
6. Time lags and uncertainties
7. Decrease
8. Increase
9. Changes in interest rates are inversely related to bond prices
10. Operational lags are the time line from the Open Market Operation to a change in National Income, and often are very long.

Post-Test

1. Consumers and firms will buy and sell less and their transactions demand will decline.
2. Consumers and firms will require less money to complete the same number of transactions.
3. Lower interest rates will increase investment and consumer demand, thus increasing national income and the overall level of consumption.
4. Price levels remained fairly constant and very slow moderate growth in the economy began.
5. Interest rates rise, decreasing the quantity of money demanded and raising the demand for bonds and the price of bonds.
6. Money supply increases, interest rates fall, investment and aggregate demand rises, increasing national income.
7. Lower transactions demand, decrease in the price level, increases in the interest rate decline in income, etc.
8. Lower interest rates will lower the value of the dollar.
9. Household = consumer durables, houses, real estate
   businesses = plant, equipment, inventories
10. Interest rates rise, aggregate demand falls with declines in investment and consumption, and national income falls.

Chapter 17

Pretest

1. Interest rates rise.
2. Crowding out
3. Deficit financing increases interest rates more
4. Interest rates increase.
5. Demand for imports increases as income rises.
6. Reduce taxes or increase government spending

7. Expansionary
8. Expansionary monetary policy
9. 7.5%
10. Inflation and unemployment

T/F		Multiple Choice		Short Answer
1. F	6. F	1. B	6. B	1. 2.5%, unemployment, 1.0%
2. T	7. T	2. C	7. B.	2. Decreases
3 T	8. T	3. A	8. D	3. Increase
4. F	9. T	4. B	9. C	4. Decrease
5. T	10. F	5. B	10. A	5. Decrease, monetary, fiscal

Problems

1. Tax cuts or government spending increases to increase output, interest rates may rise moderately resulting in small, if any, crowding out
2. Increase money supply so interest rates fall and output rises
3. Fiscal policy: when income rises, transactions demand for money rises, interest rate rise, investment is crowded out   Monetary policy: when money supply increases, interest rates fall
4. Fall
5. Increase money or government spending
6. Tax increases or government cuts
7. Decrease money supply
8. When income rise, individuals buy more imports, bringing AD down.

Post-Test

1. MV = P4, so if output rises and money supply doesn't then prices rise
2. Demand for money increases.
3. Money supply increases.
4. Lower money supply or contractionary fiscal policy
5. 7.5%
6. Net export change
7. Net exports increase as demand for imports declines.
8. Interest rates rise.
9. Those decreasing interest rates
10. Crowding out occurs later after interest rates rise.

Chapter 18

Pretest

1. Increases in the price level, increase the demand for money, increase interest rates, reduce investment, lower output levels

2. See number for why output is inversely related to P
3. It's vertical at full employment on the production possibilities frontier
4. Shifts down to the right
5. Almost horizontal at low output levels and becomes steeper as the economy reaches full employment where it becomes vertical
6. Output increases and prices only moderately rise
7. Output decreases, prices rise AS shifts up to the left
8. Economy always returns to full employment

T/F		Multiple Choice		Short Answer
1. T	6. F	1. d	6. b	1. Interest, positively
2. T	7. T	2. c	7. a	2. Shift down
3. F	8. F	3. a	8. c	3. Slowly rise, increase
4. T	9. F	4. c	9. a	4. Increase, stay at full employment
5. F	10. F	5. d	10. c	5. Prices fall

Problems

1. Unemployment rises, prices may stay at the same or fall slowly
2. Those encouraging savings and investment
3. It becomes smaller
4. Labor supply increases when interest rates rise because of the life-cycle consumption patterns.
5. Stimulate AD with government spending or money supply increases
6. Do nothing
7. Increase savings and investments
8. Oil supply shock shifts AS to the left

Post-Test

1. Those promoting savings and investment
2. New Keynesians: short-run AS is almost horizontal at output levels, then becomes vertical at full employment, LRAS is vertical   New Classical: AS is vertical at full employment
3. When prices rise, transactions mony demand rises, interest rates rise, investment falls
4. Long-term contracts, institutional factors
5. Long-term contracts, institutional factors
6. Workers will increase hours to have more to save given life-cycle model
7. Money supply increase, tax cut
8. Output decreases, prices stay the same

Chapter 19

Pretest

1. Growth in aggregate demand, state of the economy, aggregate supply shocks, and expectations of future inflation

Answer Key

2. Once economy returns to full employment, inflation stops.
3. AD shifts to the right beyond full employment, then AS shifts to the left returning the economy to the Long Run full employment output at higher prices
4. Inflationary expectations
5. Shift aggregate supply continuously up and to the left
6. Expectations based on post inflation and available information
7. Full employment output is fixed in the Long Run
8. Stopping the growth of the money supply

T/F		Multiple Choice		Short Answer
1. F	6. F	1. d	6. a	1. Growth in nominal AD; state of the economy; AS shocks; expectations of future inflation
2. T	7. T	2. d	7. b	
3. T	8. F	3. b	8. b	2. Vertical
4. F	9. T	4. d	9. c	3. Short run, long run
5. F	10. T	5. d	10. d	4. Any
				5. Aggregate supply, right

Problems

1. Expectations shift the short-run Phillips curve to the right but the long-run curve remains at full employment.
2. Stopping inflation requires a contractionary fiscal and monetary policy while the opposite policies can be used to combat unemployment.
3. AD shifts to the right driving prices up and output stays constant
4. Can solve one of the problems but not both; must weigh costs and benefits of policies. (i.e., those on fixed incomes vs. unemployed individuals)
5. Higher unemployment
6. Shift it up and to the left
7. Need shift of AD to the right pushing the economy beyond full employment
8. Shift aggregate supply to the right and down by reducing tax rates
9. Stabilize expectations about economic performance

Post-Test

1. Economy is at full employment
2. Businesses and individuals can proceed with knowledge
3. Full employment long-run equilibrium
4. Prices up, output at full employment
5. AD shifts up to the right, prices up, output up in the short run. In long run if output is beyond full employment, AS shifts up to left driving prices up and output back to full employment
6. AS shifts down to the right
7. In short run, prices up and output down. In long run, prices are up and output is at full employment
8. Unemployment will probably rise

Chapter 20

Pretest

1. Countries benefit from trade due to different opportunity costs of production
2. Differences in opportunity costs
3. Downward pressure on prices of factors used more intensively
4. Product distinctions and differing tastes of consumers
5. North American Free Trade Agreement between U.S., Canada, and Mexico to reduce trade barrier
6. General agreement on tariffs and trade is an international agreement to reduce trade barriers.
7. reduction in trade barriers will increase production efficiency.
8. Quotas, tariffs, and strategic tariffs, consumers lose, workers in protected industries may gain

T/F		Multiple Choice		Short Answer
1. T	6. T	1. c	6. a	1. Most favored nation
2. F	7. T	2. b	7. b	2. Comparative advantage, opportunity cost
3. T	8. F	3. a	8. b	3. Quota
4. F	9. T	4. d		4. Tariffs
5. F	10. F	5. c		5. Increase

Problems

1. Increases in trade, standard of living etc. are among benefits; costs are associated with loss of jobs in sectors that do not have a comparative advantage
2. Europeans win, others lose
3. A tariff shifts supply to left, driving price up and quantity down of foreign cars. Demand for domestic cars increases and price increases.

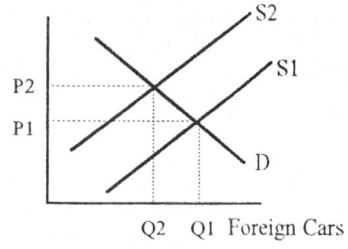 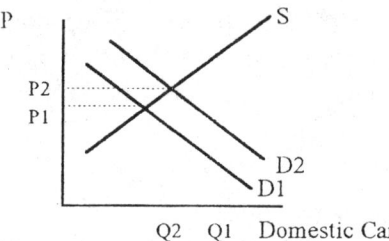

4. Imports cost more for Americans and exports cost less for foreigners
5. When exchange rates are fixed and they don't reflect the balance of trade
6. Gains from specialization, imports-exports over time, exchange rates are determined by price ratios of goods exchanged, and differences in opportunity costs determine gains from trade
7. Countries will export goods using abundant inputs and those producers will benefit (including labor)
8. Very

Post-Test

1. Differences in opportunity costs
2. Autoworkers and owners of U.S. auto interests
3. Protection of infant or new industries
4. Cheaper Chinese imports vs. political and human rights concerns
5. Product differentiation and economies of scale
6. Increase in demand for skilled labor increases wages while decreases in demand for unskilled labor lowers wages
7. Land is abundant in U.S. and in short supply in Japan
8. Decrease due to lower demand

Chapter 21

Pretest

1. Current account, capital account, official settlement accounts
2. Floating rates are determined by the market, fixed by the government
3. Increase in demand for Japanese imports increase the supply of dollars
4. Fixed exchange rates to the U.S. dollar until 1973
5. Fiscal policy becomes ineffective
6. Difference between capital inflows and outflows
7. Most stable currency with a country dedicated to low inflation rates
8. Foreign investment in the U.S. increases, and demand for dollars increases

T/F		Multiple Choice		Short Answer
1. F	6. T	1. c	6. a	1. Rise, balance
2. F	7. T	2. a	7. a	2. Increase
3. F	8. F	3. b	8. a	3. Increase
4. T		4. c		4. Eurodollars
5. F		5. b		5. Negative

Problems

1. Decrease
2. Other nations are unwilling to carry negative balances over time
3. Stability of the U.S. government
4. Markets can efficiently adjust for demand and supply of goods, services, and capital.
5. Decrease in value, when demand for Yen declines
6. Dollar increases due to demand for dollars increases, and Peso devalues due to less demand
7. Demand for imports increases when real income rises due to an increase in AD
8. Pegged to German mark

Post-Test

1. Inflation devalued currencies
2. Other countries will refuse to continue lending
3. Value increases
4. Does not reflect demand and supply of goods, services, and capital
5. To stabilize the value of their currency
6. Decrease value
7. Money investors
8. Negative with the exception of 1991

Chapter 22

Pretest

1. Measurement errors, and it ignores distribution of income
2. Labor force participation rates, savings and productive investment, choice of production technologies, and population growth rates
3. Impedes investment and growth
4. In a less developed country with low wages and a large unskilled labor supply
5. Higher in LDC's
6. Development strategy using relatively cheap labor to produce goods for the export market
7. Development strategy using relatively cheap labor to produce goods for internal markets coupled with tariffs and quotas on imports
8. Lending developing countries currency to purchase oil

T/F		Multiple Choice		Short Answer
1. T	6. F	1. d	6. a	1. Capital Flight
2. F	7. F	2. a	7. a	2. Kuznets Curve
3. F	8. T	3. c	8. b	3. Lower
4. F		4. b		4. $7,050 in 1992 dollars
5. T		5. a		5. Higher

Problems

1. Rural areas of South Asia, Sub-Saharan Africa, and parts of Southeast Asia
2. Very high, 5.8% per year between 1965-90
3. To buy needed imports
4. Differences in purchasing power
5. Infant mortality, life expectancy, literacy, access to gas, water, and electricity, political freedom and human rights
6. Warm climates allow for year-round farming and discourage saving habits in a culture.
7. Moslem laws against lending and borrowing money
8. High inflation rates in less developed countries and economic and political instability

Post-Test

1. Loans, grants, gifts used for capital investment and growth
2. Capital intensive production and high population growth
4. Shows relationship between income distribution and per capita GDP. Middle income countries have the least equal income distribution
5. Strain on savings and investment
6. Agricultural based economics and culture
7. Outward-oriented strategy
8. Inward-oriented strategy

Chapter 23

Pretest

1. Allocational, distributional, imperfect information
2. Those who start out with more resources are likely to end up with more resources in a market economy.
3. Monopoly and oligopoly power
4. Individuals have an incentive to take an action which will increase the costs to the insurer.
5. Those at higher risk are more likely to be in the insurance pool.
6. Private costs are less than social costs.
7. Private sector will not produce them because they can not exclude consumers
8. In the absence the costs are high (e.g. long periods of unemployment, etc.)
9. Defense, redistribution, and provision of public pensions and insurance
10. Education, highways, aid to poor, and hospital care

T/F		Multiple Choice		Short Answer
1. F	6. T	1. b	6. b	1. Common-use
2. T	7. F	2. d	7. c	2. Adverse selection, principal agent
3. T	8. T	3. b	8. a.	3. Externality
4. F	9. T	4. d	9. d.	4. Merit good
5. T	10. F	5. d		5. Defense, redistribution, and pensions

Problems

1. Taxes are more progressive and social programs are designed to redistribute income
2. Externalities
3. Social and private costs are different
4. Exclusive = auto, computer, stereo   non-exclusive = clean air, defense, clean water
5. Individuals will have incentives to seek unnecessary medical care, but it is hard to imagine that large numbers of people will want unnecessary medical care (e.g., how many people will want to have too many colonoscopies?).
6. Imperfect information markets, because the salesperson has an information advantage
7. Private costs are borne by individuals, but society also loses human capital, and potential productivity increases

8. Principal agent and adverse selection
9. Free rider problem
10. Both because of private and social benefits

Post-Test

1. Good on horizontal and bad on vertical equity because initial wealth determines final wealth distribution
2. Market failure re: resource use
3. Leads to various market failures such as adverse selection, moral hazard, etc.
4. Society believes everyone is entitled to health care regardless of income or wealth.
5. Re; unemployment, price stabilization, long-term growth, etc.
6. Elderly and rates will be higher due to adverse selection
7. No one owned the property rights of the sea otters, and the fur traders had no incentive to preserve them because they were a common-use resource.
8. Good that will be consumed by everyone because no one can be excluded, e.g. defense
9. Assesses social cost of pollution on the polluter, where the ideal tax is equal to the marginal cost of pollution
10. Defense, pensions, income redistribution

Chapter 24

Pretest

1. Personal income and Social Security taxes
2. Personal income, sales, property
3. Debt financing increased under Reagan
4. Progressive = taxes increase in percentage terms when income increases, regressive = taxes decrease in percentage terms as income rises, proportional = taxes are proportional to income
5. Same rate is applied to all incomes up to a ceiling of approximately $60,000
6. Eliminated capital gains tax preference and collapsed the rate structure to four tax rates with a maximum income tax of 33%
7. Produces costs for some individuals that are not necessarily consistent with economic efficiencies, also Kenneth Arrow's Impossibility Theorem, and role of lobbyists
8. Social Security taxes were raised to protect solvency of the system as boomers age
9. Can't exclude consumers, i.e. non-exclusionary good like defense
10. Ease of administration, simplicity, flexibility, efficiency, and equity

Answer Key

T/F		Multiple Choice		Short Answer
1. T	6. F	1. b	6. a	1. Deficit
2. F	7. T	2. a	7. c	2. Progressive, income
3. F	8. F	3. d	8. b	3. Same
4. F	9. T	4. c	9. d	4. Increases
5. T	10. T	5. b	10. b	5. Regressive, progressive

Problems

1. Private interests of the tobacco lobby justify lobbying expenditures to protect the benefits they receive from the subsidies while the individual costs to citizens are small and provide little incentive to lobby, even though the total costs to society are very high and justify the elimination of the subsidies.
2. Flatter tax rates and treats capital gains the same as other sources of income
3. Easy to administer, simple, flexible, adds the social cost of cigarettes to the price increasing efficiency, and equitable given cigarette smokers are likely to incur higher health care costs which will ultimately be borne by society
4. Ability to pay concerns when consumer can not forego food expenditures
5. Tax cuts were received by high as well as low income individuals, and owners of like property are taxed at different rates depending on the date of purchase violating horizontal equity
6. Payroll tax increases in 1983
7. Increased the national debt
8. Vertical equity, i.e. should higher income individuals pay higher taxes?
9. Increases the progressiveness of the tax system, ensuring a negative tax for those working and still earning less than a minimum threshold
10. Voting rules do not produce a consistent set of social preferences based on citizen preferences.

Post-Test

1. Since the poor consume more of their income it is likely to be regressive
2. Income = proportional to progressive, sales = regressive, property = regressive or progressive depending on point of view
3. Wealthy are more likely to receive income from capital gains, so preferential treatment for capital gains is biased towards the rich
4. Social security since it is a flat rate topping off near $60,000
5. Easier to collect and more difficult to evade
6. Corporate income taxes and individual income taxes on dividends
7. Pay-as-you-go system
8. Covers all types of income and treats them the same
9. Progressive = income, regressive = social security, proportional = some income taxes
10. Lobbying, logrolling, etc.

Answers to Sample Tests

Questions	I	II	III	Part IV	V	VI	VII
1.	a	b	b	c	b	d	c
2.	b	e	c	a	a	c	c
3.	b	d	b	a	d	a	c
4.	b	c	d	a	a	b	a
5.	b	b	c	a	c	d	d
6.	b	a	b	a	d	c	d
7.	a	c	b	c	b	d	a
8.	c	d	d	a	c	b	b
9.	c	b	a	a	c	c	d
10.	b	b	c	a	d	b	c
11.	b	a	a	c	a	b	b
12.	a	e	c	d	c	c	b
13.	d	c	a	c	d	d	c
14.	a	e	b	b	c	b	c
15.	c	b	d	c	b	b	c
16.	c	a	e	c	b	a	c
17.	d	d	c	c	a	d	d
18.	b	a	a	c	d	a	c
19.	a	c	a	a	a	d	b
20.	a	d	d	b	b	a	a
21.	c	b	c	d	d	b	c
22.	c	c	d	d	e	d	a
23.	b	d	c	b	c	d	b
24.	b	a	c	c	d	d	c
25.		c	b	c	c	a	a